Transnational Corporations and Labor

A Directory of Resources

Compiled and edited by
Thomas P. Fenton
and
Mary J. Heffron

Maryknoll, New York 10545

Resource Directories previously published

Third World Resource Directory
Asia and Pacific
Latin America and Caribbean
Women in the Third World
Food, Hunger, Agribusiness
Africa
Middle East
Human Rights

Graphics credits: Rachel Burger/*cpf*, 59; *China Talk*, 66; *The Copy Book*, 15, 19; Rini Templeton, 50, 83, 85, 114, 120, 137, 143, 146. All from the DataCenter Graphics Collection (dcgc).

Copyright © 1989 by Thomas P. Fenton and Mary J. Heffron
All rights reserved
Published in the United States of America by Orbis Books, Maryknoll, NY 10545
Manufactured in the United States of America

Library of Congress Cataloging-in-Publication Data

Fenton, Thomas P.
   Transnational corporations and labor : a directory of resources / compiled and edited by Thomas P. Fenton and Mary J. Heffron.
     p.   cm.
   Includes bibliographical references.
   ISBN 0-88344-635-9
   1. International business enterprises—Developing countries—Bibliography. 2. International business enterprises—Developing countries—Directories. 3. Working class—Developing countries—Bibliography. 4. Working class—Developing countries—Directories. 5. Trade-unions—Developing countries—Bibliography. 6. Trade-unions—Developing countries—Directories. I. Heffron, Mary J. II. Title
Z7164.U5F46   1989
[HD2932]
016.3388′881724—dc20   89-38860
                                                                                   CIP

ISBN for the series: 0-88344-647-2

Contents

Foreword ....*v*
Preface ....*vii*
Introduction...*xii*

Chapter 1: Organizations   *1*
   Annotated Entries   2
   Organization's name; address; telephone number; organization's self-description; keyword descriptions of the organization's political and religious affiliation, region and issue focus, activities, and resources; and title of periodical publications.
   Supplementary List of Organizations   14
   Information Sources   19

Chapter 2: Books   *21*
   Annotated Entries   22
   Author(s) or editor(s); title; place of publication; publisher; date of publication; number of pages; price; keyword description of format; description of content.
      General   22
      Bibliographies and Guides   50
      Directories and Reference Books   52
      United Nations Publications   57
   Supplementary List of Books   59
   Information Sources   66

Chapter 3: Periodicals   *67*
   Annotated Entries   67
   Title; publisher; address; number of issues per year; format (newspaper, magazine, or newsletter); size (height in centimeters); number of pages; subscription costs; keyword description of format; description of content.
   Supplementary List of Periodicals   83
   Information Sources   84

Chapter 4: Pamphlets and Articles   *86*
   Annotated Entries   87
   Author(s) or editor(s); title; publisher; name of periodical; publication

iv   CONTENTS

data (volume, number date); number of pages; price; keyword description of format; description of content.
Supplementary List of Pamphlets and Articles   114
Information Sources   119

Chapter 5: Audiovisuals   *121*

VISUAL RESOURCES
Annotated Entries   122
Title; producer(s); director(s); date; length (minutes); format; principal distributor; rental and sale price; secondary distributor(s); description of content; source of annotation.
Supplementary List of Visual Resources   137
Information Sources   142
AUDIO RESOURCES
Annotated Entries   143
Title; artist(s) or producer(s); date; length; format (record or tape); distributor; ordering number; price; description of content.

Indexes   *147*

Organizations   147
Individuals   153
Titles   156
Geographical Areas   163
Subjects   163

Foreword

A couple years ago when I first began looking for materials on organizations and resources on international labor and transnational corporations, it quickly became clear that no comprehensive resource directory existed. This book fills that void. *Transnational Corporations and Labor* is packed with gems of information about unique and ground-breaking organizations, books, periodicals, and audiovisual material that promote a progressive labor approach to the internationalization of most countries' economies. It will be invaluable to those wanting to be educated or to educate, to activists (labor and otherwise) in the First World who want to work with counterparts in the Third World, and to activists in the Third World who want to make links with sympathizers in the First World.

The rapid globalization of economies is characterized increasingly by the ability of transnational corporations, with the support of international banks, to shift production operations from county to country and region to region, from high-wage areas to low-wage areas. This pits workers in one country against workers in another and has enabled a major assault on labor to take place. For industrialized countries, the internationalization of the economy has resulted in massive job losses in the manufacturing sector, reduced wages for those who remain, and a weakened labor movement. The loss of jobs and perceived economic threat have also helped fuel a growing nationalism, if not racism, that bodes no good for anyone. In the Third World, oppression against labor unions has intensified, as efforts are made to keep labor weak and wages low. In the last year, the number of labor leaders assassinated in the Third World doubled while thousands more have been disappeared, tortured, and jailed.

Logically, the basic response to mobile, globe-trotting transnational corporations should be international labor solidarity. Historically, however, there has been more talk than action on building international labor cooperation. Of late, some official international labor bodies have begun to show signs of activism. There is growing recognition even within the U.S. labor movement of the need for workers in the First and Third Worlds to jointly confront transnational corporations, although the U.S. AFL-CIO's international apparatus still does more to implement U.S. foreign policy than build labor solidarity. Especially notable has been the work of progressive trade unionists on South Africa and Central America (e.g., the recently formed Labor Coalition on Central America, the New York Labor Committee against Apartheid, and the National Labor Committee in Support of Human Rights and Democracy in El Salvador). Such efforts need to be recognized, supported, and supplemented by other progressive activists. This resource directory helps make such action possible.

In many ways, the most vibrant labor movements in the world are those in the Third World. Despite increased oppression, labor activists are making progress in forming independent unions and are beginning to flex their muscles in a number of countries. Nationwide strikes are not uncommon, and marches turn out tens of thousands of workers in demonstrations of solidarity. This resource directory provides information on how to learn about these struggles, how to support them, and how they can seek support.

A look at the relatively sparse organizational section* indicates that too few people are working to build labor solidarity between countries, particularly between the U.S. and the Third World. This book reveals the need for networking, and serves as an essential tool to do so. In a visit to Thailand a year ago, I asked labor activists about possible U.S. solidarity actions. One Thai labor leader replied, "Just knowing that there are people in the U.S. who support our labor struggles is very important. The first step is simply to begin communicating with each other." *Transnational Corporations and Labor* is the most comprehensive resource available to make this happen.

STEPHEN COATS

---

*One addition I would recommend is the International Labor Rights Education and Research Fund, a fledgling group of labor, human rights, religious, and Third World activists (Box 68, 110 Maryland Avenue, N.E., Washington, D.C. 20002). The Fund aims to promote international labor rights, especially in the Third World, primarily by linking labor rights to U.S. trade, investment, and aid policy. Its newsletter, *Worker Rights News*, is the only independent publication in the U.S. that covers the public policy side of international labor issues.

Preface

This directory of resources on transnational corporations and labor is one in a series of twelve volumes on Third World regions and issues that is being compiled by Third World Resources, an affiliated project of the DataCenter.

OBJECTIVES

Our aim in compiling this and all the other resource guides in the twelve-volume series is to meet five objectives:

1. To strengthen the ties among organizations that oppose the injustices in foreign military and economic intervention in the Third World by helping to dismantle the institutional, issue-related, and regional barriers that now divide these groups.

Educators and activists who take a critical stance toward the impact of foreign intervention in Third World affairs are unnecessarily divided from one another and thus not as effective or as mutually supportive as they could be. They are divided institutionally, by issue orientation, and by region.

Institutional walls separate church workers from academics, community organizers from researchers, and social studies teachers from political activists. Third World Resources seeks to breach these institutional walls by publicizing the work of groups in all of these categories and by promoting their resources through a worldwide network of Third World-related progressive organizations.

Ironically, *issues* also drive wedges between activist organizations. Nuclear groups work on freeze issues, but fail to appreciate fully the urgency of the work of Central America-support organizations and vice versa. While this might make some sense tactically and while this focus of energies is perfectly understandable given the demands on the time of organizers, the lack of a network of mutually supportive progressive organizations clearly limits the impact of their work.

By putting people in touch with people—whatever the issue that may be their prime concern—Third World Resources encourages better cross-fertilization of ideas and plans. This results in more effective joint action and less duplication of effort in the production of education and action resources.

Regional barriers also fragment the resistance movement. Transnational corporations are—unfortunately—years ahead of their critics in realizing the need to have near-instantaneous communication across regional and national boundaries. Critics need to appreciate as well the importance of the broadest and quickest possible interchange of information and of plans for action.

Third World Resources transcends regional boundaries by including in this directory and in all its publications education- and action-oriented resources from all over the world. In this international aspect of our work we are helped by an international board of advisors and by our affiliation with Interdoc, an international network of research and documentation centers.

2. To legitimize and give equal time to alternative points of view on Third World affairs in general and on the involvement of the United States and other major powers in the Third World in particular.

In the United States critical analyses of the devastating impact of foreign public and private interests in the Third World are woefully under-represented on library shelves across the country, and the challenging voice of oppressed Third World peoples is heard only as a whisper in the media and in classrooms. We suspect that this criticism applies equally well to other major industrialized powers.

—Yet analytical and educational work of this nature *is* being done. The array of resources presented in this directory testifies to that fact. This work *must* be publicized more widely.

—Critical Third World voices *are* crying out for justice. These voices *must* be magnified.

Commenting on our *Third World Resource Directory* (Orbis Books, 1984), the director of the Third World Studies Center in Manila has said: "The publication of the resource directory is truly heartwarming, for it tells us abundantly that in America not everyone has been silent or silenced and that many are laboring to explain the links between the behavior of the U.S. government and multinationals and the problems that we face in our own countries."

The purpose of the present directory is to publicize the efforts of those who are explaining these links and to make certain that the victims of interventionism by the United States and other powers have an opportunity to tell their story.

3. To promote the education/action resources of Third World-related organizations in a sustained, focused, and professional manner.

DataCenter president Fred Goff described this problem in his Foreword to the *Third World Resource Directory:* "All too often the limited resources available to these [progressive] organizations are consumed by the process of producing a given book, pamphlet, newsletter, or film. Little energy or money remains for adequately publicizing these resources."

Anyone who has worked in solidarity and anti-intervention organizations knows how true this observation is. Even when the desire is there to reach beyond the institutional, issue-related, and regional barriers described above, the energy and financial resources that this outreach demands are too often just not there. This results in the underutilization of available resources and—perhaps even worse—the waste of limited time and money in the production of redundant resources.

Third World Resources furthers the promotional outreach of progressive organizations by focusing its energies on *identifying* and *acquiring* resources from all over the world on regions such as the Middle East and on issues such as transnational corporations, on *describing* and *evaluating* the resources in a careful, non-rhetorical fashion, on *presenting* them in an attractive, readily accessible format, and on *publicizing* the work of these organizations to a broad audience of educators, researchers, librarians, and political activists.

4. To put in the hands of researchers and organizers in the Third World comprehensive guides to Third World-related organizations and educational resources in other parts of the world.

DataCenter president Fred Goff spoke to this problem as well: "Researchers and organizers in the Third World have learned from experience that information critical to their struggle for social justice—information about the realities of power in their own countries—is often available only here in the United States" (Foreword, *Third World Resource Directory*).

Third World Resources responds to this need of activists and educators in the Third World by providing them with handy sourcebooks of annotated descriptions and comprehensive lists of organizations, books, magazines, films, and other resources on a wide variety of Third World regions and related issues. The *Third World Resources* newsletter keeps these references current, and the Third World Resources documentation clearinghouse at the DataCenter assures easy access to the entire collection of resources from anywhere in the world.

5. To direct concerned citizens in First World countries to the books, periodicals, audiovisuals, and other resources they need to study in order to take informed and effective action to correct injustices in the ways their governments and businesses treat Third World nations and peoples.

This directory and the others in the twelve-volume set are designed to offer immediate answers to the questions concerned citizens ask: How can I find out more about the impact of transnational corporations in Southeast Asia? What can I read to help me understand what is happening in the Middle East? What steps can I take to help people in the Philippines or to stop U.S. intervention in Central America? Where can I rent a good educational film on South Africa?

THIRD WORLD RESOURCES

The present directory and the entire twelve-volume set of resource directories update and expand the resources presented in the *Third World Resource Directory* and complement the two other facets of the

x   PREFACE

Third World Resources project: a quarterly newsletter and resource guide and a clearinghouse of Third World-related resources.

Quarterly Newsletter and Resource Guide

Third World Resources publishes a twenty-page quarterly newsletter, *Third World Resources: A Quarterly Review of Resources from and about the Third World,* with notices and descriptive listings of organizations and newly released print, audiovisual, and other educational resources from and about the Third World. Each issue of the newsletter contains a unique four-page resource guide that provides comprehensive coverage of one particular region. This resource guide is available at discounts for bulk distribution.

Clearinghouse of Third World-related Resources

In order to insure the widest possible access to the resources gathered in the course of work on the resource directories and newsletter, Third World Resources catalogs and integrates all incoming information and materials into the library collection of the DataCenter where they can be used by the hundreds of journalists, teachers, community organizers, and others who visit the center's public-access library each year. The materials are also available to the center's national and international network of Search Service clients.

In addition, bibliographical data on all of the resources are stored in a computerized data base to facilitate identification and retrieval of cross-referenced resources. Write to Third World Resources for information on how to gain access to this unique storehouse of critical information through the Interdoc or PeaceNet electronic communications networks.

APPRECIATION

The work of Third World Resources is sustained by friends all over the world who give generously of their time, money, resources, and encouragement. This directory and all our efforts are dedicated to them with heartfelt thanks for their support.

We acknowledge in a special way the assistance of our colleagues at the DataCenter. The DataCenter has a unique collection of materials on transnational corporations and labor and its staff members are expert at assembling documentation to aid activists, journalists, lawyers, and educators in all aspects of their work.

Our co-worker Raquel Sancho deserves a special word of thanks for the thorough and conscientious work she has been doing in compiling information on Third World-related audiovisuals.

John Eagleson and the late Phil Scharper deserve the credit for launching this series of publications during their time at Orbis Books.

Hank Schlau edited the manuscript of this directory with customary devotion to detail and good humor. To him and the rest of the staff at Orbis Books we extend our thanks.

The production of *Transnational Corporations and Labor: A Directory of Resources* was made possible in part by grants from the Maryknoll Fathers and Brothers and the Office of Community Development of the Presbyterian Church (USA). We are grateful for their generosity and personal support.

Introduction

The table of contents (above) is a guide to the overall structure of this directory. Each of the five chapters opens with an introduction that describes the format and contents of the particular chapter.

In this introduction we offer comments on the format and content of the directory as a whole.

FORMAT

This directory updates and expands the resources in the chapter on transnational corporations in the *Third World Resource Directory* (Orbis Books, 1984). That chapter (pp. 202-19), as well as cross-referenced entries throughout the 1984 directory, should be consulted for complementary annotated lists of organizations and their resources on transnational corporations.

Because of the obvious interplay between transnational corporations and working people in the Third World we have broadened the scope of this directory to include labor. This subject was not treated as such in the *Third World Resource Directory,* but numerous resources in that directory—and in the other directories compiled by Third World Resources—do pertain to international labor.

We have tried to include complete descriptive and ordering information for every citation in this directory. When we have judged that addresses for the organizations, publishers, and distributors would be necessary for the acquisition of resources, we have given those addresses either in the organizations index in the back of the book or with the individual entries. Library reference books should be consulted for the addresses of publishers or film distributors that do not appear in this directory.

We caution you to inquire about current prices and terms of sale or rental before placing an order for any item in this directory.

CONTENT

Our comments on the content of this directory and of the resources themselves fall into four categories: definitions, scope, limitations, and political orientation.

INTRODUCTION xiii

Definitions

We use the term *Third World* in a geographical sense to encompass the peoples and countries of Africa, Asia and Pacific (excluding Japan, Australia, and New Zealand), Latin America and Caribbean, and the Middle East. In order to limit this directory to a modest size we have not included the real and urgent concerns of persons who live in "Third World" conditions in the industrialized nations of North America, Europe, and other areas. We refer you to the sources of information in each of the chapters of this directory for indirect references to resources on those issues.

The term *transnational corporation* is not well defined in the international community. The United Nations Economic and Social Council defines transnational corporations as "all enterprises which control assets—factories, mines, sales offices and the like—in two or more countries." In compiling this directory we have narrowed this definition, for the most part, to corporations engaged in *industrial production* in two or more countries. A few resources deal with banks and other financial institutions, but these will be treated more fully in a forthcoming directory of resources.

By *labor* we mean organized labor (i.e., in trade unions), as well as *work* in the broad sense. The number of print and audiovisual resources that are available on the subject of women and work is striking. Most women workers in Third World countries, however, are not active participants in trade unions. Thus the need to work with the broadest possible definition of labor.

Many resources in this directory deal with the interplay between transnational corporations and labor (i.e., the employees of transnational corporations). Others, however, do not. These deal with transnational corporations on their own or with labor and work on their own.

Scope

In compiling this directory we endeavored to identify and acquire resources on transnational corporations and labor from organizations in all parts of the world. We looked for print and audiovisual resources that described and analyzed these issues as completely and clearly as possible. We searched also for resources that offered a progressive political perspective on these topics (see below under "Political Orientation") without being doctrinaire or rhetorical.

The heading "transnational corporations and labor" includes under it a wide array of topics, many of which are covered in this directory: foreign investment, industrial development, plant shutdowns, international debt, the international labor movement, women workers, the international division of labor, working conditions in factories owned and operated by transnational corporations, nuclear energy, production and use of pesticides and other chemicals, export processing zones, the export to Third World countries of hazardous products, international migration for work purposes, and slavery.

Some subject areas that would have been appropriate for this directory, such as the production and export of military weapons, are omitted because they will be treated in forthcoming directories in the Third World Resources series.

All of the directories in the Third World Resources series contain resources that treat transnational corporations and labor. Except in a few cases we have not duplicated resources found in other Third World Resources directories. We have included only those materials that treat aspects of transnational corporations and labor that are not covered in the directories already published (see below) or that—by definition— would not likely fall into any of the directories scheduled for publication in the series.

Readers interested in transnational corporations and labor as these issues relate to women or to food should see the two directories published by Orbis Books in spring 1987: *Women: A Directory of Resources* and *Food, Hunger, Agribusiness: A Directory of Resources.* The following directories should be consulted for resources that treat transnational corporations and labor in specific Third World regions: *Asia and Pacific* (1986), *Latin America and Caribbean* (1986), *Africa* (1987), and *Middle East* (1988).

Limitations

In attempting to meet our goals we have had to contend with limitations that are beyond our control. We call attention to these limitations here by way of explaining why some organizations and resources that meet our selection criteria do not appear in this directory and why certain aspects of the subject matter have not been given the attention they deserve.

We are limited, first of all, by what is available. We are obviously unable to include books that have not been written or films that have not been made. We were frustrated ourselves at times at not being able to find a popularly written book on this or that aspect of the subject or a good introductory film on this or that country and region. One byproduct of a directory such as this is to highlight subject and geographical areas that deserve attention from writers and filmmakers.

We are limited, next, by our own awareness of resources. Naturally we are more familiar with the resources of organizations that are based here in North America. The resources in this directory reflect that familiarity. We acknowledge that we still have a long way to go toward our goal of making this collection of resources truly international in origin. We welcome the participation of educators and activists outside of North America in helping us expand the reach of future editions of this directory.

Another limitation is the lack of access to resources that *are* available and that we *do* know about. We send survey questionnaires to organizations that we would like to include in the directory and we request review copies of or detailed information on books, periodicals, pamphlets, and audiovisual resources that we judge to be appropriate for listing. When the time comes to compile the directory we can only work with the information we have at hand.

A final limitation is that to the best of our knowledge there is at this time no other directory of this nature on transnational corporations and labor. (Where resource guides do exist on one or more aspects of this subject we acknowledge them in the directory.) Thus, we had to start virtually from scratch in identifying organizations and acquiring their resources. With the publication of this directory we — and others — have a base to build on for the future.

It should also be noted — for our sakes as well as for many of the organizations represented in this directory — that documentation work on subjects such as transnational corporations and labor is chronically underfunded by funding agencies and donors. This severely taxes the time and energy of all who are devoted to this vital work.

Political Orientation

In the preface to the *Third World Resource Directory* we described the resources in that directory as — by and large — "partisan and biased" in favor of a "radical analysis" of Third World affairs. We described this radical analysis as one that contends that:
 • reforms in the system are not enough; the crying need is for radical (that is, fundamental) changes in economic, political, and social (race, sex, and class) relations;
 • change will come about through struggles (though not necessarily violent ones) between the "powerful" and the "powerless";
 • the private and public institutional power of countries like the United States is often used to frustrate initiatives for fundamental social change in Third World countries.

Even a cursory examination of educational resources about the Third World clearly demonstrates that most resources — and certainly the bulk of what we are exposed to in the media — ignore this "radical" analysis in favor of one that:
 • stresses reforms that do not upset the present disposition of power;
 • characterizes all people in the First World countries as rich and powerful and describes all in the Third World as poor and powerless;
 • judges all struggles for radical social change to be Soviet-inspired and, therefore, to be opposed.

We situate our study of transnational corporations and labor in the "radical" political context, trying as much as possible to examine these realities from the point of view of those in the Third World who feel the impact of transnational corporations most harshly and who strive to organize themselves to combat the political and economic power of the corporations.

We take as our own this partial statement of the objectives of the UN Centre on Transnational Corporations: "To further the understanding of the nature of the transnational corporations and of their political, legal, economic, and social effects on home and host countries and in international relations, particularly between developed and developing countries; to secure effective international arrangements aimed at enhancing the contribution of transnational corporations to national development goals and world economic growth while controlling and eliminating their negative effects." Our primary concern is with the impact of transnational corporations on Third World countries, but some of the resources in this directory examine the equally important effects that the corporations have on individuals and communities in their home countries (e.g., in the case of plant closings).

While openly admitting our political orientation we feel it is also important to point out that political biases are woven into most—if not all—education and action resources on the regions and issues we are covering—whether those resources be left-wing, right-wing, or moderate in character. One cannot describe or analyze events in the Third World without betraying the lines of a political belief system regarding the means and pace of social change, the causes of social unrest, the allegiance owed one's own government, and so forth.

We have been straightforward about our own partisanship because we believe strongly that it is important for all to identify, evaluate, and admit to the biases that inform their analysis of and decisions regarding Third World affairs. Educators and librarians especially should be diligent about calling attention to the political biases in *all* of the resources on their desks and shelves—not just those that are alternative or radical in orientation.

In compiling a directory of resources we are not advocating the wholesale substitution of one body of thought for another. For one thing, as a careful study of the resources in this directory will demonstrate, there is no "one body of thought" that runs throughout the varied and numerous resources listed below—even though the political orientation of many of the resources could be labeled as alternative or radical. For another, a confession of one's political biases is not necessarily to be equated with a lack of appreciation for or openness to the truth in other points of view.

Our overriding aim is to promote the critical and responsible study of the points of view represented in the resources in this directory along with consideration of all other descriptions and analyses of Third World affairs.

1

Organizations

This chapter is divided into three parts: annotated entries, supplementary list of organizations, and sources of additional information.

Each **annotated entry** includes: organization's name, address, telephone number; organization's self-description (in quotation marks); keyword descriptions of the organization's political and religious affiliation, focus (first geographical, then according to issues), activities, and resources, and title(s) of periodical(s).

The keywords were selected, in most cases, by the organizations themselves and are intended to provide a quick overview of each organization's work. The descriptors are neither all-inclusive nor scientific.

If the name of a periodical stands alone, this means that the magazine, newsletter, or newspaper is fully annotated in the periodicals chapter below. Otherwise, pertinent descriptive information accompanies the citation.

Organizations in the **supplementary list** (pp. 14–19) are grouped under these regional headings: Africa; Asia and Pacific; Europe; Latin America and Caribbean; and North America (Canada and the United States).

The part entitled **information sources** (pp. 19–20) provides the titles of directories and guides that contain the names of other organizations concerned about transnational corporations and labor in the Third World.

All of the organizations and periodicals in this chapter are listed in the appropriate indexes at the back of this directory.

Data on many of the organizations that appear on the supplementary list were compiled by Deborah Smith, formerly of the Institute for Policy Studies, and published in *Meeting the Corporate Challenge: A Handbook on Corporate Campaigns,* published by Transnationals Information Exchange (*TIE Report* 18/19, February 1985). Entries on the TIE list are annotated, providing (when available) a short description of the organization's work, the name of any periodicals, and the name of a contact person. We have omitted organizations when we know the address is incorrect as given or when the organization is financed entirely by a government or corporation.

With allowances made for a handful of dated entries, we highly recommend the TIE resource guide and thank Deborah Smith and the Transnationals Information Exchange for granting us permission to use data from the guide in this directory.

ANNOTATED ENTRIES

■ Asia Monitor Resource Center, 444 Nathan Rd., 8/B, Kowloon, Hongkong. Tel: (3) 855319.

"The Asia Monitor Resource Center is an independent, nonprofit research and information center. The aim of the AMRC is to systematically gather, organize, analyze, and publish information on the impact of foreign economic, military, and political forces on the people and nations of Asia. The center serves individuals and organizations in Asia and abroad who believe that a critical examination of these forces is essential in working for just and equitable development. Founded in 1976, the AMRC presently focuses on Asian labor issues, transnational economic activity, and health, safety, and the environment."

FOCUS: Asia and Pacific. Health • chemical hazards • human rights • militarism, peace, disarmament • nuclear arms and energy • foreign aid and trade • labor • women • political economy • national liberation struggles • transnational corporations • food, hunger, agribusiness.

ACTIVITIES: Popular education • workshops and seminars • solidarity work • networking • training of interns • media relations • dissemination of documentation and information • publishing • research and writing.

RESOURCES: Speakers • research services • books and literature • library.

PERIODICAL: *Asia Labour Monitor*.

■ Australia-Asia Worker Links, P.O. Box 264, Fitzroy, VIC 3065, Australia. Tel: (03) 419-5045.

"The aims of Australia-Asia Worker Links are: (1) To develop solidarity networks between Australian and Asian workers and trade unions in their struggle for an independent and genuine labour movement in the region. (2) To promote an understanding of the present economic system, increasingly controlled by multinational companies, and how the system affects workers. (3) To develop strategies and internationalization to counter the centralization of power and wealth."

FOCUS: Asia and Pacific. International labor • human rights • foreign aid and trade • women • international awareness • transna-

tional corporations • native peoples.
ACTIVITIES: Education • workshops and seminars • organizing • solidarity work • networking • dissemination of documentation and information • publishing • production of audiovisuals • distribution of print matter • distribution of audiovisuals • educational research and writing.
RESOURCES: Speakers • audiovisuals • books and literature.
PERIODICAL: *Asian Workers Organizing.*
■ Center on Transnational Economy, Casilla de Correo 86, Sucursal 26 B, 1425 Buenos Aires, Argentina. Tel: 781-5159.
"CET is a nonprofit, nongovernmental regional institution that is devoted to the systematic research of various theoretical and policy matters related to the presence of transnational corporations in the economy of Latin America. CET's projects are grouped in four areas: transnationalization, finance, trade, and new technologies.
"The Center on Transnational Economy is associated with the Instituto para América Latina (IPAL) in Mexico City, a multidisciplinary institution with research programs and activities in the areas of economics, culture, and politics."
FOCUS: Global • Latin America and Caribbean. Political economy • transnational corporations.
ACTIVITIES: Workshops and seminars • political action • dissemination of documentation and information • policy-oriented research and writing.
RESOURCES: Research services • books and literature • library.
PERIODICAL: *Economia de América Latina.*
■ Centre for Research on Multinational Corporations (SOMO), Paulus Potterstraat 20, 1071 DA Amsterdam, The Netherlands. Tel: (020) 73-75-15.
"SOMO was founded in 1972 because of the growing awareness of the central role that transnational corporations play in developing countries, as well as in their home economies. The centre's aim is to document and critically research the worldwide operations of transnational corporations, especially those based in the Netherlands. The activities of SOMO consist primarily of research on the internationalization of the economy of the Netherlands and the role transnational corporations play in the international division of labor between industrialized and developing countries. The research work and documentation service of SOMO are mainly intended to support initiatives taken by the groups most directly affected by the activities of transnational corporations. In practice, this means that SOMO works mainly at the request of and together with two types of groups: workers employed by transnational corporations and their subsidiaries and organized in trade unions or works councils, and Third World solidarity groups in the Netherlands whose objective is to increase awareness of the development process and of the unequal international distribution of economic opportunities."

4 ORGANIZATIONS

FOCUS: International. Transfer of technology • foreign aid and trade • labor • transnational corporations • development • international banking.

ACTIVITIES: Library services • dissemination of documentation and information • publishing • research and writing.

RESOURCES: Documentation center • research services • books and literature • consultant services.

■ Council on Economic Priorities, 30 Irving Pl., New York, NY 10003. Tel: (212) 420-1133.

"The Council on Economic Priorities is a nonprofit organization established to disseminate unbiased and detailed information on the practices of U.S. corporations. These practices have a profound impact on the quality of American life. CEP was established so that the American public could become aware of this impact and work to ensure corporate social responsibility."

FOCUS: Global. Political economy • militarism, peace, disarmament • nuclear arms and energy • labor • transnational corporations.

ACTIVITIES: Research and writing • library services • distribution of print matter.

RESOURCES: Books and literature • studies and reports.

PERIODICAL: *CEP Research Report.*

■ Counter Information Services, 9 Poland St., London NW1, England. Tel: 439-3764.

"CIS is a collective of journalists dedicated to publishing information not covered or collated by the established media. It is their aim to investigate the major social and economic institutions that govern our daily lives in order that the basic facts and assumptions behind them be as widely known as possible. CIS is financed by sales, subscriptions, donations, and grants."

FOCUS: United Kingdom and international. Transnational corporations • women • migrant workers • nuclear arms and energy • apartheid • new technology • racism.

ACTIVITIES: Research and writing • publishing.

RESOURCES: Research services.

PERIODICAL: *CIS Anti-Reports.* Magazine. 6 issues/yr.

■ DataCenter, 464 19th St., Oakland, CA 94612. Tel: (415) 835-4692.

"The DataCenter is the leading public-interest library and research center in the United States. Since 1977, the DataCenter's extensive, specialized library and individualized client research program have served the information needs of scholars, journalists, labor and business leaders, and political activists throughout the United States and the world. The center's library contains updated files on more than seven thousand corporations. Its archives include more than 3,500 carefully selected books and directories on politics and economics—with more than three hundred newspapers and magazines clipped daily."

FOCUS: International. Corporate social responsibility • human rights

• militarism, peace, disarmament • nuclear arms and energy • foreign aid and trade • labor • women • political economy • national liberation struggles • transnational corporations • food, hunger, agribusiness • plant shutdowns • economic dislocation.
ACTIVITIES: Library services • publishing.
RESOURCES: Library • research services • books and literature.
PERIODICALS: (1) *Corporate Responsibility Monitor.* (2) *Plant Shutdowns Monitor.*

■ GATT-fly, 11 Madison Ave., Toronto, Ontario M5R 25Z, Canada. Tel: (416) 921-4615.

"GATT-fly is a project of Canadian churches and was founded in 1973 to assist popular groups and progressive church organizations in struggling for economic justice in Canada and in the Third World. GATT-fly pursues these objectives through research, political action, and popular education. GATT-fly seeks to empower those who have been kept powerless by structures of domination. One way in which GATT-fly does this is by helping to build links among popular groups sharing common interests in the struggle for economic justice.

"The name GATT-fly is a play on the words 'gadfly' and the 'General Agreement on Tariffs and Trade' (GATT), which is an international trade forum instituted by industrial capitalist countries to reduce trade barriers and enlarge global markets. To GATT-fly the General Agreement on Tariffs and Trade is a symbol of the global economic structures that work to enrich the few at the expense of the oppression of millions."

FOCUS: International • Canada. International debt • foreign aid and trade • political economy • transnational corporations • social justice • food, hunger, agribusiness • economic self-reliance • Canada-U.S. trade • textile and clothing industries • energy and resource development.
ACTIVITIES: Popular education • constituency education • workshops and seminars • political action • solidarity work • networking • Congressional testimony • media relations • justice and peace ministries • publishing • distribution of print matter • educational research and writing • policy-oriented research and writing.
RESOURCES: Speakers • study-action guides • research services • books and literature.
PERIODICAL: *GATT-fly Report.* Newsletter. 4-5 issues/yr.

■ IBASE (Instituto Brasileiro de Análises Socialis e Econômicas), Rua Vicente Souza 29, 22251, Rio de Janeiro, Brazil. Tel: (021) 286-0348.

"IBASE is a research and consultative nongovernmental development organization (NGDO) whose main objective is the democratic dissemination of reliable socio-economic information to social groups. Founded in 1981, IBASE is a nonprofit, nonpartisan institute. Its constituency is mainly rural and urban unions, church and grassroots groups, educational and community groups, and other NGDOs.

6   ORGANIZATIONS

IBASE's information and studies are circulated through regular publications, books, newsletters, radio programs, and audiovisual kits, as well as through the press. IBASE also provides computer and data communication services and is linked by computer to major NGDOs worldwide."

FOCUS: Third World general • Latin America and Caribbean. Human rights • nuclear arms and energy • foreign aid and trade • labor • international awareness • transnational corporations • social justice • native peoples • food, hunger, agribusiness.

ACTIVITIES: Education • workshops and seminars • legislative action • networking • training of interns • media relations • dissemination of documentation and information • publishing • production of audiovisuals • distribution of print matter • distribution of audiovisuals • research and writing.

RESOURCES: Speakers • study-action guides • research services • books and literature • consultant services • catalog of publications and audiovisuals (in Portuguese).

PERIODICAL: *Boletim Politicas Governamentais.* 11 issues/yr.

■ IDOC International, Via Santa Maria dell'Anima, 30, 00186 Rome, Italy. Tel: 65/68/332.

"The International Documentation and Communication Centre (IDOC) is a non-profit organization with an international membership and international staff. Over a quarter of a century IDOC has built up extensive experience in the collection, analysis, categorization, and dissemination of information coming from more than one thousand organizations, mostly from Third World countries. IDOC's computerized and manual data bases contain more than 70,000 documents dealing with political, economic, and cultural issues and problems of social, human, and ecological liberation."

FOCUS: International. Political economy • human rights • militarism, peace, disarmament • nuclear arms and energy • foreign aid and trade • labor • women • national liberation struggles • transnational corporations • social justice • food, hunger, agribusiness • development • communications technologies.

ACTIVITIES: Library services • popular education • training of interns • dissemination of documentation and information • publishing • research and writing • training in information storage and retrieval.

RESOURCES: Library • research services • books and literature.

PERIODICAL: *IDOC Internazionale.* Magazine. 6 issues/year.

■ Interfaith Center on Corporate Responsibility, 475 Riverside Dr., Rm. 566, New York, NY 10115. Tel: (212) 870-2296.

"The Interfaith Center on Corporate Responsibility is an organization of church and religious institutional investors concerned about the social impact of corporations and the application of social criteria to investments.

"ICCR assists its member agencies to express social responsibility with their investments by (1) facilitating exchange of views and sharing of research and information in an attempt to produce a more effective use of investments to support the social policy and program objectives of the participating groups; (2) developing strategies in which member groups may decide to voluntarily act together; (3) receiving and considering proposals for projects for action by one or more member groups; (4) conducting research on general issues and specific concerns relating to corporate social responsibilities; and (5) providing staff services to the various work groups of the center."

RELIGIOUS AFFILIATION: National Council of Churches.

FOCUS: Third World. Community reinvestment • racism • militarism, peace, disarmament • nuclear arms and energy • women • transnational corporations • social justice • corporate responsibility • domestic equality.

ACTIVITIES: Education • Congressional testimony • training of interns • publishing • research and writing • filing shareholder resolutions.

RESOURCES: Speakers • books and literature.

PERIODICAL: *Corporate Examiner.*

■ International Coalition of Consumers Unions (IOCU), Emmastraat 9, 2595 EG The Hague, The Netherlands. Tel: (070) 47-63-31.

"IOCU was founded in 1960 and has grown from the five founding consumer groups—Consumers' Union (USA), Consumers' Association (UK), Australian Consumers Association, Consumentenbond (Netherlands), Association des Consommateurs (Belgium)—to today's 134 groups scattered through fifty countries.

"The early aims of promoting cooperation in consumer education, information, protection; in research and testing; in acting as a clearinghouse and information center and in representing consumer interests at international bodies like the United Nations—these have been streamlined into three broad areas of work: (1) To bring together and support members, with information and training. (2) To expand the consumer movement, nurturing new and growing groups. (3) To represent the consumer interest at the United Nations and other international fora and to swing the international spotlight onto consumer issues, activating individuals and business into a positive response."

FOCUS: International. Consumer protection • foreign aid and trade • women • political economy • international awareness • transnational corporations • social justice • native peoples • food, hunger, agribusiness.

ACTIVITIES: Political action • constituency education • workshops and seminars • political action • legislative action • networking • training of interns • library services • dissemination of documentation and information • publishing • research and writing • policy-oriented research and writing.

RESOURCES: Speakers • audiovisuals • study-action guides • research services • curriculum guides • books and literature • consultant services • library.

ORGANIZATIONS

PERIODICAL: *IOCU Newsletter.* 10 issues/yr.

■ International Commission for the Coordination of Solidarity among Sugar Workers (ICCSASW), 345 Adelaide St., W., Suite 300, Toronto, Ontario M5V 2S2, Canada. Tel: (416) 597-8454.

"The aims of ICCSASW are to bring together workers in the sugar industry internationally in the interest of promoting and assisting solidarity and solidarity actions and to provide information, network facilities, contacts, and seminars and workshops to this end."

FOCUS: Third World • international. Production of sugar • human rights • foreign aid and trade • labor • transnational corporations • food, hunger, agribusiness.

ACTIVITIES: Workshops and seminars • constituency education • solidarity work • networking • training of interns • library services • dissemination of documentation and information • publishing • distribution of print matter • research and writing.

RESOURCES: Library • research services • consultant services.

PERIODICAL: *Sugar World.*

■ International Labour Organisation, CH-1211 Geneva 22, Switzerland; and 1750 New York Ave, NW, Suite 330, Washington, DC 20006. Tel: (202) 376-2315.

"The International Labour Organisation was created in 1919 and is headquartered in Geneva, Switzerland. It is the only international organization where worker and employer representatives participate directly and on an equal basis with those of governments. This tripartite structure and the international focus of the ILO have remained constant since its founding. The ILO works to eradicate poverty and unemployment in the world, and to strive for social justice and better working and living conditions everywhere. The main methods for accomplishing these goals are international labor standards, technical assistance, and studies and research in the ILO's competent fields."

FOCUS: International. International labor • women workers • development • child labor • occupational safety and health.

ACTIVITIES: Establishment of international labor standards • technical assistance • research and writing.

RESOURCES: Research services • consultant services • publications.

PERIODICAL: *International Labour Reports.*

■ Investor Responsibility Research Center, 1755 Massachusetts Ave., NW, Suite 600, Washington, DC 20036. Tel: (202) 939-6500.

"The Investor Responsibility Research Center, founded in 1972 as an independent, not-for-profit corporation, conducts research and publishes impartial reports on contemporary business and public policy issues that affect corporations and institutional investors. IRRC's work is financed primarily by annual subscription fees paid by more than 350 investing institutions."

FOCUS: International • South Africa. Corporate governance • militarism, peace, disarmament • nuclear arms and energy • labor • transnational corporations • energy and the environment.

ACTIVITIES: Research and writing • publishing.
RESOURCES: Research services • books and literature • consultant services.
PERIODICALS: (1) *News for Investors.* Newsletter. 12 issues/yr. (2) *Corporate Governance Bulletin.* Newsletter. 6 issues/yr. (3) *South Africa Reporter.* Newsletter. 4 issues/yr.

■ Labor Network on Central America, P.O. Box 28014, Oakland, CA 94604. Tel: (415) 272-9951.

"Launched in February 1983, the Labor Network consists of West Coast labor solidarity committees and trade union activists who have been active in bringing the issue of the Central American conflict to the attention of working people in the United States, and to the U.S. labor movement in particular. The network has three goals: (1) To strengthen opposition within labor to all forms of U.S. intervention in Central America. (2) To build long-lasting labor support for the workers' movements of Central America. (3) To deepen U.S. workers' understanding of what is at stake in Central America."

FOCUS: Central America • Nicaragua. Labor.
ACTIVITIES: Popular education • constituency education • solidarity work • networking • media relations • publishing • production of audiovisuals • distribution of print matter • distribution of audiovisuals • research and writing • arranging tours for labor leaders to and from Central America.
RESOURCES: Audiovisuals • books and literature.
PERIODICAL: *Labor Report on Central America.*

■ Labor Research Association, 80 E. 11th St., Suite 634, New York, NY 10003. Tel: (212) 473-1042.

"LRA's customized research services provide unions with comprehensive reports on private and public employers for use in negotiations, organizing drives, and political action campaigns. LRA's reports include detailed analyses of profits, investments, industry trends, board interlocks, budgets, subcontracting arrangements, unorganized shops, National Labor Relations Board records, and contract costs."

FOCUS: United States and international. Political economy • labor • transnational corporations.
ACTIVITIES: Research and writing • constituency education • publishing.
RESOURCES: Publications • research services • consultant services.
PERIODICALS: (1) *Economic Notes.* (2) *Trade Union Advisor.* Newsletter. 26 issues/yr.

■ NARMIC (National Action/Research on the Military Industrial Complex), 1501 Cherry St., Philadelphia, PA 19102. Tel: (212) 241-7175.

"Since its beginning in 1969 NARMIC has challenged the [U.S.] military establishment and its link to the weapons industry. NARMIC's priorities today are research and outreach on human rights and disarmament. Through technical studies, slideshows, radio programs, and articles in U.S. national magazines, members of NARMIC's staff provide facts on a wide range of topics from apartheid to antipersonnel weapons."

FOCUS: International. U.S. military-industrial complex • human rights.

ACTIVITIES: Popular education • dissemination of documentation and information • publishing • research and writing.

RESOURCES: Speakers • audiovisuals • study-action guides • books and literature.

■ Oxfam, 274 Banbury Rd., Oxford OX2 7DZ, England. Tel: (0865) 56777.

"Oxfam is a partnership of people who—regardless of race, sex, religion, or politics—work together for the basic human rights of food, shelter, and reasonable conditions of life. We believe that if shared equitably there are sufficient material resources in the world to enable all people to find fulfilment and to meet basic human needs.

"Oxfam began in 1942 in England as the Oxford Committee for Famine Relief. Today there are five Oxfams—one each in Australia, Belgium, Canada, England, and the United States. All are autonomous, but share one field network.

"Oxfam (U.K.) is engaged in development education, political action, disaster relief, and international aid-giving for social development."

FOCUS: Third World. Human rights • foreign aid and trade • women • international awareness • transnational corporations • social justice • native peoples • food, hunger, agribusiness • development.

ACTIVITIES: Networking • constituency education • legislative action • Congressional testimony • media relations • dissemination of documentation and information • publishing • production of audiovisuals • distribution of print matter • research and writing.

RESOURCES: Speakers • audiovisuals • study-action guides • curriculum guides • books and literature.

PERIODICAL: *Oxfam News.* 4 issues/yr.

■ Pesticide Action Network (PAN) International. Seven regional centers: (1) Environment Liaison Centre, P.O. Box 72461, Nairobi, Kenya. (2) Sudanese Environment Conservation Society, P.O. Box 321, Khartoum, Sudan. (3) Environment et Developpement du Tiers Monde, B.P. 3370, Dakar, Senegal. (4) IOCU, P.O. Box 1045, 10830 Penang, Malaysia. (5) PAN Europe, Stevinstraat 115, 1040 Brussels, Belgium. (6) Fundación Natura, Casilla 253, Quito, Ecuador. (7) PAN North America Regional Center, P.O. Box 610, San Francisco, CA 94101. Tel: (415) 541-9140.

"The Pesticide Action Network (PAN) is an international coalition of citizens' groups and individuals who oppose the unnecessary use and misuse of pesticides and support reliance on safe, sustainable pest control methods. Established in 1982, PAN currently links over 300 organizations in some 50 countries, coordinated by seven Regional Centers.

Because PAN is a network, no individual can direct or represent the entire coalition. Participants are free to pursue their own projects to further PAN's objectives, and benefit from their access to the information and resources of the network.

"The North American regional office (PAN) was set up in 1984 when PAN International launched its 'Dirty Dozen' campaign, targeting twelve pesticides considered particularly hazardous for Third World applications."

POLITICAL AFFILIATION: PAN International.

FOCUS: Third World. Pesticides • environment • health • international awareness • transnational corporations • social justice • native peoples • food, hunger, agribusiness • peoples' struggles to protect themselves.

ACTIVITIES: Popular education • workshops and seminars • political action • solidarity work • networking • dissemination of documentation and information • overseas project support • publishing • distribution of print matter • policy-oriented research and writing • information referrals.

RESOURCES: Speakers • books and literature • consultant services.

PERIODICAL: From PAN N.A.: *Global Pesticide Newsletter* and *Dirty Dozen Campaigner.* Each 3 issues/yr. Newsletters.

■ Philippine Workers Support Committee, P.O. Box 11208, Honolulu, HI 96828.

"The PWSC is a U.S. labor-based network of chapters, committees, and individuals united around the principle of supporting our sisters and brothers in the Philippines in their efforts to gain basic trade union and democratic rights. We are united around five principles: (1) We support the growth of a genuine labor movement in the Philippines. (2) We support the efforts of the Kilusang Mayo Uno (KMU) and others to organize a strong labor movement genuinely representing Filipino workers' interests. (3) We support the right of workers to organize, bargain collectively, and strike. (4) We support the struggle of Filipino workers against all forms of exploitation and oppression. (5) We support the efforts of workers in the United States and around the world to improve their working and living conditions."

FOCUS: Philippines. Labor movement in the Philippines • human rights • national liberation struggles.

ACTIVITIES: Study tours for labor leaders • constituency education • solidarity work • networking • media relations • dissemination of documentation and information • publishing.

RESOURCES: Speakers • books and literature • consultant services.

PERIODICAL: *Philippine Labor Alert.*

■ Taskforce on the Churches and Corporate Responsibility, 129 St. Clair Ave. W., Toronto, Ontario M4J 4Z2, Canada. Tel: (416) 923-1758.

"TCCR is a national ecumenical coalition of the major Canadian Christian churches. It assists the member churches in implementing policies adopted by the churches in the area of corporate social responsibility. Issues related to Southern Africa, Latin America (particularly Chile), and environment and energy in Canada are the current concerns of the Taskforce."

RELIGIOUS AFFILIATION: Interdenominational.

FOCUS: Third World • Latin America and Caribbean • Asia and Pacific • South Africa • Namibia. Human rights • nuclear arms and energy • foreign aid and trade • transnational corporations • environment and energy.

ACTIVITIES: Parliamentary testimony • constituency education • legislative action • research and writing • educational research and writing.

RESOURCES: Literature.

■ Third World Studies Center, University of the Philippines, P.O. Box 210, Palma Hall, Rm. 428, Diliman, Quezon City, Philippines. Tel: 97-6061.

"The center was created in 1976 under the office of the dean of the College of Arts and Sciences of the University of the Philippines in response to the need for a program of studies and research that critically analyzes the problems of underdevelopment in the Third World and of the Philippines in particular. The TWSC maintains a resource collection and public reading room and carries on a program of research and publications, seminars and lectures, as well as audiovisual presentations."

FOCUS: Third World. Human rights • militarism, peace, disarmament • nuclear arms and energy • foreign aid and trade • labor • women • political economy • international awareness • national liberation struggles • transnational corporations • social justice • native peoples • food, hunger, agribusiness.

ACTIVITIES: Popular education • workshops and seminars • political action • networking • training of interns • media relations • library services • dissemination of documentation and information • justice and peace ministries • publishing • production of audiovisuals • distribution of print matter • distribution of audiovisuals • research and writing • policy-oriented research and writing.

RESOURCES: Speakers • audiovisuals • study-action guides • curriculum guides • books and literature • library.

PERIODICAL: *Kasarinlan*. Magazine. 6 issues/yr.

■ Trade Union International Research and Education Group (TUIREG), Ruskin College, Walton St., Oxford OX1 2HE, England. Tel: (0865) 54599.

"TUIREG is a group of trade unionists who are committed to working for development through educational activities in the United Kingdom and throughout the world. Collectively their experience covers workers' education, cooperative education, educational methods, writing, research communications, industrial relations, filmmaking and video production, and development economics."

FOCUS: Third World and international. Development • transnational corporations • international labor • occupational health and safety • political economy.
ACTIVITIES: Research and writing • popular education • training • production of audiovisuals.
RESOURCES: Research services • literature • audiovisuals.

■ Transnational Corporations Research Project, Faculty of Geography, University of Sydney, Sydney, NSW 2006, Australia.

"The TCRP was established in 1975 with the objective of providing information on and initiating research into a wide range of aspects of foreign direct investment and the activities of transnational corporations in Australia, South East Asia, and the Pacific.

"There are three main areas of work: (1) The publication of books, research monographs, working papers, and data papers. (2) The building up of a library of books, articles, and relevant journals located [at the University of Sydney]. (3) The establishment of relationships with similar research projects in other countries."

FOCUS: Global • Asia and Pacific. Transnational corporations • foreign aid and trade • labor • native peoples • food, hunger, agribusiness.
ACTIVITIES: Workshops and seminars • library services • dissemination of documentation and information • publishing • research and writing.
RESOURCES: Research services • books and literature • consultant services • library.

■ Transnationals Information Exchange, c/o Transnational Institute, 20 Paulus Potterstraat, 1071 DA Amsterdam, Netherlands. Tel: (020) 66-42-191.

"Funded by the World Council of Churches and the Transnational Institute, TIE is a network of some forty action/research groups and workers' organizations. These include trade unions, shop stewards' committees, Third World groups, church organizations, labor research centers, and some local government economic planning departments.

"TIE exists in order to (1) enable the exchange of information and experience between action and research groups working on transnational corporations, mainly in Europe, but also between such groups in Europe and those in the rest of the world; (2) develop a similar dialogue between such groups and trade unions and other workers' organization in order that the type of information produced may be of most help to those whom it most affects and so that the contacts between workers' representatives from transnational corporations' subsidiaries in different countries may be strengthened and more fully informed; and (3) promote discussion and debate on the effects of growing corporate power both within Europe and other parts of the world, in order to encourage positive and practical alternatives within the labor movement."

FOCUS: International. Transnational corporations • human rights •

militarism, peace, disarmament • nuclear arms and energy • foreign aid and trade • labor • women • political economy • international awareness • national liberation struggles • social justice • native peoples • food, hunger, agribusiness • auto industry • information technology.

ACTIVITIES: Research and writing • constituency education • workshops and seminars • political action • legislative action • solidarity work • networking • Congressional testimony • media relations • overseas project support • publishing • production of audiovisuals • distribution of print matter • policy-oriented research and writing.

RESOURCES: Speakers • books and literature.

■ United Nations Centre on Transnational Corporations, United Nations Bldg., Rm. DC21344, New York, NY 10017. Tel: (212) 963-3897.

"The Centre on Transnational Corporations serves as a focal point for all matters related to transnational corporations and acts as secretariat to the UN's Commission on Transnational Corporations. Its objectives are (1) to further the understanding of the nature of the transnational corporations and of their political, legal, economic, and social effects on home and host countries and in international relations, particularly between developed and developing countries; (2) to secure effective international arrangements aimed at enhancing the contribution of transnational corporations to national development goals and worldwide economic growth while controlling and eliminating their negative effects; and (3) to strengthen the negotiating capacity of host countries, in particular the developing countries, in their dealing with transnational corporations."

FOCUS: Global. Transnational corporations.

ACTIVITIES: Policy-oriented research and writing • training of interns • library services • dissemination of documentation and information • publishing.

RESOURCES: Speakers • books and literature • library.

PERIODICAL: *The CTC Reporter.*

SUPPLEMENTARY LIST OF ORGANIZATIONS

AFRICA

Pan African Women Trade Unionists, P.O. Box 61068, Nairobi, Kenya.

ASIA AND PACIFIC

Alternative News and Features, A 1/9 Model Town, Delhi 110009, India.

Asian Bureau Australia, 173 Royal Parade, Parkville, Victoria 3052, Australia. Tel: 347-8595.

Asian Women Workers' Center, 2-3-18-34 Nishi-Waseda, Shinjuku-ku, Tokyo 169, Japan.
Australian Consumers' Association, 57 Carrington Rd., Marrickville, NSW 2204, Australia. Tel: (02) 558-0099.
Campaign against Foreign Control in New Zealand, P.O. Box 2258, Christchurch, New Zealand.
Center for Labor Studies, Gonzalez Bldg., 3rd floor, 1186 Quezon Blvd., Quezon City, Philippines.
Center for Studies in Social Sciences, 10 Lake Terrace, Calcutta, India. Tel: 95425.
Center for the Progress of Peoples, 48 Princess Margaret Rd., 1st floor, Homantin, Kowloon, Hongkong. Tel: (3) 7145123.
Centre for Society and Religion, 281 Deans Rd., Colombo 10, Sri Lanka. Tel: 595425.
Christian Conference of Asia, Urban-Rural Mission, 57 Peking Rd., 5th floor, Kowloon, Hongkong.
Citizen's Alliance for Consumer Protection, Maligaya Bldg., 430 El Rodriguez Ave., Quezon City, Philippines.
EILER (Ecumenical Institute for Labor Education and Research), P.O. Box SM 437, 2806 Manila, Philippines.
ESCAP/UNCTC Joint Unit on Transnational Corporations, UN Building, Rajadamnern Ave., Bangkok 2, Thailand. Tel: 2829161200.
IBON Documentation Center, P.O. Box SM-447, Sta. Mesa, Manila, Philippines.
Indian Institute of Public Administration, Indraprestha Estate, Ring Rd., New Delhi 110002, India.
KOGAI, Dept. of Urban Engineering, University of Tokyo, 7-3-3 Hongo, Bunkyo-ku, Tokyo 113, Japan. Tel: (03) 812-2111, ext. 7411.

16 ORGANIZATIONS

Pacific-Asia Resource Center, C.P.O. Box 5250, Tokyo International, Tokyo, Japan. Tel: 291-5901.
Peninsula Watchdog, P.O. Box 74, Coromandel, New Zealand.
Rodo Joho, 5-13-12 Shinbashi, Minatoku, Tokyo, Japan.
Save Aramoana Campaign, 320 George St., Dunedin, New Zealand.
Transnational Co-operative Ltd. (TNC Workers Research), G.P.O. Box 161, Sydney, NSW 2001, Australia. Tel: 692-1122.
Transnational Research—New Zealand, P.O. Box 10180, Wellington, New Zealand.

EUROPE

Altinform, Kloosverstraat 63-I, 2000 Antwerpen, Belgium. Tel: 234-2113.
Arbetarorslsens Internationella Centrum (AIC), Barnbusgatan 16, S-105 53 Stockholm, Sweden.
BASTA!, P.O. Box 1552, Nijmegen, Netherlands.
Bern Declaration, C.P. 81, 1.00 Lausanne 9, Switzerland.
Bern Declaration, Gartenhofstrasse 27, CH-8004 Zurich, Switzerland.
Birmingham Trade Union Group for World Development, c/o W.E.A., 9/11 Digbeth, Birmingham B5 6BH, England.
CAITS (Centre for Alternative Industrial and Technological Systems), c/o Polytechnic of North London, Holloway Rd., London NY 8DB, England. Tel: 607 2789.
Campaign against Arms Trade, 5 Caledonian Rd., London N1 9DX, England.
CEDETIM, 14 rue de Nanteuil, 75014 Paris, France.
Centre d'Information Organisation Internationale Catholique, 1, Rue de Varembe, 1211 Geneva 20, Switzerland. Tel: 34 14 65.
Centre Tricontinental (CETRI), Av. Ste. Gertrude 5, B-1348 Ottignies, Louvain-la-Neuve, Belgium.
CEREM (Centre d'Etudes et de Recherches sur l'Enterprise Multinationale), 124 rue Henri-Barbusse, 93308 Aubervilliers CEDEX, France.
CETIM, 37, quai Wilson, 1201 Geneva, Switzerland. Tel: 31 59 63.
CIDOB (Centre d'Infromacio i Documentacio Internacional), Lluria 125, 1er, Barcelona 37, Spain.
Coventry Workshop, 38 Binley Rd., Coventry CV3 IJA, England. Tel: (0203) 27772.
Dias, Singel 137, Amsterdam, Netherlands.
Ecumenical Development Week, Gottgatan 3, S-752 22 Uppsala, Sweden.
ELTSA (End Loans to Southern Africa), c/o 467 Caledonian Rd., London N7 9BE, England.
European Environmental Bureau, 29 Rue Vautier, B 1040 Brussels, Belgium. Tel: (02) 647-1099.
European Trade Union Institute (ETUI), Boulevard de l'Imperatrice

66 (Bte. 4), 1000 Brussels, Belgium. Tel: (02) 512-3070.
Gewekschaftliche Einheit Alternative, Wipplingestrasse 23, Vienna 1010, Austria.
GRESEA-Oxfam Group, Waverse Steenweg 36, 1050 Brussels, Belgium. Tel: (0) 21 511-3312.
Health Action International (HAI), c/o IOCU, Emmastraat 9, 2595 EG The Hague, The Netherlands. Tel: (070) 47 63 31.
ICAS (International Workers Solidarity Center), Tweelingenstraat 74 bus 2, 2018 Antwerpen, Belgium. Tel: (03) 235-2870.
IEPALA, Villalar 3, Madrid 1, Spain. Tel: (1) 403-0300.
INDOC, P.O. Box 11250, 2391 EG Leiden, Netherlands.
Informationsdienst Dritte Welt, Monbijoustrasse 31, CH-3001 Bern, Switzerland.
International Baby Food Action Network (IBFAN), c/o GIFA, Case 157, 1211 Geneva 19, Switzerland. Tel: (41-22) 989164.
International Foundation for Development Alternatives (IFDA), 2, Place du Marche, CH-1260 Nyon, Switzerland.
International Restructuring Education Network Europe (IRENE), c/o Centrum voor Ontwikkelingssamenwerking, Korvelseweg 127, 5025 JC Tilburg, Netherlands. Tel: (013) 351523.
IWGIA (International Work Group for Indigenous Affairs), Fiolstraede 10, DK-1171 Copenhagen K, Denmark. Tel: (01) 124 724.
Kammer fur Arbeiter und Angestellte fur Wien, Prinz Eugenstrasse 20-22, A-1041 Vienna, Austria.
Manchester Employment Research Group, 300 Oxford Rd., Manchester M13 9N5, England. Tel: (061) 273-8717.
Northwest Transnationals Project (NWTP), 300 Oxford Rd., Manchester M13 9N5, England. Tel: (061) 273-8717.
OSACI, Prins Hendrik Kade 48, 1012 AC Amsterdam, Netherlands.
Partizans, 218 Liverpool Rd., London N1, England.
Raw Materials Group, P.O. Box 81519, S10282 Stockholm, Sweden. Tel: (468) 42 75 77.
Research Group MOL, Passeerdergracht 32, 1016 XH Amsterdam, Netherlands. Tel: (020) 223-493.
Research Policy Institute, University of Lund, Magistratsvagen 55 N, S-222 44 Lund, Sweden. Tel: (046) 10 70 00.
Seeds Action Network, c/o CIDOB, Lluria 125, 08037 Barcelona, Spain.
SOBE, Kruisstraat 82, 5612 CK Eindhoven, Netherlands.
Social Audit Limited, P.O. Box 111, London NW1 8XG, England. Tel: (01) 734-1561.
SOLAGRAL, 12, Ave. de la Soeur Rosalie, 75013 Paris, France.
Third World Action Group, Postfach 1007, 3001 Bern, Switzerland.
Voedings Bond FNV, Postbus 9750, 3506 GT Utrecht, Netherlands.
War on Want, 467 Caledonian Rd., London N7 9BE, England. Tel: (01) 609-0211.
War on Want International, Women's Group, 300 Oxford Rd., Manchester M13 9N5, England. Tel: (061) 273-7767.

18 ORGANIZATIONS

Wereldsolidariteit Group, V.Z.W., Wetstraat 121, 1040 Brussels, Belgium. Tel: (02) 735-6050.

Women and Work Hazards Group, c/o British Society for Social Responsibility in Science, 9 Poland St., London WC1, England.

Women Working Worldwide, c/o War on Want, 476 Caledonian Rd., London N7 9BE, England. Tel: (01) 609-0211.

LATIN AMERICA AND CARIBBEAN

CAPPS (Centro de Assessoria Pesquisas e Publicacoes Sindicais), Rua Major Diogo 135, Bela Vista, CEP 01324, São Paulo, Brazil. Tel: (011) 32-8629.

CEDAL, Avenido Guzman Blanco 465, Oficina 402, Lima, Peru. Tel: (14) 234349.

Center on Transnational Culture, Apartado 270031, Lima 27, Peru. Tel: 466-332.

DESCO, Avenida Salaverry 1945, Lima, Peru. Tel: (14) 724712.

DIEESE (Inter-Union Department for Statistics and Socio-Economic Research), Rua das Carmelitas 149-3, Andar, Brazil. Tel: (011) 32-4823.

ILET (Institutu Latinoamericano de Estudios Transnacionales), Apartado Postal 85-025, Mexico 20 DF, Mexico.

IPAL (Instituto para América Latina), Apartado 270031, Lima 27, Peru. Tel: 466-322.

NORTH AMERICA

American Labor Education Center, 1835 Kilbourne Pl., NW, Washington, DC 20010. Tel: (202) 387-6780 or 462-8925.

Center for Alternative Mining Development Policy, 210 Avon St., No. 9, La Crosse, WI 54603. Tel: (608) 784-4399.

The Center for Ethics and Corporate Policy, 637 South Dearborn St., Chicago, IL 60605. Tel: (312) 922-1512.

East-West Centre Project on Women and Transnational Corporations, East-West Culture Learning Institute, 1777 East-West Rd., Honolulu, HI 96848. Tel: (808) 944-7555.

INFACT, 310 E. 38 St., Minneapolis, MN 55409. Tel: (612) 825-6837.

Institute for Labor Education and Research, 853 Broadway, Rm. 207, New York, NY 10003.

Institute for Policy Studies/Transnational Institute, 1601 Connecticut Ave., NW, Washington, DC 20009. Tel: (202) 234-9382.

Interfaith Action for Economic Justice, 110 Maryland Ave., NE, Washington, DC 20002. Tel: (202) 543-2800.

Labor Campaign for Unions in El Salvador, % Local 111-IBT, 111 Broadway, Suite 800, New York, NY 10006. Tel: (212) 732-5411.

Labor Committee on the Middle East, P.O. Box 421429, San Francisco, CA 94142-1429.

ORGANIZATIONS 19

Latin American Working Group, P.O. Box 2207, Sta. P, Toronto, Ontario M5S 2T2, Canada. Tel: (416) 533-4221

Midwest Center for Labor Research, 3411 W. Diversey Ave., Suite 14, Chicago, IL 60647. Tel: (312) 278-5418.

NACLA, 475 Riverside Dr., Rm. 454, New York, NY 10115. Tel: (212) 870-3146.

Nationwide Women's Program, Project on Women and Global Corporations, 1501 Cherry St., Philadelphia, PA 19102. Tel: (215) 241-7000.

Pacific Studies Center, 222B View St., Mountain View, CA 94041. Tel: (415) 969-1545.

The Resource Center, P.O. Box 4506, Albuquerque, NM 87196. Tel: (505) 266-5009.

Social Investment Forum, 711 Atlantic Ave., Boston, MA 02111. Tel: (617) 423-6655.

INFORMATION SOURCES

In addition to the TIE resource guide mentioned above in the introduction to this chapter another source of information on organizations concerned with the impact of transnational corporations is the *Consumer Directory* published annually by the International Organization of Consumers Unions, Emmastraat 9, 2595 EG The Hague, The Netherlands. The 1987 edition (248pp., $18) listed and described twelve international organizations (e.g., the UN Centre on Transnational Corporations) and consumer groups in more than ninety countries around the world.

The guides and reference books listed in chapter 2 below should be consulted for additional lists of organizations. See also the organizations whose periodicals are described in chapter 3.

ORGANIZATIONS

We have intentionally omitted entries on official trade unions around the world because information on such organizations is readily available in other reference books such as F. John Harper's *Trade Unions of the World* (see books chapter below). Three major global labor organizations are excellent sources of information and are, therefore, worth including. They are:

- International Confederation of Free Trade Unions (ICFTU), 37-41 rue Montagne aux Herbes Potagères, 1000 Brussels, Belgium. Tel: (2) 217 8085.
- World Confederation of Labor (WCL), 33 rue de Trèves, 1040 Brussels, Belgium, Tel: (2) 230-6295.
- World Federation of Trade Unions (WFTU), Vinohradská 10, 12147 Prague 2, Czechoslovakia. Tel: 235-35-65.

See the publications from **Third World Resources** described in the preface to this directory. The "Feature Insert" in the summer 1987 issue of *Third World Resources* contained resources on transnational corporations and labor. The spring 1987 edition described reference guides — such as those from Human Rights Internet (Cambridge, Mass.) — that will prove of value in locating other organizations concerned with transnational corporations and labor. Send a stamped, self-addressed envelope to Third World Resources, 464 19 St., Oakland, CA 94612, USA, for a free copy of either or both of the 4-page guides.

2

Books

This chapter is divided into three parts: annotated entries, supplementary list of books, and sources of additional information on books related to transnational corporations and labor.

The part called **annotated entries** is divided into four sections: general; bibliographies and guides; directories and reference books; and United Nations publications. Information in the annotated entries is given in the following order: author(s) or editor(s); title; place of publication; publisher; date of publication; number of pages; price; keyword description of format; description of content.

Books in the **supplementary list** (pp. 59–66) are grouped under these headings: general; Africa; Asia and Pacific; Latin America and Caribbean; and Middle East. Information in the entries in this section is given in the following order: author(s) or editor(s); title; place of publication; publisher; date of publication; number of pages; price.

The appearance of a book in the supplementary list does not imply that it is necessarily less noteworthy than the books in the annotated section. Some books appear in the supplementary list only because they were received too late for inclusion in the annotated section or if we were unable to obtain a review copy of the publication.

The part entitled **information sources** (p. 66) provides the names of directories and guides that contain the titles of other books related to transnational corporations and labor. All titles are integrated into the titles index at the back of this directory. The addresses for most of the publishers and distributors appear in the organizations index. (We have omitted addresses when we judged that a particular book could be easily acquired through a bookstore or library.) We have given the North American distributors for books published outside the United States. Readers in other countries should check with publishers for local distributors. All books are paperback unless we indicate that they are clothbound.

ANNOTATED ENTRIES

General

■ Alschuler, Lawrence R. *Multinationals and Maldevelopment: Alternative Development Strategies in Argentina, the Ivory Coast, and Korea.* New York: St. Martin's Press, 1988. 218pp. $37.50. Cloth. Notes, figures, index, references, tables.

The question—in its most basic and academically precise formulation—is: does multinational presence *vary* with economic growth and stagnation? Less rigorously put: does the involvement of multinational corporations in a developing nation's economy enhance opportunities for economic growth, equality, liberty, and personal growth or does it engender economic stagnation, inequality, repression, and alienation?

Political scientist Lawrence Alschuler searches for answers to this question by studying three Third World nations—Argentina, the Ivory Coast, and Korea—from 1946 to 1976. These three countries were selected for examination because they were judged to be "maximally different" (in terms of size, location, colonial heritage, etc.). The differences set in bold relief whatever points of commonality are discovered vis-à-vis multinational corporations. "What is tenable for these countries," Alschuler believes, "is likely to be valid generally for much of the Third World."

In chapter 1 Alschuler defines his terms and constructs an elaborate research model. He then uses this model to analyze each of the three countries chapter-by-chapter: Argentina ("from egalitarian stagnation to authoritarian growth"), Ivory Coast ("libertarian growth without equality"), and Korea ("authoritarian growth with equality").

In chapter 5 the author draws the findings from each of the country studies and concludes that "the principal explanatory condition for maldevelopment [is] the development strategy of the state." "Multinational strategies," Alschuler explains, "reinforce the impact of the state's development strategy on maldevelopment without having their own qualitatively distinct and independent impact."

■ Barry, Tom, Beth Wood, and Deb Preusch. *The Other Side of Paradise: Foreign Control in the Caribbean.* New York: Grove Press, 1984. 405pp. $9.95. Map, glossary, index, notes, statistical tables, tables.

The thrust of this readable study is to demonstrate how the increasing flow of corporate investments into the Caribbean is failing to better in any way the condition of the majority of the people in the region. In fact, foreign control in the Caribbean frequently exacerbates local social and economic problems. The authors cite many examples, among them: U.S. firms doing business in the Virgin Islands are legally permitted to dump human and manufacturing wastes directly into the sea; unregulated foreign-owned manufacturing has made Puerto Rico the most polluted island in the Caribbean; eighty-one cents of every tourist dollar finds its way back to the United States from the Bahamas; and only two of every three children born in Haiti survive their first year — despite massive amounts of U.S. aid and the infusion of substantial corporate investments.

The first part of the book is given to industry surveys (including agriculture, tourism, manufacturing, finance, and mining), while the second part examines the external relations and internal situation of each country in the region — from the Netherlands Antilles to St. Vincent and the Grenadines.

The authors' writing style is inviting and their documentation is copious and clearly presented. Chapters on French, British, and Canadian relations with the nations of the Caribbean expand the relevance of the book beyond just the United States.

■ Bergquist, Charles. *Labor in Latin America: Comparative Essays on Chile, Argentina, Venezuela, and Colombia.* Stanford, Calif.: Stanford University Press, 1986. 398pp. $39.50. Maps, figures, index, notes, photographs, tables.

"Workers, especially those engaged in production for export," writes Charles Bergquist, "have played a determining role in the modern history of Latin American societies. Their struggle for material well-being and control over their own lives has fundamentally altered the direction of national political evolution and the pattern of economic development in the countries of the [Latin American] region."

The author, Professor of History and Director of International Studies at Duke University, explains how and why this opening statement — the central thesis of *Labor in Latin America* — flies in the face of his personal experience of organized labor and his academic studies of U.S. and Latin American history. "Through concrete experience and formal education," Bergquist writes, "I learned to discount the role of labor in the history of the modern world." Bergquist describes experiences that led him to reevaluate the importance ascribed to labor in popular and academic understandings. These experiences ranged from Peace Corps work in rural areas of Latin America to involvement in the anti-Vietnam War movement.

This work represents Bergquist's attempt to elevate labor to the "central place" he believes it merits in the national histories of four Latin American countries and — by extension — in other nations as well. "If the essays in this volume," Bergquist writes, "succeed in showing that workers' struggles fundamentally influenced the course of the national histories of Chile, Argentina, Venezuela, and Colombia, if they demonstrate how those struggles illuminate the central issues in the historiography of these nations, if they unveil the democratic goals of working people and the complexity of the reasons for their failure to realize fully their aspirations in the past, they reveal to us concretely how working people make their own history."

Labor in Latin America opens with a chapter on "Modern Latin American Historiography and the Labor Movement" and then provides chapter-length studies of each of the four countries. The book closes with cautionary statements about the "limits" of this study and speculation about the "promise" of the author's approach for labor studies elsewhere. Given the path-breaking character of *Labor in Latin America*, a bibliography would have added immensely to the value of this book.

■ Branford, Sue, and Bernardo Kucinski. *Debt Squads: The U.S., the Banks, and Latin America.* London and New Jersey: Zed Books, 1988. 142pp. $15. Glossary, figures, index, maps, notes, tables.

In the five-year period, 1976-1981, Latin America borrowed $272.9 billion on the world market. The authors of *Debt Squads* illustrate the magnitude of Latin America's debt problem by detailing what happened to that enormous sum. "Almost all (91.6 per cent) of this money went straight back to the banks: in debt-servicing (62.2 per cent); in other outflows, particularly capital flight (20.5 per cent); and in the building up of international reserves (8.9 per cent). Only a tiny proportion—8.4 per cent ($22.9 billion)—was brought into [Latin America], possibly (but not always) to be used in development projects."

In *Debt Squads* journalists Branford and Kucinski examine the role of international banks in creating and perpetuating Latin America's debt crisis. They study the crisis "from the point of view of ordinary Latin Americans, who reaped few, if any, benefits from the huge borrowing, but are today being forced to pay for it, through either their labour or their poverty." The authors describe the human dimensions of Latin America's debt burden, concluding that "the scale of the confiscated income and the fall in living standards and investment have been dramatic, far greater than is suggested by the bankers' figures...."

The authors argue that the Latin American debt crisis arose as part of a crisis in the U.S. economy in the 1960s and was continued by "two leading characters": "the international bankers, with their chaotic euromarket, the result of American expansion, and the dictators of the debt, the generals who, trained by Washington and encouraged by the local elites, came to power across much of the [Latin American] continent."

Both Branford and Kucinski, the latter a Brazilian journalist, have written for international financial magazines and newspapers. They analyze and write about Latin America's debt crisis with honesty and rationality. At the same time, they state, "we have not given up our right—indeed, we see it as our obligation—to take a position, as indeed we do in the conclusion when we say that, given the right external conditions, Latin America should default on its debt." "Unlike those who say that the Latin American people are under a moral obligation to honour the debt," Branford and Kucinski conclude, "we say that their only obligation is to stop paying it."

■ Bunster, Ximena, and Elsa M. Chaney. *Sellers and Servants: Working Women in Lima, Peru.* New York and London: Praeger Publishers,

1985. 258pp. $35.95. Cloth. Glossary, bibliography, index, photographs, tables.

Nearly one-third of all employed women in Latin America are sellers or servants. In Lima, Peru—the site of this study—nearly one-half of the employed women work in those occupations. The occupations are critical subjects of study not only because of their numerical importance but also because those jobs occupy the lower tiers of the traditional labor market both in terms of wages and conditions of work. Yet, until this study, little was known about the women who labored as sellers and servants in Latin America.

"Why are so many Third World women and men still earning their livelihood in such seemingly haphazard fashion, after more than two decades of intensive development activity?" the authors ask. And what about the evidence that shows that even when Third World women do get jobs in the modern sector, they are condemned to work in crowded, unsanitary, and noisy conditions at repetitive jobs in the branches of transnational corporations?

Using a pioneer "talking pictures" interviewing technique, Bunster and Chaney (the former a Chilean anthropologist and the latter an international development specialist) have amassed a fascinating body of information on poor working women in Lima and—it is to be hoped—have made a considerable contribution to the emancipation of the subjects of their study and of women in other Third World cities as well.

■ Caporaso, James A., ed. *A Changing International Division of Labor.* Boulder, Colo.: Lynne Rienner Publishers, 1986. 250pp. $26.50. Cloth. Tables, bibliography, figures, index.

Why a peanut farmer in Nigeria earns one-tenth the income of a sheepherder in New Zealand is just one of the many questions about the international role of labor—and about contemporary divisions between rich and poor in the global system—that gave rise to the compilation of the articles in this second volume of the *International Political Economy Yearbook.*

In his preface, lengthy opening chapter, and concluding essay, the editor clearly defines his terms and situates labor within the process of international production and within the larger society.

Five additional chapters take up themes such as the consequences of automation in the North for developing nations' exports, the changing internationalization strategies of multinational firms, and Australia and the international division of labor in the Asia-Pacific region.

The final chapter of the book identifies and analyzes what Caporaso believes to be "the most salient trends relevant to labor and production in general." These are: the migration of capital from core to periphery (i.e., from industrialized to developing nations), the rise of global production sharing, the peripheralization of labor in core countries, the growing reliance on female labor in both periphery and core, and the growing scope of the use of industrial policy.

Caporaso's work closes with a 21-page bibliography of books and articles—as up-to-date as 1987.

For a related study, see *Labor in the Capitalist World Economy*, edited by Charles Bergquist (Beverly Hills, Calif.: Sage, 1984).

- Chaney, Elsa M., and Mary Garcia Castro, eds. *Muchachas No More: Household Workers in Latin America and the Caribbean.* Philadelphia: Temple University Press, 1989. 486pp. $34.95. Cloth. Bibliography, figures.

A significant proportion, 20 percent, of all the women in the paid workforce of Latin American and the Caribbean are domestic workers. Little value is put on their work and little notice is paid to them. A survey in Peru showed that women considered only two other occupations less desirable than domestic work: prostitution and begging.

This book documents the struggle of women domestic workers for recognition of their role and their rights. As the title states, these women no longer see themselves as "girls" (*muchachas*), but as professional workers.

The editors have purposely chosen articles that are descriptive rather than theoretical. They see this whole area as a "new field of research [that] first needs to establish a solid base upon which theorizing can be built." The articles come from and describe workers and their situations throughout the region (Jamaica, Brazil, Colombia, Peru, the Caribbean, the West Indies, Mexico, Chile, Cuba), present a historical survey (from Spanish colonial times), and treat many themes, including the relation of feminism to domestic work, the *patrona* and the worker, domestic workers' organizations, and the union movement. Five of the authors themselves are domestic workers.

Margo Smith's bibliography is noteworthy. She describes a computerized database linking workers across cultures and provides twenty-four pages of articles, studies, and books related to this important topic.

- Chapkis, Wendy, and Cynthia Enloe, eds. *Of Common Cloth: Women in the Global Textile Industry.* Washington, D.C.: Institute for Policy Studies, 1983. 141pp. $5.95.

This book is the fruit of a three-day meeting held at the Transnational Institute in Amsterdam; the meeting brought together women from several First and Third World countries—researchers, trade unionists, activists, and others—"to exchange experiences and information on the fast-changing global textile industry." Basic to the meeting was the knowledge that women supply much of the labor power—in unskilled, low-paid, deadend jobs—in one of the world's "oldest and most fundamental industries," the textile industry, and the belief that women need to get a "clearer understanding of how their exploitation is rooted in the structures and mythologies of sexism."

In compiling this reader, the editors explain, "we had before us the images of women—separated by country and culture—each working her bit of fabric." "This book," they state, "is intended to take those separate experiences and begin to weave them into a piece of common cloth."

Of Common Cloth addresses such topics as the myths about women as workers (that they are docile, that they don't need to earn as much as men, that they don't mind monotony, that they have naturally nimble fingers); women's place in the international division of labor ("cheap labor" means women's labor); the patriarchal thread running through the history of the textile industry; conditions in India, the Philippines, Mexico, and South Korea; women as workers in the home and in the factory; technology; occupational safety; racism; organizing strikes and strategies; and union-busting.

Important issues are raised, but they are not developed. *Of Common Cloth* merely whets one's appetite as it introduces issues related to the role of women in the textile industry and in labor in general. The resource section supplies useful suggestions for further reading and action.

■ Christian Conference of Asia, Urban Rural Mission. *Minangkabau: Story of People vs. TNCs in Asia.* Hongkong: CCA, URM, 1981. 154pp. $2. Maps, bibliography, illustrations, photographs.

This book takes its title from an Indonesian folk tale that expresses the hope and aspirations of people who struggle against the unjust demands of tyrannical oppressors. The Urban Rural Mission division of the Christian Conference of Asia produced *Minangkabau* in order to inspire people to action vis-à-vis transnational corporations (TNCs). For "in the final analysis," writes CCA-URM secretary A. George Ninan, "it is the people—victims—who have to rise up and defend their rights, for the very process of such a rising up itself is a movement towards a just and creative society."

Using case studies, *Minangkabau* describes in simple terms the motives and mechanisms of West German, Japanese, U.S., and other transnational corporations in Asia and then offers as counterpoint successful stories of resistance to the TNCs by industrial and agricultural workers in Malaysia, Hongkong, South Korea, and other countries in the region.

■ Christian Conference of Asia, Urban Rural Mission. *Struggling to Survive: Women Workers in Asia.* Hongkong: CCA, URM, 1983. 162pp. $1. Maps, illustrations, photographs, tables.

This short book contains stories of Asian women who are industrial workers in Hongkong, Thailand, Malaysia, Sri Lanka, and the Philippines. Case studies describe the low wages, long working hours, and inhumane treatment that are the lot of these women. Each section opens with a short essay that puts the stories into a national and historical context.

■ Clarke, Robert, and Richard Swift, eds. Development Education Centre. *Ties That Bind: Canada and the Third World.* Toronto: Between the Lines, 1982. 240pp. Notes, appendixes, bibliography, illustrations, tables.

This study analyzes transnational corporations in the context of worldwide development and underdevelopment and of Canada's role in the global economic system.

The editors—both staff members of the Development Education Centre in Toronto—identify five interrelated areas that they believe are key to an understanding of international development: "the question of how Canadians perceive the Third World and what this means; the political geography of the North-South debate and the 'New International Economic Order'...; the role of transnational corporations; foreign aid; [and] militarism." Richard Swift, Brian Tomlinson, Robert Carty, and Michael Klare each, respectively, wrote a chapter on the first, second, fourth, or fifth topic. Labor educator D'Arcy Martin handled chapter 3: "Facing the Octopus—The Transnational Corporation."

Martin provides a popular introduction to the subject of transnational corporations, offering numerous examples of how our everyday lives are inextricably tied to workers in Third World nations. His aim is not to do away with transnational corporations, but "to identify the sources of their strength, and to explore options for holding them more socially accountable." Canada has a big stake in debating the issue of corporate social accountability, Martin explains, "both because [Canada] acts as host to many foreign-based companies and because increasingly its economy is being used as the home for companies, in areas such as mining and banking, which are active on a world scale."

Martin recognizes that *accountability* can be a buzzword that lulls activists—Canadians and others—into thinking that this consumer boycott or that shareholder action is going to right all that is wrong with transnational corporations. "Ultimately," he states, "the tension [between transnational corporations and 'the rest of us'] is a political one, since present inequalities among nations and within Canada itself have provided the motor for transnational expansion. Any serious efforts to hold the transnationals socially accountable must deal with these inequalities." Martin's chapter is an excellent introductory essay on transnational corporations and on the varieties of ways in which activists in host and home countries are dealing with these political inequalities.

■ Cohen, Robin, Peter C. W. Gutkind, and Phyllis Brazier, eds. *Peasants and Proletarians: The Struggles of Third World Workers.* New York: Monthly Review Press, 1979. 505pp. $16. Cloth. Notes, bibliography, tables.

Editors Cohen, Gutkind, and Brazier compiled this reader in order to establish "a corpus of shared knowledge and understanding between scholars and activists interested in the study of workers in Africa, Asia, and Latin America, and between workers from the three continents [living] in the advanced capitalist countries and their... counterparts [in their countries of origin]." Though dated to some degree, the reader remains a unique and valuable reference for contemporary studies of the struggles of Third World workers. (An example of the datedness of the book is the editors' insistence that Third World workers are industrial as well as agricultural—a fact that is now taken for granted.)

The twenty-one essays in *Peasants and Proletarians* are divided into five parts, each of which opens with an essay by the editors: (1) early forms of resistance; (2) workers on the land; (3) strategies of working-class action; (4) migrant workers and advanced capitalism; and (5) contemporary struggles. The essays provide empirical data, as well as theoretical speculations. They examine the nature of workers in the Third World, the forms of consciousness that they express, and the forms of action they are able to undertake to pursue their class interests.

The editors tried for a regional balance in their selection of articles. Countries covered include Chile, China, Nigeria, Southern Rhodesia (in the early 1900s), Peru, Jamaica, Algeria, Ceylon (Sri Lanka), India, Puerto Rico, and South Africa. The obvious regional omission is the Middle East (or West Asia). Broader articles treat subjects such as "rural women's subsistence production in the capitalist periphery" and "the rural proletariat and the problem of the rural proletarian consciousness."

For a more recent treatment of this subject see *International Labour and the Third World: The Making of a New Working Class,* edited by Rosalind Boyd, Robin Cohen, and Peter Gutkind (Hampshire, England: Gower Publishing Co., 1987). $54.95. Cloth.

■ Dembo, David, et al., eds. *Nothing to Lose But Our Lives: Empowerment to Oppose Hazards in a Transnational World.* New York: New Horizons Press, 1988. 207pp. $13.50. Appendixes, references, tables.

This book, co-published in cooperation with Asian Regional Exchange for New Alternatives (Hongkong) and the Indian Law Institute (New Delhi), is designed to represent "a transnational effort of individuals and organizations . . . to make science and technology more socially accountable and responsible."

The causes and consequences of three recent industrial disasters are analyzed: (1) the gas leak at Union Carbide's chemical plant in Bhopal, India; (2) the fire and explosion at the nuclear power plant in Chernobyl in the Soviet Union; and (3) the chemical leaks at plants along the Rhine River. The existing national and international systems for dealing with such catastrophes are analyzed and alternative methods for coping effectively with transnational industrial disasters are discussed.

In the chapter from which the title of this book is derived Clarence Dias explains how and why the workers are predominantly the "risk bearers" in hazardous industries worldwide. He urges the development of effective strategies "for worker empowerment and industry disempowerment" in this area and offers a twelve-point draft charter of rights for workers in hazardous industries as a starting point.

The fifth and final section of the book examines "new approaches" in coping with industrial hazards. These go beyond self-regulation by industry and government policing to include participative policing systems, worker and community hazard indemnity funds, the codification of international liabilities for transnational industrial accidents, and more.

■ Deyo, Frederic C., ed. *The Political Economy of the New Asian Industrialism.* Ithaca and London: Cornell University Press, 1987. 252pp. Notes, index, references, tables.

How can critics of transnational corporations explain the apparent success of the newly industrializing countries of East Asia (South Korea, Taiwan, Singapore, and Hongkong) — the NICs? Economic growth in these countries has been heavily dependent on foreign capital, markets, and technology. Their productive development has been export-oriented. These — according to critics — are the telltale signs of skewed development, evidence of economies at the beck and call of foreign economic interests and operating for the benefit of the few.

The fact is, however, that the East Asian NICs have "sustained continuing and relatively equitable industrial growth over two decades," according to editor Frederic Deyo. And "this growth," Deyo states, "has been paralleled by a favorable pattern of income equality, low unemployment, and the near elimination of the grinding poverty that debilitates the poorest social strata in other Third World countries." "Most remarkable of all," he concludes, "this 'economic miracle' has occurred in small countries bereft of the natural and physical resources that have fostered growth elsewhere."

The eight essays in this book probe the East Asian NICs searching for elements in their development that could be replicated elsewhere and identifying those aspects of the "economic miracle" that are unique. The essays seek to answer three questions, in particular: How have sociopolitical and institutional forces contributed to the success of state-led export-oriented industrialization in South Korea, Taiwan, and Singapore? In what ways has industrial development affected the bourgeoisie, labor, and other social groups in these countries? How useful are modernization and dependency perspectives for understanding East Asian growth?

Articles are contributed by Richard Barrett, Tun-jen Cheng, Soomi Chin, Bruce Cumings, Frederic Deyo, Peter Evans, Stephan Haggard, Chalmers Johnson, and Hagen Koo. With the exception of Soomi Chin, all the contributors are professors at U.S. universities.

■ Dinham, Barbara, and Colin Hines. *Agribusiness in Africa.* London: Earth Resources Research, 1983. 224pp. £4.95. Notes, figures, indexes, maps, tables. Available in North America from Africa World Press.

"Throughout the world," the authors of this study begin, "agricultural production, formerly largely in the hands of peasants or small farmers, is increasingly dominated by big corporations." *Agribusiness in Africa* describes the role that transnational corporations have assumed in Africa (exclusive of South Africa) — particularly in relation to cash crops such as sugar and coffee — and explores the impact they have had.

The opening chapter describes the role of transnational corporations in Africa; the chapter begins by focusing on the corporations' origins as plantation companies, or purchasers of peasant-produced cash crops, and then moves on to discuss the adaptations they have been forced to make in independent Africa. The authors ask: Can agribusiness increase Africa's wealth? Who benefits from their presence? What happens when companies become involved in processing food for consumption in Africa? What conflicts arise between the companies and governments or between governments and peasant farmers?

Chapter-length studies follow on two cash crops (sugar and coffee) and on two countries "with different approaches to development" (Kenya and Tanzania).

Finally, the authors study the implications of the increasing role of agribusiness in African domestic food production and look critically at the trend toward investment in modern large-scale food production schemes. *Agribusiness in Africa* closes with profiles of four British companies that have a life-and-death impact on the peoples of Africa: Unilever (an Anglo-Dutch group), Tate & Lyle, Booker McConnell, and Lonrho.

■ Finch, Ron. *Exporting Danger: A History of the Canadian Nuclear Energy Export Programme.* Montreal and Buffalo: Black Rose Books, 1986. 236pp. $14.95. Notes, appendixes, bibliography, figures, tables.

"Canada has never produced an atomic bomb of its own," writes Ron Finch, "but it has played a major role in the proliferation of nuclear technology throughout the world." *Exporting Danger* describes and analyzes that role.

The book opens with a lengthy description of Canada's development as a nuclear power. In chapter 2 the scene shifts to the Third World where we read about Canada's efforts (beginning in the late 1960s) to support its domestic nuclear power industry by stimulating sales of nuclear reactors in Taiwan, Argentina, South Korea, Mexico, and other Third World nations. Finch describes how Canada's limited profits were due in large part to "generous supplier terms" and bribes and how its use of Canadian tax dollars to push sales overseas meant less money at home to search for energy sources other than nuclear power. In addition, Finch notes, "it was not coincidental that right-wing dictatorships tended to import nuclear reactors." "The decision to import reactor technology," he explains, "coincided with the specific form of economic development in Third World countries, with the neo-colonial regime the most likely to import nuclear technology. The ready access to foreign capital and the receptivity of a neo-colonial regime to the importation of foreign technology to offer an energy source for foreign-owned companies served to perpetuate the repressive regimes."

Finch turns next to an examination of how Canadian nuclear exports have contributed to the proliferation of nuclear weapons. India, Pakistan, Taiwan, South Korea, and Argentina figure largely in this chapter.

Chapter 4 explains how Canada's stake in foreign sales went beyond the marketing of nuclear technology and equipment and included, as well, the export of uranium. Canada is the world's largest producer of uranium and is second only to the United States in uranium exports. The final chapter in *Exporting Danger* describes the Canadian government's plans to "rescue the Canadian nuclear reactor program" and, in the process, further stimulate the development of the domestic uranium industry. Finch expresses his concern that the control of Canada's energy programs is in the hands of those who benefit most from a continuation of the failed policies of the past: "government bureaucrats and private profit-makers."

■ Foner, Philip S. *U.S. Labor Movement and Latin America. Vol. 1: 1846-1919.* South Hadley, Mass.: Bergin & Garvey Publishers, 1988. 228pp. $39.95. Cloth. Notes, index, references.

This is the first in a two-volume reference work on "the reaction of labor unions and Socialists in the United States" to events in Latin America from the Mexican War of 1846 up to the present.

Much of volume 1, which concludes with the founding of the Pan-American Federation of Labor in 1918, is devoted to the Mexican Revolution of 1910 and to a description of efforts by U.S. trade unionists and socialists to prevent U.S. intervention aimed at crushing the revolution.

Foner's study reveals that important elements in both the labor union and socialist movements "opposed imperialism as practiced by [the U.S.] government." "At the same time," Foner writes, "[the study] discloses that in seeking closer ties with Latin American labor, sections of the U.S. labor movement, especially the American Federation of Labor under the leadership of its long-time president, Samuel Gompers, consciously sought to aid U.S. economic and political domination over the area."

Other published works have examined the foreign policy perspectives and activities of U.S. labor unions. Notable among these are: *American Labor and United States Foreign Policy: The Cold War in the Unions from Gompers to Loveston* by Ronald Radosh (New York: Random House, 1969), and *Labor Organizations in the United States and Mexico: A History of Their Relations* by Harold Levenstein (Westport, Conn.: Greenwood Press, 1971).

Foner's two volumes are unique in that they trace the development of organized labor's relations with Latin America from the middle of the nineteenth century and their coverage is not confined to just one or two countries.

■ Frundt, Henry J. *Refreshing Pauses: Coca-Cola and Human Rights in Guatemala.* New York: Praeger Publishers, 1987. 269pp. $34.95. Cloth. Bibliography, index, notes.

Sociologist Henry Frundt examines the 1975 organizing drive and subsequent strike at the Coca-Cola bottling plant in Guatemala City, actions that "contributed to the democratization of Guatemala's politics and [changed] forms of international organization that address human rights issues." (The "international" reference is to the international labor unions, Coca-Cola shareholders, and international churches and human rights organizations that mobilized in support of the Coca-Cola workers in a manner never seen before.)

Frundt maintains that there is much to be learned in this one case study: the need for integration between national and international organizing forces, the impact that international labor union affiliates (as opposed to labor union bureaucrats) can have, the way in which global organizations can cooperate in spite of their different agendas, and how transnational corporations can modify their structures and operating procedures to make them more responsive to the needs and rights of their workers.

Frundt personalizes his account as much as possible to enliven the historical record, but the terrible typewriterlike setting of the text works against him at every turn. The print is faint and the letter spacing is spread too wide to induce any but the most dedicated to venture into what is in fact a story rich in significance and personal and organizational courage. *Refreshing Pauses* deserved much more attention from its publisher than it obviously received.

■ Green, Mark, ed. *The Big Business Reader: On Corporate America.* New York: Pilgrim Press, 1983. 514pp. $12.95. Tables.

This collection of close to fifty articles deals with U.S. corporations and the consumer, organized labor, natural resources, the community, politics, government ("as partner"), regulation, and markets. One section examines the "culture of the corporation" (free speech within the corporation, executive salaries, etc.) and another the issue of corporate governance (social accountability, shareholder activism, etc.).

The section devoted to "the impact of multinationals" contains four articles: "The Global Shopping Center" by Richard J. Barnet and Ronald Müller, "How American Banks Keep the Chilean Junta Going" by Isabel Letelier and Michael Moffitt, "Babies, Bottles and Breast Milk: The Nestlé Syndrome" by Leah Margulies, and "The Dumping of Hazardous Products on Foreign Markets" by Mark Dowie and writers at *Mother Jones.*

The final section examines what alternatives there may be "to business as usual" as far as corporate power is concerned. Editor Mark Green teams up with Jules Bernstein, Vic Kamber, and Alice Tepper Marlin to offer the "Conceptual Draft of a Corporate Democracy Act" that attempts to make corporations more accountable to their constituencies by insisting that executives share more of their power with directors, shareholders, workers, consumers, and local communities.

While much of this book is focused on the impact of U.S. corporations on U.S. society, the relevance of the essays in *The Big Business Reader* to the peoples and nations of the Third World is plain to see.

■ Grunwald, Joseph, and Kenneth Flamm. *The Global Factory: Foreign Assembly in International Trade.* Washington, D.C.: Brookings Institution, 1985. 260pp. $10.95. Tables, figures, index.

This study from the liberal Brookings Institution examines internationalization in the semiconductor industry and transnational assembly operations in Mexico, Haiti, and Colombia. *The Global Factory* weighs the impact of this internationalization of production on the United States and the developing countries. The book's concluding chapter offers policy suggestions for home and host countries.

Three broad sets of questions concern the authors: (1) What is the importance of overseas production? What are its characteristics? Is coproduction a universal phenomenon, or is it confined to a limited array of regions, countries, or products? (2) What have been the causes of growth in overseas production? and (3) What have been the effects of overseas production on home and host economies? Can the arguments made by proponents and critics of these arrangements be evaluated reasonably?

The negative data and examples the authors reveal are all the more damning of transnational corporations for having come from an organization as "balanced" and prestigious as the Brookings Institution.

In measured tones Grunwald and Flamm describe the impact of economic dislocation in the United States and the lack of linkages in Third World countries between the assembly operations of foreign corporations and local economies. As an example of the latter, they admit that "Mexican inputs into assembly plants tend to be confined primarily to janitorial supplies and packing materials." Regarding the former they write: "The workers [in the United States] who suffer most in the two industries most strongly affected by foreign production, apparel and electronics, especially in the least-skilled assembly jobs, are women."

■ Harrod, Jeffrey. *Power, Production, and the Unprotected Worker.* New York: Columbia University Press, 1987. 347pp. $40. Cloth. Notes, appendix, index.

This is the second in a series of four original studies that analyze power relations in societies and in world politics from the standpoint of social relations of production. Others in the Columbia University Press "Power and Production" series are: *Power, Production and the Established Worker* (also by Jeffrey Harrod); *Production, Power, and World Order* (by Robert W. Cox); and *Power, Production, and Redistributive Social Relations* (also by Robert W. Cox).

This study examines "unprotected" workers (i.e., the least powerful producers in the world labor force) in six categories: subsistence farmers, peasants, urban marginals, unorganized wage workers, self-employed, and housewives.

Each form of labor is discussed from the standpoint of power relations (e.g., peasant versus landowner) for—the author recognizes—"the political economy of international change begins with the consciousness and dynamics of power relations in production, [that is,] of forms of social relations." (Harrod acknowledges at the same time, however, that political change is filtered through "the teeming diversity of culture, religion, history, and tradition.")

More than half of the world's labor force is made up of workers at the lowest level of the production hierarchy—and this percentage is growing. The author is certainly correct in arguing that "any social scientist or general observer of the human condition" who ignores, or fails to analyze rigorously, the variety of patterns of power relations in the labor force "is likely to produce at best uneven and at worst self-defeating results."

■ Hawes, Gary. *The Philippine State and the Marcos Regime: The Politics of Export.* Ithaca and London: Cornell University Press, 1987. 196pp. $25. Cloth. Illustrations, appendix, bibliography, chronology, documentation.

From his personal experience as a Peace Corps volunteer with the Philippine government's Department of Agriculture (1972–74) and his research studies and investigations since that time, Professor Hawes fashions this study of export-oriented development (especially in the agriculture industry) during the twenty-year reign of Ferdinand Marcos. Unsparing in his criticisms of the personal avarice of Marcos and his "crony capitalists," Hawes does not, however, see these individuals—or even the Marcos "regime"—as *the* source of the nation's economic problems.

Throughout this study, Hawes argues that "political economy must be concerned with two levels of analysis, the regime and the state." The Marcos regime is gone, but "the pattern of class domination, while no longer so harshly repressive, remains relatively unchanged." In fact, of the four class segments that Hawes analyzes in this book—state capitalists, crony capitalists, producers for the domestic market, and producers for the international market—"the only segment to have suffered immediate damage because of the fall of Marcos," Hawes notes, "is that of the crony capitalists."

Liberals who look to the personal charisma of Corazon Aquino or to an ill-focused "people's power" to redirect the Philippine economy in favor of the interests of the Philippine majority will benefit from Hawes's careful study of the origins and nature of the political economy of the Philippines.

Hawes devotes a chapter each to the coconut, sugar, and fruit products industries, and then closes with an analysis of "state" and "regime" in the Philippine context.

■ Howard, Michael C. *The Impact of the International Mining Industry on Native Peoples.* Sydney: University of Sydney, Transnational Corporations Research Project, 1988. 258pp. Notes, tables.

As state and private interests push into the "last frontiers" in search of the mineral resources that are needed for modern military and industrial development, national and international movements of native peoples concerned about the human and environmental costs of this development are growing apace. The interplay between intensified mineral exploitation and the developing political consciousness of tribal peoples is the focus of this study from the Transnational Corporations Research Project.

In his introduction, author Michael Howard identifies the principal actors in the international mining industry. Private corporations include Rio Tinto Zinc, Anglo American, Broken Hill Pty., Inco, Amax, and Kennecott. State-owned enterprises include copper companies such as CODELCO (Chile), ZIMCO (Zambia), and Gecomines (Zaire). Howard describes as well the involvement of other actors—banks and other lending agencies, for example—in mining development around the world.

Howard next turns his attention to the tribal peoples who have borne the brunt of the intensive exploitation of minerals and other natural resources. "The last few remnants of tribal peoples living beyond the frontier," Howard writes, "have now been brought within the precincts of the capitalist world-economy." "For those [tribal peoples] living on lands containing mineral wealth or some other significant natural resource or in the path of a highway or the floodwaters of a hydroelectric dam," he explains, "the situation has been especially traumatic."

The major part of this book consists of four case studies: (1) the development of Brazil's Amazon Basin; (2) mining development in the Philippines under Ferdinand Marcos; (3) mining developments in several small island nations in the South Pacific; and (4) an examination—from the corporate and tribal peoples' points of view—of the worldwide activities of Amax, a mining company "that received a great deal of notoriety during the 1970s and 1980s, largely as a result of its relations with native peoples."

■ Innes, Duncan. *Anglo American and the Rise of Modern South Africa.* New York: Monthly Review Press, 1984. 352pp. $12.50. Notes, appendixes, figures, statistical tables, charts, bibliography, index.

The Anglo American Group of companies, author Duncan Innes explains, is involved "in virtually every major sphere of mining, financial and industrial activity in South Africa." "Overall," he states, "the consolidated value of the Group's investments makes it easily the largest single company in the country." Innes's study attempts to measure and analyze Anglo's power "in order to enhance our understanding of the nature of the Group's role in South African society and, in the process, to throw some light on the nature of that society itself." His book, then, has a dual purpose: to trace the historical development of the Anglo American Group and to study the South African society in which Anglo has developed.

"To understand the nature of South African society," Innes writes, "we need to be able to identify its motivating forces: how it develops, what form it takes and, most important of all, why it develops." And this demands an understanding of "the fundamental laws of motion of capitalist society."

Anglo American opens with two chapters devoted to the history of the capitalist development of the diamond and gold industries in South Africa. Next we read of the "birth of Anglo American" in the midst of the brutal suppression of workers' rights in the mining industry. Five historical chapters lead up to the final summary analysis of "the Anglo monopoly in industry and finance."

Approximately one-third of this book—which had its origins in a doctoral thesis—is given to appendixes, a 16-page bibliography, and a detailed index. The appendixes provide surveys of the Anglo American Group of companies and of the international links of the group.

The author, a South African, is a senior lecturer in sociology at the University of Witwatersrand in South Africa.

■ Ives, Jane H., ed. *The Export of Hazard: Transnational Corporations and Environmental Control Issues.* Boston: Routledge & Kegan Paul, 1985. 230pp. $19.95. Map, bibliography, index, notes, tables.

In his foreword to *The Export of Hazard* Ralph Nader identifies the contribution that this powerful book makes: " . . . it brings, for the first time, definition to a pattern of international corporate damage whose long history and more recent intensification have been seriously overlooked by most scholars and social activists."

Based on work done around an international conference on "U.S. Hazard Exports to the Developing World" in late 1979, this collection of essays by prominent scholars and social activists treats subjects such as problems of workplace hazards and the regulating process in the United States, Europe, and developing countries; the economic and political impact of exporting hazardous industries and products to nations with less strict regulating systems; the role of professionals and institutions in the regulation of international trade in hazardous and toxic materials; and the institutional level best suited to address/correct the problem.

A lengthy introductory bibliography to the literature on export of hazardous products from the United States and an analysis of the Bhopal disaster close this ground-breaking book.

■ Jenkins, Rhys. *Transnational Corporations and the Latin American Automobile Industry.* Pittsburgh: University of Pittsburgh Press, 1986. 270pp. $32.95. Notes, bibliography, illustrations, index, tables.

"The motor industry," Rhys Jenkins writes, "has played a key role in capitalist development for most of the twentieth century. It was the leading sector in the United States in the inter-war years, it played the same role in Western Europe in the fifties and the sixties, and in Latin America it became a crucial barometer of economic progress in a number of countries in the sixties and seventies." This globe-spanning industry is dominated by a handful of transnational corporations—U.S., European, and Japanese.

This study focuses on the development of the motor industry in Latin America, but Jenkins insists that this industry and economic change in general in Latin America "can only be understood in the context of developments in the international economy to which the [Latin America] region has been linked since the Conquest." One such international development, Jenkins notes, is the internationalization of capital that blossomed in the seventies and early eighties. This restructuring of international capital resulted in the formation of "a true world industry with growing interpenetration of capitals and increasing similarities of products and processes world-wide." Jenkins sets his study of the Latin American auto industry in the context of such international developments.

Jenkins broadens his field of study in yet another way. Whereas most studies of this industry confine their attention to the terminal industry, that is "those firms which assemble cars and commercial vehicles," this book includes the distribution network of authorized dealers and the sale of parts to the replacement market, as well as repair shops and garages. (Ancillary industries, such as plastics and textiles, are excluded because the motor industry does not account for a major share of their output.)

Jenkins considers the strategies of corporations and Latin American governments vis-à-vis the auto industry and weighs the impact the industry has and is likely to have on industry workers and the Latin American people in general.

- Jenkins, Rhys. *Transnational Corporations and Uneven Development: The Internationalization of Capital and the Third World.* London and New York: Methuen, 1987. 229pp. Tables, bibliography, figures, glossary, index.

Transnational Corporations and Uneven Development is an outstanding introductory text on the subject of the impact of transnational corporations on the peoples and nations of the Third World. It is written with students in mind; it provides an overview of the historical development of transnational corporations; it offers documentation that is comprehensive without being intrusive; it situates transnational corporations in an appropriate international framework (i.e., "the internationalization of capital"); and it describes and analyzes the theoretical perspectives of both critics and supporters of transnational corporations. Each chapter closes with a short bibliographical survey of related readings.

Jenkins's own conclusions about the impact of transnational corporations is that it is "uneven and contradictory," just as capitalist development itself is uneven and contradictory. He argues that portrayals of transnational corporations as knights on white chargers "coming to the rescue of Third World countries" or as "the evil genius" behind all the problems of the Third World do not square with the complexity of Third World realities. Jenkins states his case for a study of transnational corporations that includes both the sphere of *circulation* (i.e., relations of exchange and distribution) and the sphere of *production* and that integrates the analysis of transnational corporations within "a broader analysis of the capitalist system."

Jenkins builds the case for his point of view in six chapters, each of which is devoted to one of the following subjects: transnational corporations and competition and monopoly; technology; capital flows, accumulation, and the balance of payments; labor; local capital in the Third World; and the state.

■ Khan, Kushi M., ed. *Multinationals of the South: New Actors in the International Economy.* New York: St. Martin's Press, 1986. 250pp. $29.95. Notes, index, references, list of contributors, tables.

This volume of twelve essays had its origins in a November 1985 conference sponsored by the German Overseas Institute (Hamburg) on the subject of multinational corporations *from* Third World countries.

In *Multinationals of the South* contributors from the Federal Republic of Germany, England, India, Yugoslavia, Mexico, and the United States examine a variety of aspects of this relatively new phenomenon. Editor Kushi Khan, a senior research fellow at the German Overseas Institute, opens the book with a descriptive chapter on the origins and identity of these new economic actors. Other writers take up issues such as the investment development cycle and Third World multinationals; Third World multinationals and trade expansion among the countries of the South; Arab multinationals: problems, potential, and policies; multilateral finance institutions of developing countries as promoters of financial cooperation; practices and policies of host countries toward Third World multinationals; and so forth.

Specialists in political economy will find this book to be an up-to-date compendium of data and analytical thought, as well as a useful source for bibliographical references from a wide range of authors.

■ McDonnell, Kathleen, ed. *Adverse Effects: Women and the Pharmaceutical Industry.* Penang, Malaysia: International Organization of Consumers Unions, Regional Office for Asia and the Pacific, 1986. 217pp. Notes, list of contributors, photographs, tables.

"The world is littered with inappropriate, wasteful and even unsafe medical remedies aggressively promoted by those hungry for profits and careless of life," writes IOCU officer Anwar Fazal in his foreword to *Adverse Effects.* "Women in particular," he continues, "because of their own special health needs and their role in providing for the health care of others, are victims of violence and targets for manipulation by both the pharmaceutical industry and population control policy-makers." This book, Fazal states, "sets out to examine and expose, through a series of case studies, how women the world over are exploited and injured by drugs." The book describes, as well, the varied ways in which women are organizing themselves in opposition to this violence and manipulation.

The four articles in part 1 consider women as consumers of hormonal drugs, such as estrogen-progesterone combinations (EP drugs), diethylstilbestrol (DES), and "mood-modifiers." Part 2, on pharmaceuticals and population control, assesses the impact of the pharmaceutical industry's drugs and devices in Third World family planning programs. The use of injectable contraceptives in India, the promotion of DepoProvera in Southeast Asia, and the "rise and fall of the IUD" are given special attention. In part 3 the authors look at international efforts that have been made to challenge the power of the transnational pharmaceutical companies and to return control of health to women themselves.

Case histories and personal stories bring all of these issues to life for the reader. Copious footnotes and tables serve the needs of researchers and those who desire to study these issues further.

- MacShane, Denis, Martin Plaut, and David Ward. *Power! Black Workers, Their Unions, and the Struggle for Freedom in South Africa.* Boston: South End Press, 1984. 196pp. $8. Maps, appendixes, list of abbreviations, list of resources, tables.

More than half a million black workers in South Africa are organized, and in the three years leading to 1984 organized labor staged an average of one strike a day in South Africa. Clearly, no attempt to describe or analyze the tumultuous events that rock South Africa can escape reference to these startling statistics.

Power! is a groundbreaking guide to the trade union movement in South Africa. Based on research and interviews with workers and union leaders in South Africa, this book examines the history of the black working-class struggle, its achievements, its internal differences, its politics, and its international links.

Labor union activists in England, the United States, and other countries with heavy investments in South African industry will be better able to forge solidarity links with organized labor in South Africa thanks to the efforts of Plaut, MacShane, and Ward. That such concerted action is the intent of the authors is obvious in their provision of addresses and telephone numbers for more than fifty black unions throughout South Africa.

- Mattelart, Armand. *Transnationals and the Third World: The Struggle for Culture.* South Hadley, Mass.: Bergin & Garvey, 1985. 184pp. $12.95. Notes, index.

Mattelart describes the focus of this United Nations-sponsored study as "the sociocultural impact of transnational firms on developing nations." Mattelart, the author of an earlier work on this subject (*Multinational Corporations and the Control of Culture,* 1979) was charged by the UN's Centre of Transnational Corporations to prepare a report on the "negative impact" on transnational corporations in sociocultural terms to complement another UN-sponsored study that analyzed the "positive impact of transnational firms."

After defining his terms and the scope of his study in chapter 1 Mattelart moves in chapter 2 to a description of the "principal features of the cultural networks." Here he looks at film, television, advertising, publishing products, education, and tourism. In the next chapter he weighs the sociocultural impact of transnational corporations in four areas: television, consumption patterns, the world of work, and the role of women. In the fourth chapter Mattelart examines advertising codes and regulations, national communication policies, and self-reliance and communication technologies. Self-reliance is the theme of Mattelart's final chapter. Given the enormous reach and resources of transnational corporations, how can Third World nations pursue self-reliant policies of cultural development?

Mattelart's study presumes a fair amount of familiarity with terminology and with concepts such as the New International Economic Order and the New International Information Order.

■ Mies, Maria, Veronika Bennholdt-Thomsen, and Claudia Von Werlhof. *Women: The Last Colony*. London and New Jersey: Zed Books, 1988. 185pp. $15. Notes, sources, index, notes, tables.

The thrust of this Marxist analysis is that virtually every recent model or blueprint for development—even ones offered by the ecology and alternative political movements—"remain trapped within the mental—and real life—horizons of the White Man" because they "systematically exclude two areas of reality which continue to serve as the unseen foundation for the entire social edifice of industrialism: women and the colonies or underdeveloped societies." "Our view," Mies writes, "is that no comprehensive, valid, and hence realizable alternative theory of science will emerge as long as the question of women and of the colonies continues to be shut out of both public discussion and the development of models for future societies." "This book," she concludes, "is intended as a contribution towards making these spheres visible and incorporating their interrelations and their connection to the whole into the development of a new social theory."

What do women and the colonies have in common? "Both are defined out of so-called social production," Mies states, "and placed within—or more accurately demoted to—the 'realm of nature'." This "systematic exclusion" of women and subjugated peoples from the work-a-day world of wage earners and capitalists results in their being treated "as if they were means of production or 'natural resources' such as water, air and land." In the logic of the capitalist mode of production resources are to be appropriated, possessed, and exploited.

The nine essays in this collection describe the effects of this relegation of women and subjugated peoples to the status of natural resources in three sections: (1) women's work and capitalism; (2) colonization of women and nature; and (3) politics against women and women's struggles. The third section includes an essay by Maria Mies on "class struggles and women's struggles in rural India."

■ Muller, Mike. *The Health of Nations: A North-South Investigation*. London: Faber and Faber, 1982. 224pp. $15.95. Note on terminology, diagrams, index, list of abbreviations, notes, references, tables.

The literature on the controversial policies and practices of pharmaceutical companies in Third World nations has grown considerably since the early 1970s when—as Mike Muller notes—"there were perhaps five key documents to read." Given the level of interest in this issue today, Muller sets himself the task of charting the course the international debate is taking, "illustrating some of the life-and-death issues which literally underlie its often dry language, and indicating which issues will grow in importance in the 1980s." (Actually Muller's reach extends "Towards the Year 2000," as the title of his final chapter indicates.)

Muller's aim is to push the debate to a deeper level of criticism. Many abuses by the pharmaceutical corporations, he contends, have already been identified. It is now time to ask whether even the positive contributions of the drug companies "are not in fact outweighed by, and are incidental to, the damage they do and the bad health care they promote" and, "in economic terms, whether the resources they have captured would not generate more benefit to their consumers if applied in other ways."

Muller's judgments regarding the depth and breadth of the worldwide debate regarding this subject are, perhaps, overstated. There is still much to uncover, to document, and to publicize on this subject. Fortunately, Muller's more sophisticated purposes do not keep him from providing readers new to this subject with numerous examples of the abusive practices that—in his judgment—are already well-known. His assessment of his contributions to this debate are, by contrast, understated. Muller was born in Africa and has traveled extensively in Africa, Asia, Europe, and the United States. He continually draws on his personal experiences, as well as his considerable depth of theoretical knowledge, to enliven and clarify what in the hands of others could be a very dry and esoteric study.

■ Munck, Ronaldo. *The New International Labour Studies: An Introduction.* London and Atlantic Highlands, N.J.: Zed Books, 1988. 233pp. $15. Bibliography, index, notes, tables.

The Third World is no longer "the simple agricultural reserve of the advanced industrial countries," writes Ronaldo Munck in this introduction to international labor studies. In the Third World today, he explains, "one-third of the population lives in cities and over half the labour force are engaged in non-agricultural activities." The author contends that beyond the significance of their numbers, workers in the Third World are developing "new forms of struggle" and for this reason, as well, a study of labor's experience in the Third World is necessary.

Munck cautions against an examination of Third World workers divorced from the international economic, political, and social processes of which they are an integral part. At the same time, as Robin Cohen points out in the foreword, the organized struggles of Third World workers cannot be presumed to be "simplified extensions of the experience of labour movements and industrial relations in Europe and North America."

Argentinian Ronaldo Munck, professor of industrial sociology at the University of Ulster, is singularly capable of giving the study of Third

World labor the importance it merits, situating it in its international context and, at the same time, making the necessary distinctions vis-à-vis labor in the industrialized nations. He has written *Argentina, from Anarchism to Peronism: Workers, Unions and Politics, 1855-1985*; *Politics and Dependency in the Third World*; *Revolutionary Trends in Latin America*; and *The Difficult Dialogue: Marxism and Nationalism*.

■ Nash, June, and Maria P. Fernandez-Kelly, eds. *Women, Men, and the International Division of Labor*. Albany: State University of New York Press, 1983. 464pp. $14.95. Notes, index, references, statistical tables, list of contributors.

Part of the SUNY series on the anthropology of work, this book examines in its eighteen varied articles the "emerging contradictions in the new international division of labor." The editors note that gender plays a distinct role in these contradictions, and that, just as in the Industrial Revolution in England and Europe during the nineteenth century, young women and children — in developing countries this time around — are the prime labor force because they are the "lowest paid segment of those countries paying the lowest wages."

This book is divided into four sections, each of which contains one or more articles focusing specifically on Third World women. The first section presents an overview of the global economy as it has developed over the past thirty years; the second deals with problems of "production, reproduction, and the household economy"; the third addresses the implications that shifts in industrialization have for migration; and the last section consists of case studies from California's "Silicon Valley," the Caribbean, Taiwan, Malaysia, and the Southeast Asia region. The case studies all pertain either to the electronics or the textile industries, both of which have historically used women in dead-end, low-paying jobs.

Women, Men, and the International Division of Labor appears on the surface to be a study that would be of interest only to scholars — with its charts, notes, and list of eminent contributors, but that is not the case. The editors have produced an engrossing collection of readings that are accessible to all who have an interest in this timely topic.

■ Niosi, Jorge. *Canadian Multinationals*. Trans. Robert Chodos. Toronto: Between the Lines, 1985. 200pp. Notes, bibliography, tables.

Canadian multinationals, i.e., those owned by Canadian stockholders and directors, have not been given the attention they deserve by researchers and activists. There are many reasons for this. Critics often associate foreign investment with imperialism, yet Canada has never had a colonial empire, not even much of a sphere of foreign economic influence. Overseas investors are often thought to be the corporations that are in the forefront technologically, yet Canada is one of the world's leading importers of technology. Finally, analysts have been more preoccupied with the impact of foreign investment in Canada than they have been with Canada's involvement overseas.

Despite this lack of attention the fact remains that Canada is one of the world's largest capital exporting countries and Canadian corporations are among the world leaders in a wide variety of industries including mining and refining, aluminum, distilling, rubber, telecommunications equipment, farm machinery, and shoes.

Canadian Multinationals measures the extent of Canadian direct investment in foreign countries and compares these investments with those of U.S., Australian, Japanese and other investors. Thirteen Canadian multinationals, in three sectors, are studied in depth: utilities (Brascan and International Power), mining (Inco, Falconbridge, Noranda Mines, Alcan, and Cominco), and manufacturing (Seagram, Hiram Walker, MacMillan Bloedel, Massey-Ferguson, Polysar, and Northern Telecom).

Norge's first chapter is given to an analysis of "theories of multinational corporations" and "imperialism, dependency, and multinational corporations." This analysis leads him to an elaboration of major propositions regarding multinational corporations that provide the conceptual framework for the remainder of *Canadian Multinationals.*

■ Phizacklea, Annie, ed. *One Way Ticket: Migration and Female Labour.* London, Boston, Melbourne: Routledge & Kegan Paul, 1983. 162pp. $8.95. Bibliography, index, list of contributors, notes, tables.

For millions of women the transition from unwaged to waged work since the early 1970s has come about through migration, whether it be from rural to urban areas or migration of an international kind. "In this book," writes editor Phizacklea, "we address both types of migration, but focus in particular on the migration of women from the European periphery and Third World to the advanced industrial nations of Western Europe."

Phizacklea describes the dimensions of the issue in her introduction. Then in the first chapter Mirjana Morokvasic distinguishes and classifies various trends in the literature concerning women and migration. Succeeding chapters treat "Motherhood and Waged Work: West Indian, Asian, and White Mothers Compared"; "The Second Generation: West Indian Female School-leavers"; "Sexual Divisions and Ethnic Adaptation: The Case of Greek-Cypriot Women"; and "Living in Between: Turkish Women in Their Homeland and in the Netherlands."

In the final chapter, Mary Hancock claims that "much of the current literature" ignores the ways in which transnational corporations have targeted women worldwide as cheap and exploitable labor. She attempts to redress "the conspiracy of silence" by examining the issue of transnational production and the exploitation of women workers through a case study of the United States electronics industry in South East Asia and the Pacific—an industry heavily dependent on a low-wage, predominantly migrant, female workforce.

■ Plant, Roger. *Sugar and Modern Slavery: A Tale of Two Countries.* London: Zed Books, 1987. 177pp. $11.50. Notes, bibliography, chronology, glossary, index, list of abbreviations, maps.

In 1982 the Anti-Slavery Society asked investigative journalist Roger

Plant to look into reports that Haiti's then president Jean-Claude Duvalier was selling more than 10,000 of his fellow citizens to the government of the Dominican Republic each year to cut cane on the Republic's twelve nationalized sugar plantations. The Haitian cane cutters, the reports charged, were not free to leave the plantations during the six months of the harvest season, were padlocked in barracks at night, and were left with only a few dollars of savings to take back to Haiti at the end of the harvest. There were also reports, Plant states, "that Haitians illegally resident in the Dominican Republic were being kidnapped by army officers and troops and sold for profit to state-owned or privately owned sugar enterprises."

In *Sugar and Modern Slavery* Plant offers evidence to support every one of these charges: forced labor, traffic in persons, secret monetary transactions for the effective sale of workers, brutality against Haitian workers, and subhuman living conditions on the sugar plantations. In a word: slavery.

He goes further and analyzes why the two countries, which share the same island in the Caribbean, are in the predicament in which they find themselves. The Dominican Republic cannot provide enough employment for its own urban and rural poor, Plant explains, and yet it imports "tens of thousands of cane cutters from a neighboring country—an even poorer one—because its own nationals, with some reason, equate the life and work of cane cutters in the sugar industry with slavery."

Plant's goal in this book is to examine "the total mess in which a country which has traditionally relied on agricultural exports for its foreign exchange earnings finds itself today." Like so many other countries that have opted for this model of development the Dominican Republic is caught in a vicious downward spiral: forced to produce and sell more and more cash crops at depressed world market prices in order to import food to feed a population that rightly balks at working as slaves to produce the cash crops in the first place. The results are increased poverty, political repression, and—in the case of Haiti and the Dominican Republic—modern-day slavery.

■ Sheridan, Mary, and Janet W. Salaff, eds. *Lives: Chinese Working Women*. Bloomington, Ind.: Indiana University Press, 1984. 258pp. $8.95. Notes.

Using the "life history" research method (a blending of history and biography) the writers in this anthology present vivid and intimate portrayals of the life and work of women in Hongkong, Taiwan, and the People's Republic of China.

After an introduction to the subject and to the life history method the editors divide their study into three sections: (1) the lives of the older generation in pre-1949 China, (2) the lives of younger women in Hongkong and Taiwan, and (3) the lives of women in revolution and reconstruction in modern-day China.

Lives introduces the reader to a Hakka stevedore and a revolutionary hero in pre-liberation China, a waitress and a garment worker in Hongkong, an electronics worker in Taiwan, and a pigsty keeper in today's China.

As diverse as the portraits are, they share common themes: the responsibilities of eldest daughters, violence in the family, sibling affection and rivalry, and the primacy of men in private affairs. Other lesser themes also surface: moral regulations and personal codes, loyalty, self-interest, sacrifice, and the importance of food and diet.

■ Silverman, Milton, Philip R. Lee, and Mia Lydecker. *Prescriptions for Death: The Drugging of the Third World.* Berkeley and Los Angeles: University of California Press, 1982. 186pp. $16.95. Cloth. Tables, appendix, index, references.

The major part of this study by three members of the Institute of Health Policy Studies at the University of California School of Medicine is devoted to a comparative analysis of drug company performance in the United States, England, Japan, and more than twenty countries in Africa, Asia, and Latin America. The authors focus their attention on families of drugs, including antibiotics, anti-diarrhea medications, pain and fever fighters, anabolic hormones, tonics, and "the pill." Proceeding drug-by-drug Silverman, Lee, and Lydecker explain and illustrate on charts how warnings and prescriptions for the different drugs vary from country to country—with the most marked differences being between First and Third World nations in general.

Their analysis leads the authors to these conclusions: (1) "Many products ousted from the market in such industrialized nations as the United States and Great Britain, or never approved for marketing, are readily available and widely promoted in the Third World." (2) "With many important products, the dangers of serious or lethal side effects are minimized, glossed over, or totally ignored." (3) "With many of these drugs, claims of effectiveness are wildly exaggerated." (4) "In the developing countries, the reliability of drug-labeling practices is not necessarily related to the size or type of company." On this latter point the authors offer evidence of "irrational and potentially dangerous promotion" of drugs by firms large and small, foreign and domestic, known and unknown. Most are based in capitalist countries, some in socialist countries. "The offending drug companies seem to demonstrate one characteristic in common," the authors conclude, "an acute deficiency of social responsibility."

In five other chapters the authors describe other facets of "the drugging of the Third World," but it is the drug-by-drug analysis in chapter 3 that makes this book unique.

■ Soldon, Norbert C., ed. *The World of Women's Trade Unionism: Comparative Historical Essays.* Westport, Conn.: Greenwood Press, 1985. 256pp. $35. Cloth. Tables, bibliography, index, list of contributors, notes.

This collection of essays contains histories of women's trade union movements in industrialized and developing nations of the world.

Argentina is the only Third World country to merit an entire chapter: "Hidden, Silent, and Anonymous: Women Workers in the Argentine Trade Union Movement" by Marysa Navarro, Professor of History at Dartmouth College. The organization of this book, however, compensates somewhat for the underrepresentation of women's labor union activities in the Third World. For each author was asked to research and respond to a set of similar questions about the subject of women in trade unionism, and comparisons are thus made possible across national and North-South boundaries.

The questions put to the eight contributors include: What is the role of women in the work force? What is the prevailing definition of work? When and for what reason did the percentage of women in the work force increase and decrease? What is the attitude of men toward women in trade unions? What is the nature and quality of leadership in the unions? Do women favor redress of their grievances by collective bargaining or legislative action? What factors govern their choice? What is the relationship between the labor bureaucracy (female or male) and the political structure of the time? What developments have taken place in women's trade unionism since World War II?

Essays in this volume cover women's trade unionism in these industrialized nations: England, France, the United States, Italy, Germany, Sweden, and Japan.

■ Southall, Roger, ed. *Trade Unions and the New Industrialization of the Third World.* London: Zed Books, 1988. 378pp. $39.95. Cloth. Co-published by University of Pittsburgh Press and University of Ottawa Press. Tables, list of contributors, notes.

The fourteen papers in this volume were all originally presented to a conference on "Third World Trade Unionism: Equity and Democratization in the Changing International Division of Labour" organized by the Institute of International Development and Cooperation of the University of Ottawa in October 1984. All of the papers seek to gauge the capability of Third World unions for protecting and promoting the interests of workers as more and more labor-intensive manufacturing is shifted to Third World countries from the industrialized nations.

Editor Roger Southall identifies these key issues regarding this new international division of labor: "Do third world unions possess the capacity for offensive as well as defensive activities within a changing global capitalist order? Is organized labour doomed to submission at the behest of the capital logic of the world market? What are the prospects for international labour solidarity?"

The papers are divided into three sections: (1) "Organized Labor and the Industrialization of the Contemporary Third World." (2) "Industrial Restructuring, Repression, and the Third World Union Response." (3) "Comrades or Competitors? Capital Restructuring and the Prospects for Labor Internationalism?" Third World countries given special attention in the second of the three sections are Argentina (the article by Ronaldo Munck), Nigeria (Nicholas Van Hear), Sri

Lanka (Laksiri Fernando), Iran (Valentine Moghadam), and Malaysia (Peter Wad). Rhoda Howard brings this section to a close with an analysis of "Third World Trade Unions as Agencies of Human Rights: The Case of Commonwealth Africa."

This is an outstanding collection of essays—all from a progressive political viewpoint—on a subject that needs and deserves much more attention.

■ Tavis, Lee A., ed. *Multinational Managers and Poverty in the Third World.* Notre Dame: University of Notre Dame Press, 1984. 288pp. $9.95. Appendix.

The papers in this anthology issued from a seminar organized at the University of Notre Dame to identify "ways in which socially conscious multinational managers (executives of firms whose products or services are both produced and sold in underdeveloped as well as developed countries) might respond to poverty in Third World countries where their firms have investments." Corporate managers, missionaries, academicians, and policy advisers took part in one or more aspects of the seminar, which lasted from October 1978 through 1981.

Rev. Theodore Hesburgh, then president of Notre Dame, sets the tone of the book by declaring "I cannot accept the extreme view so often espoused by many of my religious colleagues that multinationals are monsters, debilitating and ruining the poorer countries." Taking his cue from Fr. Hesburgh, editor Tavis skirts the question of whether multinationals themselves are responsible (to whatever degree) for the poverty that is so evident in the Third World and defines the aim of the seminar as finding ways for executives "to respond to the living conditions of people attempting to survive at the boundaries of physical existence, while continuing to ensure the profitability of their firms' operations."

Fortunately the debate reflected in the fourteen articles in this book is more wide ranging, open, and critical than the opening remarks by Hesburgh and Tavis would suggest. And this—more than anything else—is the virtue of *Multinational Managers.* The lines of argument may not be as carefully drawn or as persuasively advanced as they could be, but the book does give the reader a feel for the way the debate is framed.

■ Taylor, Peter. *The Smoke Ring: Tobacco, Money, & Multinational Politics.* New York: Pantheon Books, 1984. 330pp. $18.95. Cloth. Notes, appendixes, bibliography, index.

This book, says journalist Peter Taylor, "is not intended to be an anti-smoking treatise but an investigation of the political questions which the growing of tobacco and the production and consumption of cigarettes pose for governments all over the world." Taylor's stated purpose is "to consider why governments place wealth before health" and "to examine the political and economic mechanisms of the power of tobacco."

Two chapters (14 and 15) are given to an examination of the role of tobacco in Third World societies and economies. "To many Third World governments," Taylor explains, "tobacco offers a lifebelt [in times of economic crisis]. It provides jobs, revenue, exports, foreign exchange, education, training and prosperity. It creates wealth and aids development—assuming of course that 'development' is the creation of a consumer society which offers the West a market for its goods and services. Tobacco is a cash crop which, unlike cotton, cocoa, coffee, tea, sugar and groundnuts, is not subject to the fluctuations of world commodity prices: that is why for years international organisations such as the United Nations Food and Agriculture Organisation (FAO) and the World Bank (whose criterion for development is return on investment) have supported tobacco as a cash crop in Third World countries."

This extended quotation suggests the complexity of this topic as far as Third World nations are concerned (First World nations, too, for that matter, as Taylor illustrates throughout the book). Tobacco is unquestionably a killer, but the product is surrounded by a ring of special interests—notably the industry itself and the U.S. government—that will fight tooth and nail to keep this simple truth from penetrating and influencing the lives of consumers throughout the world.

■ Williams, Robert G. *Export Agriculture and the Crisis in Central America.* Chapel Hill: University of North Carolina Press, 1986. 258pp. $9.95. Notes, bibliography, diagrams, illustrations, list of abbreviations, statistical tables.

Export Agriculture was researched in the field and composed without the benefit of research assistants or of financial security. These humble origins do not detract in any way from the impact of Williams's study. On the contrary, they infuse what could have been a dry economic investigation with a flesh-and-blood vitality and sense of urgency that characterize the Central American region itself.

Williams's study challenges the widely held view "that the economic cure for instability in Central America is another program of export expansion and diversification." He establishes his case by critically examining "the two most important new exports from Central America since the end of World War II"—cotton and cattle.

In three chapters devoted to each commodity Williams describes how exports of cotton and cattle did, indeed, expand and diversify the foreign exchange earnings of the region, fill the tax coffers of the governments of Central America, generate profits for transnational corporations and local investors, and help modernize agriculture. But all at a terrible price that included the poisoning of the coastal environment (cotton), irreversible destruction of tropical forests (cattle), confiscation of land that peasants had used for food production, and, ultimately, the social instability that marks the region today.

By the early 1970s, Williams concludes, "the five countries of Central America were exposed to the world system in much the same way. All five relied on a handful of agricultural commodities whose prices were

to suffer from worldwide recessions. All five were dependent on imported inputs whose prices were to surge with uncharacteristic force. All five were habituated to borrowing from the international financial system whose interest rates were to explode. Most important, all five had social fabrics that had been weakened by more than a decade of agricultural modernization and export expansion." Chapter 8 provides a survey of the ways in which the governments of Central America have responded in different ways to the crisis brought about—in part—by the adoption of the export-oriented model of economic development.

Bibliographies and Guides

■ Anant, Suchitra, S. V. Ramani Rao, and Kabita Kapoor, comps. *Women at Work in India: A Bibliography.* New Delhi and Beverly Hills, Calif.: Sage Publications, 1986. 238pp. $22.50. Cloth. Appendixes, indexes.

This bibliography, which was compiled by staff members of the nonprofit Institute of Social Studies Trust under the sponsorship of the Indian government's Ministry of Labour, covers books, periodicals, doctoral theses, research monographs, discussion papers, and seminar papers (published and unpublished) produced on Indian women up to December 1985.

Entries are divided into seventeen subject areas, such as the general employment situation; women in the informal sector; women and labor legislation; organization and unionization; education and training of women; women and the household; and women and prostitution. Section 6, "Women Workers: Studies by Occupation/Industry," is subdivided into 47 categories from "agarbatti making" to "zari."

The appendixes list the organizations that cooperated in the production of the bibliography and the periodicals that appear in the bibliography. Addresses are provided for the organizations, but not, unfortunately, for the periodicals.

■ Garver, Paul. *Bibliography on the AFL-CIO's Foreign Policy.* November 1987. 10pp. Available from the author, 7728 Edgerton Ave., Pittsburgh, PA 15221.

This bibliography of materials related to the foreign policy of the AFL-CIO is "designed for the trade unionist who has a serious interest in the international activities of U.S. labor, but is not a specialist."

■ Ghosh, Pradip K., ed. *Multi-National Corporations and Third World Development.* Westport, Conn.: Greenwood Press, 1984. 473pp. $45. Tables, bibliography, list of resources, appendix, index, figures, list of abbreviations, notes.

This is one in Greenwood's series of International Development Resource Books, all prepared under the auspices of the Center for International Development, University of Maryland, College Park, and the World Academy of Development and Cooperation, Washington, D.C.

Like the other volumes in the series *Multi-National Corporations and Third World Development* is divided into four sections: (1) Current issues, trends, analytical methods, strategies and policies, country studies. (2) Statistical information and sources. (3) Resource bibliography. (4) Directory of information sources.

Section one, which covers more than two-thirds of the book, contains fourteen articles reprinted from publications such as the *Journal of International Affairs, International Social Science Journal, Trade and Development, Management International Review, International Labour Review,* and the *Journal of Developing Areas.* All of the articles date from the late 1970s and early 1980s.

The second section (38 pages) contains an annotated bibliography of information sources and a collection of statistical tables and figures. The bibliography is of more lasting value than the statistics, which are more than a decade old.

The resource bibliography in section 3 lists books (on development in general and on the role of multinational corporations in Third World development in particular), selected articles from periodicals, and specialized publications (reports, documents, and directories). A three-page subject index serves as a guide to the contents of the resource bibliography.

The final section of the book lists United Nations information sources, bibliographies of bibliographies, periodicals, and research institutions. This section is, unfortunately, not of much use because its contents are unfocused and dated.

■ Lifschitz, Edgardo. *Bibliografía Analítica Sobre Empresas Transnacionales/Analytical Bibliography on Transnational Corporations.* Mexico City: Instituto Latinoamericano de Estudios Transnacionales, 1980. 607pp. Cloth. Appendixes, indexes.

This bibliography of books, articles, documents, and papers on transnational corporations contains 3,815 entries arranged in alphabetical order. Key words, grouped under five headings (subject matter, geographical location, economic sectors, corporations, and institutions) enable the reader to identify items of interest in the bibliography.

Lifschitz drew on eleven other bibliographies (French, Spanish, and English) in compiling this volume.

ILET intends to update and revise the bibliographical database acquired as a result of this project on a regular basis.

■ Mekeirle, Joseph O., comp. and ed. *Multinational Corporations: The E.C.S.I.M. Guide to Information Sources.* Brussels: European Centre for Study and Information on Multinational Corporations, 1977. 454pp. Cloth. Indexes.

The entries in this comprehensive bibliography are divided into sections covering primary and secondary sources of information.

Under the heading of primary sources are: (1) Sources reporting on new and forthcoming books on multinational corporations. (2) "Less-conventional" literature sources on multinational corporations (e.g., working papers, dissertations). (3) Periodicals that frequently contain information about multinational corporations.

The second section, covering secondary information sources, is divided into five subsections: (1) Bibliographies of bibliographies on multinational corporations. (2) Multinational "company information" sources. (3) Current secondary sources covering the literature on multinational corporations. (4) Databases covering the literature on multinational corporations. (5) Sample pages from selected current secondary sources covering the literature on multinational corporations.

The final section contains eighty pages of indexes covering authors, titles, periodical titles, organizations, and subjects.

Entries are listed in their original language (principally English, Spanish, French, and German). Fewer than one-fifth of the items are annotated.

See also:

■ Mikkelsen, Britha. *Industrial Labour in Africa: A Partially Annotated Bibliography.* Uppsala: Scandinavian Institute of African Studies, 1979.

■ United Nations Centre on Transnational Corporations. *Bibliography on Transnational Corporations.* New York and Geneva: United Nations, 1978. $29. UN sales number: EF.78.II.A.4.

Directories and Reference Books

■ *British Companies Operating in the Philippines.* London: Catholic Institute for International Relations, 1984. 49pp. £1.50. Indexes, appendixes.

"Britain plays a more important role in the Philippines than is probably realized," state the editors of this directory. This list demonstrates that fact. It shows that nearly every economic sector in the Philippines has a British corporate presence. (A sectoral index enables the reader to see which companies are invested in which sectors.) "In 1981," the editors write, "the British Overseas Trade Board revealed that, while very much smaller than U.S. and Japanese investment, British investment in the Philippines was greater than that from all the other European countries put together."

This CIIR booklet opens with an eight-page overview of "the economic and political context" in the Philippines, discussing labor conditions, wages, trade unions, and living standards.

In the body of the booklet forty-eight corporations are listed in alphabetical order, with address, name of local affiliate, percentage of ownership, place of registration, and a paragraph-length description of activities. No parent banks or insurance companies or their affiliates are included.

■ *Corporate Activity Catalogue: 1986.* Hongkong: Asia Monitor Resource Center, 1988. 96pp.

This booklet is a register of foreign corporate activity in Asia during 1986. Compiled from information in public sources such as English-language newspapers and business magazines from the region, the list covers direct investments, equipment supply and installation, trade deals, subcontracts, engineering projects, technology transfer, licensing, and franchising. In addition, information on labor and legal disputes involving foreign corporations is included. All of the information is stored in computerized form, permitting electronic sorting and searches by corporate name, host country, type of business, and national origin.

A five-page introduction summarizes the year's corporate activity in Asia.

■ Dunning, John H., and Robert D. Pearce. *The World's Largest Industrial Enterprises: 1962–1983.* New York: St. Martin's Press, 1985. 186pp. Cloth. Notes, appendixes, tables.

This oversized volume presents detailed data on the structure, growth, performance, and international involvement of more than 800 of the largest companies in the world. Information is provided for 1983 and—for comparative purposes—for 1982, 1977, 1972, 1967, and 1962. The data, which are drawn from *Fortune* magazine's annual surveys, are classified into twenty industrial sectors and then by country or region.

Corporations do not appear by name except in one table and in an appendix that ranks the world's largest industrial enterprises for three years: 1962, 1972, and 1983.

■ *European Companies in the Philippines.* London: Catholic Institute for International Relations, 1987. 194pp. £8.95. Tables, bibliography, index.

This CIIR booklet provides a survey of 227 direct investments in the Philippines by corporations from fourteen European countries. Direct investment is defined as either a Philippine company partly or wholly owned by a European company, or a European company with a branch office or other permanent presence in the Philippines. In addition to direct investments, the survey identifies a range of other involvement, including the supply of large amounts of industrial equipment to local companies, manufacturing under license, and a significant amount of cross-border lending by European banks to a variety of Philippine companies and government bodies.

The introduction offers an overview of the economic situation in the Philippines under Ferdinand Marcos and Cory Aquino, with an emphasis on the role of foreign investments and loans and on the activities of the labor movement in the Philippines.

Chapters 1 through 6 discuss European corporate involvement in traditional exports (e.g., sugar), nontraditional exports (e.g., electronics, garments), other manufacturing and trading, energy, major industrial projects such as a copper smelter and an integrated steel mill, and service industries.

The bibliography lists many recent studies on foreign corporate activity in the Philippines from organizations in the Philippines such as the Alternate Resource Center, AKAP Research, the Center for Labor Studies, IBON Databank Phil Inc., and the University of the Philippines.

■ Gassert, Thomas, and the staff of the Asia Monitor Resource Center. *Health Hazards in Electronics: A Handbook.* Hongkong: Asia Monitor Resource Center, 1985. 430pp. $10. Glossary, illustrations, index, list of resources.

This handbook represents the fruit of more than five years of research and field investigations by the AMRC staff. Designed as an educational tool for community health workers, trade unionists, social workers, educators, and women's groups, this comprehensive, easy-to-use, fully illustrated manual provides access to action-oriented scientific data on specific health hazards in electronics work and describes methods for dealing with them.

The handbook also probes the root causes of work-related problems in the electronics industry, concentrating on Asia as a case study.

The handbook's list of companies gives the local subsidiary and foreign parent for electronics investors in China, India, Indonesia, Malaysia, Thailand, and seven other Asian nations and territories. A complementary list gives the parent name, home address, and name of Asian countries where transnational corporations have offshore electronics manufacturing and assembly investments.

■ Hansen, Lynn, and Maria Riley, comps. *Women Workers' Resource Directory.* Washington, D.C.: Center of Concern, 1985. 51pp.

Resources in this looseleaf directory are arranged in four categories: topics· of interest (e.g., industrial health hazards, church involvement with labor issues); industries; international labor activities; and regions (Americas, Asia, Europe). Contents include organizations, books, periodicals, articles, and occasional papers.

■ Harper, F. John, ed. and comp. *Trade Unions of the World.* Harlow,

England: Longman Group UK Ltd., 1987. 503pp. Index of trade union acronyms, statistical tables.

This reference book is the most up-to-date and comprehensive guide available on the status of trade unionism throughout the world. Nearly all the material was collected in 1985-86, according to the editor. Much of the information was supplied by trade union organizations themselves, in response to questionnaires and other approaches.

Organized country-by-country (from Afghanistan to Zimbabwe) the directory provides notes on the general political and economic context within which trade unions function in each nation. Trade unions active in the country are then described. When available the description includes address, telephone number, telex number, leadership, membership profile, names of publications, and international affiliations.

Harper's aim was to provide data on all national trade union centers affiliated with the three global organizations, the International Confederation of Free Trade Unions (ICFTU), the World Confederation of Labour (WCL), and the World Federation of Trade Unions (WFTU). He notes that "affiliation" in the case of some trade unions is ambiguous, but his policy was to record the affiliation (as reported by the international) unless clear evidence existed to indicate that the local has severed its ties with the parent union.

Harper refers to an earlier "exhaustively researched compendium" on this same topic, acknowledging that it proved "indispensable to an understanding of the worldwide historical development of trade unions to the late 1970s"; the work he refers to is *The International Directory of the Trade Union Movement* by A. P. Coldrick and Philip Jones (London: Macmillan, 1979).

■ *International Business in South Africa 1988.* Washington, D.C.: Investor Responsibility Research Center, June 1988. 250pp. $150.

This unique directory profiles all of the major multinational corporations in Europe, Asia, and Australia that have direct investments or non-equity ties in South Africa. For each company the directory gives the names, locations, and principal lines of business of its South African operations and, where available, a breakdown of its work force by race. In the case of a company that is found to have only a nonequity tie, such as a licensing or distribution agreement, the directory provides a brief description of the arrangement.

■ Lydenberg, Steven D., Alice Tepper Marlin, Sean O'Brien Strub, and the Council on Economic Priorities. *Rating America's Corporate Conscience: A Provocative Guide to the Companies Behind the Products You Buy Every Day.* Reading, Mass.: Addison-Wesley, 1986. 502pp. $14.95. Charts, lists of resources, appendixes, references, index.

The staff of the Council on Economic Priorities has compiled these profiles and charts of major U.S. corporations in order to help the reader "cast an economic vote on corporate social responsibility" during trips to the supermarket to buy everything from toothpaste to condensed milk. Also included are tips on big-ticket items such as cars, airplane tickets, and refrigerators.

The profiles and charts, which take up almost four hundred pages of the book, rate the "social responsibility" of individual corporations in these areas: relations with South Africa, nuclear- and conventional-arms contracting, charitable contributions, representation of women and minorities on boards of directors and in top management, and disclosure of information on social issues. Other vital issues, the authors explain, had to be omitted in order to keep the book to its present size.

For the second printing of *Rating America's Corporate Conscience* in April 1987 the authors updated information concerning the withdrawal of companies from South Africa and related to major mergers, sales, and corporate acquisitions.

■ Moskowitz, Milton. *The Global Marketplace: 102 of the Most Influential Companies Outside America.* New York: Macmillan Publishing Co., 1987. 708pp. $24.95. Cloth. Charts, illustrations, index, statistical tables, appendix, bibliography.

The Global Marketplace profiles 102 corporations with headquarters outside the United States. Two-thirds of these are based in five countries: Japan (19), Britain (19), France (13), West Germany (10), and Italy (7). Two—Unilever and Shell—have dual nationalities (British and Dutch). Five are government-owned entities; eight are privately owned companies (i.e., they do not offer stock to the public). Most are big; some—like Club Med and the Hard Rock Cafe—are small, but deserving of attention.

Moskowitz, a journalist and syndicated columnist, offers his thoughts on multinational corporations in a five-page introduction to the book. "This book is not a polemic on the tired old subject of multinationals subverting national sovereignties," Moskowitz writes. "The world, to my way of thinking, is more complicated than that." "These companies," he says, "are creatures of their times, subject to the same mindless passions that have wreaked such havoc and destruction during this century." Moskowitz concludes his introduction with short descriptions of corporate power in the United States ("Who Owns America?") and in the socialist economies ("For Sale: The Private Sector").

Moskowitz writes in a colorful style, bringing the human element into corporate histories whenever possible.

■ Moskowitz, Milton, Michael Katz, and Robert Levering, eds. *Everybody's Business: An Almanac. The Irreverent Guide to Corporate America.* New York and London: Harper & Row, 1980. 916pp. $9.95. Indexes, charts, illustrations, photographs, statistical tables.

This directory offers profiles of 317 large U.S. corporations, presented in a style that the editors insist is "without jargon or technical language." *Everybody's Business* is, after all, a book that is meant to be for everyone whose life is touched by these corporate giants.

Nearly all of the companies profiled in the directory take in more than $1 billion annually; well over half take in more than $2 billion.

But size and other statistical indicators are not what the editors focus their attention on. "There are other useful keys to the corporate personality," they write. "Sales figures tell you one thing, the presence (or absence) of minorities and women on the board of directors tells you something else. The number of brand names or companies they own gives you one picture of the corporation, the amount of time the company spends in courtrooms reveals still another."

Corporate profiles are divided into industrial sectors, such as food, clothing and shelter, automobiles, advertising, and communications.

■ *U.S. and Canadian Business in South Africa 1987.* Washington, D.C.: Investor Responsibility Research Center, October 1987. 182pp. $150.

This IRRC directory profiles the U.S. and Canadian companies that have either a direct investment or employees in South Africa, as well as many U.S. companies that have only nonequity links there, such as licensing and distribution agreements. For each company with equity or employees in South Africa, the directory gives the names, locations, and principal lines of business of its South African operations, the sales and assets of each (where available), and a breakdown of its work force by race. Where the company has signed the Statement of Principles (formerly the Sullivan principles), the entry shows its recent ratings.

United Nations Publications

■ United Nations Centre on Transnational Corporations. *Transnational Corporations in South Africa and Namibia: United Nations Public Hearings.* New York and Geneva: United Nations, 1986-. $200 for four-volume set. Volumes 1 and 4 available separately at $65 each.

In 1985 the Secretary-General of the United Nations appointed an eleven-member Panel of Eminent Persons to conduct public hearings on the activities of transnational corporations in South Africa and Namibia. The aim of the study was "to contribute to a greater understanding of the critical relationship between transnational corporations, the elimination of apartheid, and independence for Namibia," according to the executive director of the United Nations Centre on Transnational Corporations.

The panel issued a four-volume record of its findings.

Volume 1 (242pp.): *Reports of the Panel of Eminent Persons and of the Secretary-General.* In addition to the report and recommendations of the panel and background reports from the Secretary-General, this volume also contains a 74-page bibliography on foreign investment in South Africa and Namibia.

Volume 2 (282pp.): *Verbatim Records.*

Volume 3 (518pp.): *Statements and Submissions.* This is a compilation of written statements prepared for the hearings or other written material submitted to the panel for its consideration.

Volume 4 (444pp.): *Policy Instruments and Statements.* This reference volume includes the texts of policy instruments and official statements dealing with economic measures against South Africa's policies of apartheid and its occupation of Namibia. The texts were issued by intergovernmental bodies (e.g., the United Nations), groups of states (e.g., the League of Arab States), more than sixty national governments, and selected states and cities in the United States.

- United Nations Centre on Transnational Corporations. *Transnational Corporations in the Man-made Fibre, Textile and Clothing Industries.* New York and Geneva: United Nations, 1987. 154pp. UN sales number: E.87.II.A.11. Notes, appendixes, diagrams, tables.

The UNCTC has undertaken numerous studies on the role and activities of transnational corporations in selected industries of special interest and significance to host countries, particularly developing countries. The stated purpose of the studies is "to contribute to a better understanding of the participation and strategies of transnational corporations in those industries and to enhance the ability of host countries to establish appropriate policies and improve their negotiating capability in dealing with transnational corporations."

The UNCTC industry studies provide an overall analysis of the structure and production characteristics of the industry concerned and examine issues such as market concentration, competitive structure, forms of investment, and trends in the role and involvement of transnational corporations.

The UNCTC study of the man-made fibre, textile, and clothing industries is representative of all of the others. It opens with a six-page summary of the study. In the four following chapters the study covers: (1) Production trends and international trade in the textile and clothing industries. (2) Growth patterns. (3) Technological change in the textile and clothing industries and its implications for developing countries. (4) Strategies of developing countries and their policy implications. There are twenty-five tables scattered throughout the text and nineteen gathered together into the appendix.

Titles of similar publications from the United Nations Centre on Transnational Corporations are:

Transnational Corporations in the International Semiconductor Industry. New York and Geneva: United Nations, 1986. 471pp. $41. UN sales number: E.86.II.A.1.

Transnational Corporations in the Pharmaceutical Industry of Developing Countries. New York and Geneva: United Nations, 1984. 223pp. $21. UN sales number: E.84.II.A.10.

Transnational Corporations in the International Auto Industry. New York and Geneva: United Nations, 1983. 223pp. $21. UN sales number: E.83.II.A.6.

Transnational Corporations in the Agricultural Machinery and Equipment Industry. New York and Geneva: United Nations, 1983. 134pp. $17. UN sales number: E.83.II.A.4.

Transnational Corporations in the Fertilizer Industry. New York and Geneva: United Nations, 1983. 69pp. $8. UN sales number: E.82.II.A.10.

Transnational Corporations in International Tourism. New York and

Geneva: United Nations, 1982. 113pp. $10. UN sales number: E.82. II.A.9.

■ United Nations Conference on Trade and Development. *Technology and Development Perspectives of the Pharmaceutical Sector in Ethiopia.* New York and Geneva: United Nations, 1984. 126pp. $16.50. UN sales number: E.84.II.D.6. Notes, appendixes, diagrams, figures, tables.

Building on the knowledge gained from a series of earlier studies, country case analyses, and reports on pharmaceuticals in developing countries the United Nations Conference on Trade and Development launched an investigation into the pharmaceutical industry in Ethiopia. This report, prepared together with the Ethiopian Development Projects Study Agency/Ethiopian Centre for Technology, analyzes the present structures and policies of the industry in Ethiopia and then outlines a program for the development of the pharmaceutical sector in the country.

UN studies such as this will be of interest only to serious students of transnational corporations or to those with a focused interest in the impact of one particular industry, such as pharmaceuticals, on the peoples and nations of the Third World.

SUPPLEMENTARY LIST OF BOOKS

GENERAL

Berberoglu, Berch. *The Internationalization of Capital: Imperialism and Capitalist Development on a World Scale.* Westport, Conn.: Praeger, 1987. 224pp. Cloth.

Bergquist, C., ed. *Political Economy of the World-System Annuals: Vol. 7. Labor in the Capitalist World Economy.* Beverly Hills, Calif.: Sage, 1984.

Bluestone, Barry, and Bennett Harrison. *Deindustrialization of America.* New York: Basic Books, 1984. 323pp. $9.95.

Bornschier, Volker, and Christopher Chase-Dunn. *Transnational Corporations and Underdevelopment.* New York: Praeger, 1985.

Bull, David. *A Growing Problem: Pesticides and the Third World.* Oxford: Oxfam, 1982. 192pp. £4.95.

Burawoy, Michael. *Politics of Production, Factory Regimes under Capitalism and Socialism.* London: Verso/New Left Books, 1985. 272pp. £6.95.

Butler, Nick. *The International Grain Trade: Problems and Prospects.* New York: St. Martin's Press, 1986. 176pp. $29.95. Cloth.

Cavanagh, John, and Frederick Clairmonte. *The Merchants of Drink.* Washington, D.C.: Institute for Policy Studies, June 1988. $10.

Clairmonte, Frederick, and John Cavanagh. *The World in Their Web: The Dynamics of Textile Multinationals.* London and New Jersey: Zed Books, 1981. 278pp. $11.50

Clarke, Ian M. *The Spatial Organisation of Multinational Corporations.* New York: St. Martin's Press, 1985. 287pp. Cloth.

Cox, Robert W. *Production, Power, and World Order: Social Forces in the Making of History.* New York: Columbia University Press, 1987. 500pp. $45. Cloth.

Enderwick, P. *Multinational Business and Labour.* London: Croom Helm, 1985.

Frank, I. *Foreign Enterprise in Developing Countries.* Baltimore: Johns Hopkins University Press, 1980.

Frieden, Jeffry A. *Banking on the World: The Politics of American International Finance.* New York: Harper & Row, 1987. 264pp. $19.95. Cloth.

Frobel, Folker, et al. *New International Division of Labour: Structural Unemployment in Industrialised Countries and Industry.* Cambridge, Eng.: Cambridge University Press, 1981.

Gereffi, Gary. *Pharmaceutical Industry and Dependency in the Third World.* Princeton, N.J.: Princeton University Press, 1983.

Graham, Ronald. *The Aluminium Industry and the Third World: Multinational Corporations and Underdevelopment.* London and New Jersey: Zed Books, 1982. 278pp. $11.50.

Greenaway, David, ed. *Economic Development and International Trade.* New York: St. Martin's Press, 1988. 211pp. $45. Cloth.

Hoffman, J., and R. Rush. *Microelectronics and Clothing: The Impact of Technical Change on a Global Industry.* Geneva: International Labour Organization, 1983.

Holloway, Steven Kendall. *The Aluminium Multinationals and the Bauxite Cartel.* New York: St. Martin's Press, 1988. 98pp. $45. Cloth.

Ives, Jane H. *The Exportation of Hazardous Industries to Developing*

Countries. Rockville, Md.: National Institute for Occupational Safety and Health, 1982.

Klare, Michael T. *American Arms Supermarket*. Austin: University of Texas Press, 1984. 312pp. $10.95.

Kolko, Joyce. *Restructuring the World Economy*. New York: Pantheon Books, 1988. 390pp. $14.95.

Kumar, K., ed. *Transnational Enterprises: Their Impact on Third World Societies and Cultures*. Boulder, Colo.: Westview Press, 1980.

Kumar, Krishna, and Maxwell G. McLeod, eds. *Multinationals for Developing Countries*. Lexington, Mass.: Lexington Books, 1981.

Lal-Sanabary, Nagut M., ed. *Women and Work in the Third World: The Impact of Industrialisation and Global Economic Interdependence*. Berkeley: University of California Press, 1983.

Lall, S., ed. *The New Multinationals: The Spread of Third World Enterprise*. New York: John Wiley & Sons, 1984. 268pp. $38.95. Cloth.

Lall, Sanjaya. *The Multinational Corporation*. New York: Holmes & Meier, 1980.

Lessard, Donald R., and John Williamson. *Capital Flight and Third World Debt*. Washington, D.C.: Institute for International Economics, 1987. 260pp.

Marcussen, Henrick Secher, and Jens Erik Torp. *The Internationalization of Capital: Prospects for the Third World*. London and New Jersey: Zed Books, 1982. 181pp. $11.50.

Mattelart, A. *Multinational Corporations and the Control of Culture*. Atlantic Highlands, N.J.: Humanities Press, 1979.

Melrose, Dianna. *Bitter Pills: Medicines and the Third World Poor*. Oxford: Oxfam, 1982. £4.95.

Mezger, Dorothea. *Copper in the World Economy*. New York: Monthly Review Press, 1980. 282pp. $8.

Mitter, Swasti. *Common Fate, Common Bond: Women in the Global Economy*. London: Pluto Press, 1986. 224pp. £4.95.

Munslow, B., and H. Finch, eds. *Proletarianisation in the Third World*. London: Croom Helm, 1984.

Nore, Petter, and Terisa Turner, eds. *Oil and Class Struggle*. London and New Jersey: Zed Books, 1980. 307pp. $11.50.

Norris, Ruth, ed. *Pills, Pesticides and Profits: The International Trade in Toxic Substances*. Croton-on-Hudson, NY: North River Press, 1982. 168pp. $10.95.

Nothing To Lose but Our Lives: Empowerment To Oppose Industrial Hazards in a Transnational World. New York: New Horizons Press, 1988. 207pp. $13.50. Available from the Council on International and Public Affairs, 777 United Nations Plaza, Suite 9A, New York, NY 10017.

Odle, Maurice A. *Multinational Banks and Underdevelopment*. New York: Pergamon Press, 1981.

Perrucci, Carolyn C., et al. *Plant Closings: International Context and Social Costs*. Hawthorne, N.Y.: Walter de Gruyter, 1988. 193pp.

Robinson, J. *Multinationals and Political Control.* London: Gower, 1983.

Ruggie, J. G., ed. *Antinomies of Interdependence: National Welfare and the International Division of Labor.* New York: Columbia University Press, 1983.

Rugman, A., and L. Eden, eds. *Multinationals and Transfer Pricing.* London: Croom Helm, 1985.

Sampson, Anthony. *The Money Lenders: Bankers and a World in Turmoil.* New York: Viking Press, 1982.

Sassen, Sashia. *The Mobility of Labor and Capital.* New York and Cambridge, Eng.: Cambridge University, 1988.

Stauffer, Robert B., ed. *Transnational Corporations and the State.* Sydney: Transnational Corporations Research Project, 1986. 269pp. $16.95.

Tanzer, Michael. *The Race for Resources: Continuing Struggles over Minerals and Fuels.* New York: Monthly Review Press, 1980. 285pp. $6.50.

Taylor, June H., and Michael D. Yokell. *Yellowcake: The International Uranium Cartel.* New York: Pergamon Press, 1979.

Torrie, Jill, ed. *Banking on Poverty: The Global Impact of the IMF and World Bank.* Toronto: Between the Lines, 1983. 336pp.

Turner, L. *Oil Companies in the International System.* London: George Allen & Unwin, 1983.

United Nations Centre on Transnational Corporations. *Transnational Corporations in World Development: Third Survey.* New York and Geneva: United Nations, 1983. 386pp. $38. UN sales number: E.83.II.A.14. Fourth survey is forthcoming.

Villamil, Jose J., ed. *Transnational Capitalism and National Development: New Perspectives on Dependence.* Atlantic Highlands, NJ: Humanities Press, 1979.

Waterman, Peter, ed. *For a New Labour Internationalism: A Set of Reprints and Working Papers.* The Hague: International Labour Education Research and Information Foundation, 1984.

Wells, Louis T., Jr. *Third World Multinationals: The Rise of Foreign Investment from Developing Countries.* Cambridge, Mass.: MIT Press, 1983.

AFRICA

Biersteker, Thomas J. *Multinationals, the State, and Control of the Nigerian Economy.* Princeton, N.J.: Princeton University Press, 1988. $12.50

Bolton, Dianne. *Nationalization: A Road to Socialism? The Case of Tanzania.* London and New Jersey: Zed Books, 1985. 178pp. $10.95.

First, Ruth. *Black Gold: The Mozambican Miner, Proletarian and Peasant.* New York: St. Martin's Press, 1983.

Langdon, S. *Multinational Corporations in the Political Economy of Kenya.* London: Macmillan, 1981.

Leslie, Winsome J. *The World Bank and Structural Transformation in Developing Countries: The Case of Zaire.* Boulder, Colo. and London: Lynne Rienner, 1987. 208pp. $30. Cloth.

Mhone, Guy C. Z. *Political Economy of a Dual Labor Market in Africa: The Copper Industry and Dependency in Zambia, 1929-1969.* Rutherford, N.J.: Fairleigh Dickinson University Press, 1982. 256pp. $25.

Nyangoni, Wellington. *OECD and Western Mining Multinational Corporations in the Republic of South Africa.* Boston: University Press of America, 1982.

Quamina, Odida T. *Mineworkers of Guyana: The Making of a Working Class.* London and New Jersey: Zed Books, 1987. 118pp. $35. Cloth.

Seidman, Ann. *The Roots of Crisis in Southern Africa.* Trenton, N.J.: Africa World Press, 1986. 210pp. $8.95.

Southall, Roger, ed. *Labor and Unions in Asia and Africa: Contemporary Issues.* Hampshire, England: Macmillan Press, 1987. 272pp. £9.50.

ASIA AND PACIFIC

Asia-Pacific Peoples' Environment Network. *The Bhopal Tragedy: One Year After.* Penang: Sahabat Alam Malaysia, 1986. 236pp. $16.

Björkman, James Warner, ed. *The Changing Division of Labor in South Asia: Women and Men in India's Society, Economy, and Politics.* Riverdale, Md.: Riverdale Company, 1986. 152pp. $19. Cloth.

Cavanagh, John, Frederick Clairmonte, and Robin Room. *The World Alcohol Industry with Special Reference to Australia, New Zealand, and the Pacific Islands.* Sydney: Transnational Corporations Research Project, 1985. Rev. ed. 231pp. $16.95.

Clancey, Jack, Filo Hirota, and Denis Murphy, eds. and comps. *Labor and the Church in Asia.* Hongkong: Center for the Progress of Peoples, 1983. 138pp.

Holmstrom, Mark. *Industry and Inequality: The Social Anthropology of Indian Labour.* Cambridge, Eng.: Cambridge University Press, 1984. 342pp.

Jones, Tara. *Corporate Killing: Bhopals Will Happen.* New York: Columbia University Press, 1988. 352pp. $50. Cloth.

Morehouse, Ward, and M. Arun Subramaniam. *Bhopal Tragedy: What Really Happened and What It Means for American Workers and Communities at Risk.* New York: Bhopal Action Research Center, 1986. 204pp. $13.50.

Nemetz, Peter N., ed. *The Pacific Rim: Investment, Development and Trade.* Vancouver: University of British Columbia Press, 1987. 320pp. $12.75.

Owen, Norman G., ed. *The Philippine Economy and the United States: Studies in Past and Present Interactions.* Ann Arbor: University of Michigan, Center for South and Southeast Asian Studies, 1983.

Southall, Roger, ed. *Labor and Unions in Asia and Africa: Contemporary Issues.* Hampshire, England: Macmillan Press, 1987. 272pp. £9.50.

Stauffer, Robert B. *Transnational Corporations and the Political Economy of Development: The Continuing Philippine Debate.* Sydney: Transnational Corporations Research Project, 1980.

Thorbek, Susanne. *Voices from the City: Women of Bangkok.* London and New Jersey: Zed Books, 1987. 168pp. $12.50.

Turner, H. A. *Last Colony: But Whose? A Study of the Labour Movement, Labour Market and Labour Relations in Hong Kong.* Cambridge, Eng.: Cambridge University Press, 1980.

Utrecht, Ernst, ed. *Transnational Corporations in South East Asia and the Pacific.* Sydney: Transnational Corporations Research Project, 1978-85. 7 vols.

Yoffie, David B. *Power & Protectionism: Strategies of the Newly Industrializing Countries.* New York: Columbia University Press, 1983. 282pp. Cloth.

LATIN AMERICA AND CARIBBEAN

Angel Reyes, Miguel, and Mike Gatehouse. *Soft Drink, Hard Labour: Guatemalan Workers Take on Coca-Cola.* London: Latin America Bureau, 1987. £1.50.

Bennett, Douglas, and Kenneth Sharpe. *Transnational Corporations vs. the State: The Political Economy of the Mexican Automobile Industry.* Princeton, N.J.: Princeton University Press, 1985.

Blanchard, Peter. *The Origins of the Peruvian Labour Movement, 1883-1919.* Pittsburgh: University of Pittsburgh Press, 1982. 214pp. $23.95.

Collins, Jane L. *Unseasonal Migrations: The Effects of Rural Labor Scarcity in Peru.* Princeton, N.J.: Princeton University Press, 1988. 200pp. $27.50. Cloth.

Coote, Belinda. *The Hunger Crop: Poverty and the Sugar Industry.* Oxford: Oxfam, 1987. 160pp. £3.50.

de Shazo, Peter. *Urban Workers and Labor Unions in Chile, 1902-1927.* Madison: University of Wisconsin Press, 1983. 351pp.

Edquist, Charles. *Capitalism, Socialism and Technology: A Comparative Study of Cuba and Jamaica.* London and New Jersey: Zed Books, 1985. 182pp. $9.95.

Evans, Peter. *Dependent Development: The Alliance of Multinational, State and Local Capital in Brazil.* Princeton, N.J.: Princeton University Press, 1979.

Gerardi, R. E. *Australia, Argentina and World Capitalism, 1930-1945.* Sydney: Transnational Corporations Research Project, 1985.

Gwynne, Robert N. *Industrialization and Urbanization in Latin America.* Baltimore: Johns Hopkins University Press, 1986. 259pp. $30. Cloth.

Humphrey, J. *Capitalist Control and Workers' Struggle in the Brazilian Auto Industry.* Princeton, N.J.: Princeton University Press, 1982.

Jenkins, R. *Transnational Corporations and Industrial Transformation in Latin America.* London: Macmillan, 1984.

Kronish, R., and K. Mericle, eds. *The Political Economy of the Latin*

American Motor Vehicle Industry. Cambridge, Mass.: MIT Press, 1984.

Lernoux, Penny. *In Banks We Trust.* New York: Penguin, 1986. 352pp. $7.95.

Maxcy, G. *The Multinational Motor Industry.* London: Croom Helm, 1981.

Melrose, Dianna. *Bitter Pills: Medicines and the Third World Poor.* Oxford: Oxfam, 1982. 277pp. £4.95.

Montavon, R. *The Role of Multinational Companies in Latin America: A Case Study in Mexico.* Farnborough, Eng.: Saxon House, 1979.

Munck, Ronaldo, with Ricardo Falcon, and Bernardo Galitelli. *Argentina from Anarchism to Peronism: Workers, Unions and Politics, 1855-1985.* London and New Jersey: Zed Books, 1987. 261pp. $15.

Nash, June. *We Eat the Mines, the Mines Eat Us: Dependency and Exploitation in Bolivian Tin Mines.* New York: Columbia University Press, 1979.

Newfarmer, Richard. *Transnational Conglomerates and the Economics of Dependent Development.* Greenwich, Conn.: JAI Press, 1980. $45. Cloth.

Newfarmer, Richard S., ed. *Profits, Progress and Poverty: Case Studies of International Industries in Latin America.* South Bend, Ind.: University of Notre Dame Press, 1985.

Poverty Brokers: The IMF and Latin America. London: Latin America Bureau, 1983. 138pp. £3.25. Distributed in North America by Monthly Review Press.

Ramsaran, Ramesh F. *U.S. Investment in Latin America and the Caribbean.* New York: St. Martin's Press, 1985. 196pp. $35. Cloth.

Roxborough, I. *Unions and Politics in Mexico: The Case of the Automobile Industry.* New York: Cambridge University Press, 1984.

Ruiz, Vicki L., and Susan Tiano, eds. *Women on the U.S. Mexico Border: Responses to Change.* Winchester, Mass.: Allen & Unwin, 1987. 248pp. $14.95.

Scott, Rebecca J. *Slave Emancipation in Cuba: The Transition to Free Labor.* Princeton, N.J.: Princeton University Press, 1986. 337pp. $14.95

Tamarin, David. *The Argentine Labor Movement, 1930-1945: A Study in the Origins of Peronism.* Albuquerque: University of New Mexico Press, 1985. 273pp. $27.50. Cloth.

Thorup, Cathryn L., ed. *The United States and Mexico: Face to Face with New Technology.* New Brunswick, N.J.: Transaction Publishers, 1987. 224pp. $19.95.

MIDDLE EAST

Bayat, Assef. *Workers and Revolution in Iran: A Third World Experience of Workers' Control.* London and New Jersey: Zed Books, 1987. 224pp. $12.50.

Ladjevardi, Habib. *Labor Unions and Autocracy in Iran.* Syracuse: Syracuse University Press, 1985. 328pp. $29.95. Cloth.

Semyonov, Moshe, and Noah Lewin-Epstein. *Hewers of Wood and Drawers of Water: Noncitizen Arabs in the Israeli Labor Market.* Ithaca, N.Y.: ILR Press, 1988. $10.95.

Woodward, Peter N. *Oil and Labor in the Middle East.* New York: Praeger, 1988. 208pp. $39.95. Cloth.

INFORMATION SOURCES

For lists of other books on the subject of transnational corporations and labor see the bibliographies and directories described above in this chapter, as well as the periodicals annotated in chapter 3, below, that carry book review columns on a regular basis.

Particularly noteworthy are the topical bibliographies that Matty Klatter contributes regularly to the *Newsletter of International Labour Studies.* These bibliographies are drawn from *International Labour Studies: A Third World and Labour-Oriented Bibliography,* an occasional publication that Klatter produces and distributes free-of-charge. Write: The Library, Institute of Social Studies, 251 Badhuisweg, 2597 JR The Hague, Netherlands. Issue 40-41 (1989) of NILS contained a noteworthy bibliography and resource listing compiled by Peter Waterman: "Beyond Trade Union Imperialism in the USA."

For the names of additional publications from UN agencies, such as the Centre on Transnational Corporations, write for a copy of the annual publications catalog: United Nations, NY 10017. The International Labour Office issues a quarterly catalog of its publications: ILO Publications, CH-1211 Geneva 22, Switzerland, or 1750 New York Ave., NW, Washington, DC 20006.

See also the publications from **Third World Resources** described in the preface to this directory and the reference to the 4-page guide to resources on transnational corporations and labor in the information sources section of chapter 1 above.

3

Periodicals

This chapter is divided into three parts: annotated entries, supplementary list of periodicals, and sources of additional information on periodicals related to transnational corporations and labor in the Third World.

Information in the **annotated entries** is given in the following order: title; publisher; address; frequency of publication; format (magazine, newsletter, newspaper); size (height in centimeters and number of pages); subscription costs; keyword description of format; and description of content.

Quotation marks in the annotations enclose the words of the periodical's publisher, editor, or promotional materials.

Periodicals in the **supplementary list** (pp. 83–84) are listed alphabetically and the entries include title; address; frequency of publication; and type of periodical. Additional data are provided when available.

The **information sources** part (pp. 84–85) provides information about directories and guides that contain the names of other periodicals on these subjects.

All periodical titles and related organizations in this chapter are listed in the appropriate indexes at the back of the directory. Check through the annotated entries section of the organizations chapter above for the names of additional periodicals.

Note that this chapter does not contain periodicals that are published by governments, corporations, or official trade union organizations. Nor does it contain names of the many periodicals that have issued forth from the "socially responsible investment" movement. See the information sources section below for information on how to locate publications such as these.

ANNOTATED ENTRIES

■ *AMPO: Japan-Asia Quarterly Review,* Pacific-Asia Resource Center (PARC), C.P.O. Box 5250, Tokyo International, Tokyo, Japan. 4 issues/

yr. Magazine. 24 cm. 56pp. Individual subscription: $24/yr. Institutional subscription: $36/yr. Inquire for overseas airmail rates. Feature articles, advertisements, illustrations, notes, photographs. Available in North America from the Asia Resource Center (Washington, D.C.).

AMPO had its origins in late 1969 with the Japanese "Peace for Vietnam Committee" and an affiliated organization of foreign residents in Japan. The magazine focused considerable energies at the start on opposition to the 1970 Japan-U.S. Security Treaty. (*AMPO* is an abbreviated form of Japan-U.S. Security Treaty.) The review is designed "to overcome the fact that the Japanese left, one of the most articulate and active movements in the world, is covered by a blanket of silence in all languages but Japanese."

AMPO presents well-documented radical analyses of political, economic, and military issues in Asia in a jargon-free style. Typical articles are about workers and labor unions in Thailand, challenges to French nuclear colonialism in the South Pacific, human rights in Korea, and the International Monetary Fund in the Philippines. Literature, drama, and art are also covered.

See the two issues of *AMPO* reviewed in the pamphlets and articles chapter below: *Japan's Human Imports: As Capital Flows Out, Foreign Labor Flows In* (vol. 19, no. 4. 1988), and *Japanese Industry Moves Out* (vol. 19, no. 1. 1987).

From time to time *AMPO* devotes an entire issue to one theme. Vol. 8, no. 4 (1977), for instance, was a major study of free trade zones and the industrialization of Asia.

■ *Asia Labour Monitor,* Asia Monitor Resource Center (AMRC), 444-46 Nathan Rd., 8-B, Kowloon, Hongkong. 6 issues/yr. Magazine. 21.5 cm. 102pp. Individual subscription: $20/yr. Institutional subscription: $40/yr. Trade unions and non-profit organizations qualify for the individual subscription rate. Notes, feature article, photographs, charts, statistical tables.

In 1988 the Asia Monitor Resource Center changed the format of its publication from abstracts from the press in the Asia and Pacific region on labor-related topics to topical booklets devoted to one theme.

The first issue in the new series was entitled *Min-ju Nojo: South Korea's New Trade Unions.* (See pamphlets and articles chapter below.) The spring 1988 booklet deals with workers and unions in China's market socialism (*Smashing the Iron Rice Pot*).

The booklets are attractively designed and well-documented. They are based on field studies and on the AMRC's own clippings files and are compiled with the assistance of regional and international labor organizations and unions.

■ *Asian Migrant,* Scalabrini Migration Center, P.O. Box 10541, Broadway Centrum, Quezon City, Philippines. 6 issues/yr. Magazine. 28 cm. 32pp. Individual and institutional subscriptions: $15/yr. Subscriptions: Mass Media Scalabrinian Fathers, P.O. Box 41, Fitzroy, Victoria 3065, Australia. Editorial, documentation, feature articles, news reports, book reviews.

"Asia and refugee have become almost synonymous," note the editors of this new bimonthly. *Asian Migrant* aims to examine this phenomenon and to provide answers to questions such as these: What is it that makes people pull up stakes and journey to foreign lands? What of the families left behind by the refugees? Does the export of native labor really reduce unemployment at home? What are the hopes and expectations of the migrants?

And a final question: "What is our own relationship to this event transpiring before our very eyes, an event so colossal that no one in the developed or underdeveloped world is not touched by it in one way or another?"

The "trial issue" of *Asian Migrant* (Oct.-Nov. 1987) contained lengthy articles on Asian migrants in the Middle East and in the United States, an overview of the situation of refugees throughout the Asia region, a study of the "flesh trade" between the Philippines and Japan, and numerous newsbriefs submitted by correspondents in fifteen Asian cities, as well as Rome and Zurich. The magazine takes its inspiration from the work of Bishop John Baptist Scalabrini, who founded a society a century ago to "serve migrants of all races and religions."

■ *Asian Women Workers Newsletter,* Committee for Asian Women, 57 Peking Rd., 4th floor, Kowloon, Hongkong. 4 issues/yr. Newsletter. 29.5 cm. 14pp. $4/year outside of Asia. $3/year in Asia. Feature articles, figures, illustrations, news reports, photographs, statistical tables.

Asian newspapers and other publications are the sources for the articles and news items in this newsletter. Its editors also welcome firsthand reports "on the living and working conditions of Asian workers and their struggles for equality and liberation."

Recent issues featured articles on "retrenchments"—plant closures, worker layoffs, and dismissals—in electronic firms in Malaysia and other parts of South Asia, on workers' efforts to organize, and on the effect on women of labor laws in Asia.

"Newsbits," a regular column, reports on, for example, women's career prospects in Korea, jobs for women in India, unions and women's rights in China, and a woman's successful suit against a Japanese trade union for discrimination.

The resources section of the newsletter is of particular interest. Books, audiovisuals, reports—all are annotated carefully and full ordering information is included.

■ *CEP Research Report,* Council on Economic Priorities, 30 Irving Place, New York, NY 10003. 12 issues/yr. Newsletter. 28 cm. 6pp. Individual and institutional subscriptions: $25/yr. With membership. Feature article, charts, illustrations, network news, photographs.

Articles in this newsletter do not deal with corporate affairs in Third World countries as such, but the topics covered in the *Research Report,* such as weapons sales and the handling of nuclear wastes, have obvious implications for the developing nations.

Each issue of the newsletter contains a major article on one topic, with supporting charts and sidebar material. Articles have dealt with selective purchasing ordinances enacted by cities across the United States (prohibiting, for instance, purchases from companies tied to apartheid South Africa), the comprehensive ban on nuclear weapons tests, the economics of President Reagan's Strategic Defense Initiative, corporate responsiveness to women in the workplace, corporate responsibility in Japan, and stockholder resolutions filed by socially concerned institutional investors.

CEP's annual summary of shareholder resolutions (in the March issue of the *Research Report*) identifies corporate activities with regard to South Africa, "other international justice issues" (such as policies to prevent receipt of unlawful "capital flight" from developing countries), nuclear and conventional arms contracting, energy and the environment, equal opportunity, and more.

The back page of the newsletter is devoted to short reports on activities at the Council on Economic Priorities.

■ *Corporate Examiner,* Interfaith Center on Corporate Responsibility, 475 Riverside Dr., Rm. 566, New York, NY 10115. 10 issues/yr. Newsletter. 28 cm. 8pp. Individual and institutional subscriptions: $35/yr. Feature article, editorial, illustrations, news reports, book reviews.

The subtitle to this long-established publication of the Interfaith Center reads: "A Publication Examining Policies and Practices of Major U.S. Corporations on Apartheid, Star Wars [the Strategic Defense Initiative], Nuclear Weapons, Minorities, Women, Alternative Investments, Energy, Environment, and International Marketing."

Page one of the *Examiner* is given to a regular column entitled "Corporate Action News" and to short reviews of new publications. Both sections spill over onto later pages of the newsletter. Subjects covered in the "Corporate Action News" column include nuclear weapons, protests against General Electric, an offer by Merck & Co. to distribute for free its newly developed drug for treatment of river blindness, the firing of 4,000 Namibian mineworkers by Newmont Mining, and Citibank's departure from South Africa.

Guest editorials, reports on ICCR activities, and news reports fill out the body of the newsletter.

Each issue of *The Corporate Examiner* contains a four-page *ICCR Brief* that deals in depth with one subject. Available at bulk rate discounts, these "briefs" are handy summaries for group study and workshops. Subjects examined in recent issues include the militarization of space, U.S. corporations and economic conversion, the immorality of apartheid, and Shell Oil's reactions to criticisms of its involvement in South Africa.

■ *Corporate Responsibility Monitor,* DataCenter, 464 19th St., Oakland, CA 94612. 12 issues/yr. Magazine. 28 cm. 100pp. Individual subscription: $200/yr. Institutional subscription: $300/yr. Single issue: $35. $420/yr. for corporations. News clippings.

For professionals engaged in research and action regarding the domestic and international policies of major corporations this DataCenter publication provides full-text reproductions of selected articles from more than 100 publications representing a wide range of political viewpoints. Sources include *Mother Jones, Business Week, In These Times, Journal of Commerce, People's Daily World, Christian Science Monitor,* and the *New York Times.*

Articles are divided into nine sections: general; corporate performance; environmental issues; consumer issues; suits and investigations; corporate philanthropy; weapons production; foreign investment; and labor relations.

The full title of each article is given in the table of contents, along with the name of the publication in which it originally appeared. The name of the publication and the date of the article are provided with each of the entries.

Each issue of the *Corporate Responsibility Monitor* contains between sixty and seventy articles.

■ *The CTC Reporter,* United Nations Centre on Transnational Corporations. Order from United Nations Publications, Room DC2-0853, United Nations, New York, NY 10017, or Palais des Nations, 1211 Geneva 10, Switzerland. 2 issues/yr. Magazine. 28 cm. 60pp. Individual and institutional subscriptions: $20/yr. Single issue: $9. Sales: Room DC2-0853. Feature article, documentation, figures, illustrations, notes, charts, interviews, photographs, book reviews, statistical tables.

This official journal of the UNCTC reports on activities of the Commission on Transnational Corporations (for which the Centre on Transnational Corporations functions as secretariat), traces the progress that is made on the UNCTC's Code of Conduct for transnational corporations, and carries articles that pertain to the two institutional divisions of the CTC's work: policy analysis and research, and advisory and information services.

The magazine regularly describes work on transnational corporations that is being done at other research institutes such as the Center on Transnational Economy (Argentina) and the Transnational Corporations Research Project (Australia) and in international labor union organizations such as the World Federation of Trade Unions (WFTU) and the International Confederation of Free Trade Unions (ICFTU).

The autumn 1987 issue of *The CTC Reporter* (no. 24) included an index for issues 17-23; issues 1-16 were indexed in the spring 1984 edition (no. 17).

■ *Economic Notes,* Labor Research Association, 80 East 11 St., Rm. 634, New York, NY 10003. 6 issues/yr. Newsletter. 28 cm. 16pp. Subscription: $30/yr. Single issue: $3. Foreign: $23/year. Bulk rates available. Feature article, charts, comment and analysis, illustrations, notes, statistical tables.

Economic Notes offers one major article in each issue, with accompanying charts and statistical material. Articles routinely concern themselves with domestic U.S. economic issues, but the newsletter will occasionally explore subjects that are international in scope, such as transnational corporations and international trade, labor movement support for peace, and building trade union unity across international borders.

Two regular features of the newsletter, "Economic clips" and "Trends," provide summaries of economic activities in a readable and appealing style.

Economic Notes is written for a U.S. audience of union officers, staff, and LRA members. The editors intend their economic analyses and statistical data to be used in labor negotiations, public testimony, and membership educational programs.

The Labor Research Association also publishes a biweekly, the *Trade Union Advisor,* that offers trade union leaders current information on wages, contract settlements, corporate strategies, government spending, investments, and labor markets. As a regular feature, the *Advisor* carries exclusive interviews with individuals whom the editors regard as "the most prominent and forward-looking trade union leaders in the United States today."

■ *Global Electronics,* Pacific Studies Center, 222B View St., Mountain View, CA 94041. 12 issues/yr. Newsletter. 28 cm. 4pp. Individual and institutional subscriptions: $12/yr. Canada and Mexico: $14/yr. Overseas: $17. Back issues available. Comment and analysis, news reports, illustrations, statistical tables.

Editor Lenny Siegel packs plenty of information and commentary on the global electronics industry into this four-page newsletter. Articles occasionally run longer than one page, but most are short and to the point.

Global Electronics highlights developments in the global electronics industry as these are reported on in newspapers and industry journals such as *Electronics, San Jose Business Journal, SEMI Outlook, Silicon Valley Toxics News, Datamation, Business Week,* and the *San Jose Mercury News.*

Subjects covered include labor strife in the South Korean electronics industry, the semiconductor industry's proposal for Pentagon subsidization of a "manufacturing research consortium," AFL-CIO support for the denial of trade preferences to Third World governments ruled by reactionary regimes, health hazards in electronics assembly plants, and the paucity of women in top management positions in the electronics industry.

"Watchdogging 'High Tech' " is the way *Global Electronics* defines its mission. Readers with similar interests will appreciate the way in which this newsletter keeps them abreast of developments in this critical industry and alerts them to aspects of these developments — such as their impact on labor—that ordinarily go unreported in the business-oriented press.

■ *IECON Newsletter,* Interreligious Economic Crisis Organizing Network, 815 Second Ave., 5th floor, New York, NY 10017. 4 issues/yr. Newsletter. 28 cm. 8pp. Individual and institutional subscriptions: $20/yr. Inquire for group and bulk subscription rates. News reports, calendar, comment and analysis, documentation, essays, illustrations, network news, photographs, list of resources.

"As members of religious communities dedicated to the cause of justice," write the organizers of the Interreligious Economic Crisis Organizing Network, "we count it our responsibility to respond to the disastrous effects of economic dislocation." This newsletter chronicles IECON's efforts to meet its responsibilities to those across the United States who have suffered as a result of plant shutdowns, layoffs, and wage cutbacks.

The newsletter carries news of network activities (divided regionally), reports on meetings of the IECON steering committee, action alerts, notices of print and audiovisual resources, legislative updates, the texts of church statements on economic dislocation, and occasional descriptive articles on topics such as the use of eminent domain to prevent plant shutdowns.

The frequency of publication has varied since the foundation of IECON in 1983 as the demands of organizing sapped the limited resources of the national staff, but quarterly publication is still the aim.

■ *International Labour Review,* International Labour Organization Publications, CH-1211 Geneva 22, Switzerland, or 1750 New York Ave., NW, Washington, DC 20006. 6 issues/yr. Magazine. 120pp. Individual and institutional subscriptions: $42/yr. (surface mail). Feature articles, advertisements, bibliography, notes, reference notes, book reviews, statistical tables.

The stated purpose of this ILO publication is "to contribute to wider understanding of questions of labour and social policy and administration related to the programmes of the ILO by publishing the results of original research, international comparative studies, articles analysing experience of international interest in different countries, and reviews or notes on new publications in fields of concern to the ILO."

The technical nature of many of the articles in the *International Labour Review* limits the appeal of the journal to professionals in the field.

■ *International Labour Reports,* Mayday Publications, P.O. Box 45, Stainborough, Barnsley, Yorkshire S75 3EA, England. 6 issues/yr. Magazine. 29.5 cm. 28pp. Individual subscription: £12/$28/yr. Institutional subscription: £25/$50/yr. Apply for special rates for labor movement organizations. North American address: P.O. Box 5036, Berkeley, CA 94705. Feature articles, advertisements, comment and analysis, illustrations, news reports, columns, book reviews, list of resources, photographs.

Launched in 1984 this polished magazine covers the international labor scene with lively reporting from the field and in-depth, critical analyses of transnational corporations in Third World and industrialized nations.

Topical areas include the world of the global corporations and their strategies for the international workforce; the policies and struggles of international trade union organizations; women working worldwide; the migrant and immigrant workforce; trade union prisoners of conscience; and labor law and the international labor movement.

Third World countries and regions covered in issues of *International Labour Reports* during 1987-88 included South Africa, the Philippines, South Korea, Namibia, Brazil, Guatemala, Jamaica, India, Tunisia, Gaza and the Occupied Territories, Nicaragua, and Singapore.

The November/December 1987 edition of the magazine (no. 24) carried a four-page index of the companies, industries, countries, and topics covered in *International Labour Reports* in 1986.

This magazine is highly recommended for consistently good descriptions and analyses of international labor-related issues.

■ *Labor and Development: A Monthly Review of African Socio-Economic Events of Interest to Trade Union Leaders,* Regional Economic Research and Documentation Center, P.O. Box 7138, Lomé, Republic of Togo. Newsletter. 12 issues/yr. 30 cm. 26pp. News reports, documentation, book reviews.

This journal was launched in the early 1970s as "a response to a fundamental need recognized by African trade union organizations for a rapid exchange of news and information concerning important labor, economic, and social events." The mimeographed newsletter contains abstracts of news stories and short reports on economic issues such as prices and wages, employment and labor power, and economic development strategies. Other sections of the newsletter are entitled: "Documents"; "Research Reports"; "Trade Union History"; and "Trade Union Forum."

The Regional Economic Research and Documentation Center was established in 1972 under the sponsorship of the African-American Labor Center. A statement in *Labor and Development* contends, however, that control of the RERDC is now in the hands of the Organisation of African Trade Union Unity.

Labor and Development, which was called *Labor in Perspective* when it was first established, has a sister publication entitled *African Trade Union News,* which reports on "specific union events" on a biweekly basis.

■ *Labor Notes,* Labor Education and Research Project, 7435 Michigan Ave., Detroit, MI 48210. 12 issues/yr. Newsletter. 28 cm. 16pp. Individual subscription: $10/yr. Institutional subscription: $20/yr. Bulk rates available. Inquire for rates outside the United States. Feature articles, columnists, comment and analysis, editorial, illustrations, letters to the editor, network news, news reports, list of resources.

"Let's put the *movement* back in the labor movement" is the rallying cry of the obstreperous publishers of this newsletter. *Labor Notes* takes on undemocratic and hidebound unions with as much energy as it devotes to reports and analyses of the evil doings of corporations. Reports from Teamsters for a Democratic Union and grievances regarding the "one-party" nature of the United Auto Workers stand side-by-side in the newsletter with indictments of Chicago's social service system by union activists and updates on labor actions against a coal mining company in Wyoming.

Most of the newsletter's coverage is U.S.-focused, but international topics are treated as well. The June 1988 issue, for instance, carried a front page story on the "disappearance" of labor unionists in El Salvador and an interview with a former officer of Poland's Solidarity labor union. The August 1988 edition described the ideological battles at the 1988 convention of the Service Employees International Union concerning the forging of solidarity ties with unions in Central America that do not belong to the International Confederation of Free Trade Unions (the international body to which the AFL-CIO belongs).

Regular columns in the newsletter, such as "Resources" and "News Watch," often carry items that are international in scope.

■ *Labor Report on Central America,* P.O. Box 28014, Oakland, CA 94604. 6 issues/yr. Newspaper. 44.5 cm. 4pp. Individual and institutional subscriptions: $5/yr. Bulk rates available. Feature articles, comment and analysis, network news, news reports, list of resources.

Labor Report reports on the harsh conditions facing trade unionists in El Salvador, Guatemala, and Honduras, the situation of workers and unions in Nicaragua, the foreign policy of the United States, and the solidarity activities and positions taken on Central America by unions all over the world.

"The proliferation of labor committees, caucuses, and political action committees that are taking up the Central America issue underscores the need for regular information and analysis," writes Mark Warschauer, coordinator of the Labor Network on Central America. "In publishing the *Labor Report,*" he says, "we in the Labor Network . . . hope to contribute to meeting this need by becoming a resource to inform and help build the anti-intervention movement within labor."

■ *Labor Today: The Rank and File in Action,* National Center for Trade Union Action and Democracy, 7917 S. Exchange, Chicago, IL 60617. 4 issues/yr. Newsletter. 27.5 cm. 16pp. Individual and institutional subscriptions: $6.50/yr. Single issue: $1.75. Airmail outside the United States: $15/yr. Bulk rates available. Advertisements, comment and analysis, editorial, feature articles, illustrations, interviews, letters to the editor, news reports, photographs, book reviews.

This "independent labor journal," which was established in Detroit, Michigan, in 1962, offers coverage of international labor issues that is exceptional. Articles discuss the need for international trade union unity, the International Labour Organisation's "Declaration of Principles Concerning Multinational Enterprises," the shutdown of Todd Shipyards in California and Oregon, working conditions in assembly plants in the El Paso/Juarez area on the U.S.-Mexican border, U.S. labor's response to the Iran-contra affair, and the ties between U.S. and Salvadoran workers.

The newsletter often devotes one full page to international solidarity news. Updates on ongoing boycotts usually involve corporations with affiliates in Third World countries.

■ *Labour, Capital and Society,* Centre for Developing-Area Studies, McGill University, 3715 Peel St., Montreal, Quebec H3A 1X1, Canada. 2 issues/yr. Magazine. 21 cm. 160pp. Individual subscription: Canadian $12/yr. Institutional subscription: Canadian $18/yr. Subscriptions to developing nations: Canadian $7/yr. Advertisements, bibliography, editorial, feature articles, figures, notes, book reviews.

This influential theoretical journal completed its twentieth year of publication in 1987. It regularly carries two or three major articles—in French or English, with an abstract—on issues such as the plantation economy and forced labor in French Guinea, structural change and the organizational development of small manufacturers in Ecuador, and health and safety in the labor process.

Twenty-five pages in each issue of *Labour, Capital and Society* are given to a long-running bibliography on national and international aspects of unemployment.

Review articles, research reports, and book reviews complement the articles and bibliography.

■ *Middle East Labor Bulletin,* Labor Committee on the Middle East, P.O. Box 421429, San Francisco, CA 94142-1429. 4 issues/yr. Newsletter. 28 cm. 16 pp. Individual subscription: $7.50/yr. Institutional subscription: $15/yr. Outside North America: add $3 (surface mail), $5 (air mail). News reports, action suggestions, documentation, editorial, network news.

The Labor Committee on the Middle East was organized four months before the beginning of the Palestinian Uprising in December 1987. This, their quarterly, began publication in 1988 and is intended to play an important role in carrying out the organization's goal of bringing to American unionists "an increased awareness of the key role played by U.S. labor 'leaders' in maintaining domestic and international support for Israel's continued occupation and repression of 1.5 million Palestinians in the Israeli-occupied West Bank and Gaza." Many feature articles focus on the Israeli Labor Federation, the Histadrut, its function, organization, and influence. Other articles have considered such issues as Israeli arms sales to South Africa and Arab workers' attempts to protest unjust conditions.

Shorter articles and a regular column called "Union Roundup" serve to keep readers updated on labor news from around the world relative to the Middle East, an area, note the editors, largely ignored by the leadership of American labor and by the U.S. media.

■ *Multinational Monitor,* P.O. Box 19405, Washington, DC 20036. 12 issues/yr. Magazine. 28 cm. 26pp. Individual subscription: $22/yr. Institutional subscription: $25/yr. Single issue: $2. Businesses: $35/year. Inquire for postage outside the United States. Feature article, charts, illustrations, notes, departments, photographs, interviews, statistical tables.

This popularly written magazine is "for people who believe that the decisions made by giant corporations are everybody's business." For more than eight years *Multinational Monitor* has tracked the "new and largely secretive ways" that multinational corporations profit from their global activities. The magazine examines the impact of these corporations on working people and their communities in the United States and in Third World countries.

Each edition of the monthly magazine features one cover story with accompanying charts, tables, photographs, and sidebar materials. Short news reports, resource lists, and commentary fill out each issue.

Several back issues of *Multinational Monitor* are reviewed in the pamphlets and articles chapter below. Titles of other issues are "High-Tech Hazards: Chipping Away at Workers Health," "Levi's in Arabia," "Latin America in Crisis," "Haitian Hell," "Indigenous People: The Struggle for Land and Equality," "Cashing in on the Debt Crisis," "Labor in El Salvador," "The Nuclear Quagmire," and "Genetic Roulette."

An index of the contents of the previous year's issues normally appears in one of the summer issues. Back issues of *Multinational Monitor* are available from February 1980.

■ *National Boycott News,* 6506 28 Ave., NE, Seattle, WA 98115. Irregular. Magazine. 28 cm. 100pp. Individual subscription: $10/4 issues. Two of the four issues are "updates." Feature articles, advertisements, documentation, illustrations, letters to the editor, network news, news reports, book reviews.

One of the tactics that has proven effective in curbing or eliminating undesirable activities and policies of transnational corporations is the boycott. The tactic is so popular, in fact, that it now has its own publication: *National Boycott News.*

The *NBN* covers every conceivable boycott—national and international. Issues range from mistreatment of animals in professional rodeos and in laboratory testing, to the funneling of corporate funds to support the *contras* in Nicaragua; from cultural performances in South Africa, to the production and sale of war toys for children. Reading through the magazine makes one appreciate the range of issues in which corporations are involved, as well as the vast potential for corporate abuse.

When a boycott is first announced, *NBN* provides in-depth coverage of the issues involved. Thereafter, the magazine offers handy summaries of the companies involved, their addresses, who called for the boycott, when the boycott began, what products are involved, what the reasons are for the boycott, what the company's reply is, and what progress has been made. When a boycott is called off, *NBN* reports that news as well.

Formerly a tabloid newspaper, the *NBN* became a magazine in 1988. It has had a rough time sticking to its quarterly publication—time and money have not been equal to the editor's lofty ambitions—but those responsible for the publication feel that a format of two issues plus two updates per year is now manageable.

■ *Newsletter of International Labour Studies,* Galileistraat 130, The Hague 2561 TK, The Netherlands. 4 issues/yr. Magazine. 21 cm. 40pp. Individual subscription: $14/yr. Institutional subscription: $31/yr. Single issue: $1.40. Feature articles, bibliography, comment and analysis, documentation, list of resources, book reviews.

This newsletter was launched in March 1978 "to facilitate an exchange of information among scholars concerned primarily with the working class of Latin America, Africa, Asia, the Caribbean, and the Middle East." The activities of workers in other areas of the world are examined "insofar as they have a bearing on workers internationally." The newsletter was also intended to track and analyze "developments in the areas of transnational capital, the international division of labour, labour conditions and struggles in Third World countries, and international migration."

NILS identifies and describes research work in progress, reports on meetings, conferences, and publications in the field, issues requests for information, and publishes short articles on labor-related themes. Matty Klatter, the librarian at the Institute of Social Studies (The Hague), regularly contributes a bibliography of books and articles on a theme such as Indian labor studies or international labor migration.

The editor, Peter Waterman, has performed a valuable service in struggling to keep *NILS* alive and publishing. The newsletter is a unique networking tool filled with helpful information on contacts, notices, and resources. It is a barometer, as well, indicating the present level of development of the independent international labor movement.

Many issues of *NILS* concern themselves with one theme or one country or region. Examples are labor internationalism (nos. 30-31), African labor studies and African labor struggles (nos. 26-27), homeworking on a world scale (no. 21), Indonesia (no. 18), Brazil (no. 15), Asia (no. 13), women and wage labor (no. 7), and labor studies in Tanzania (no. 5). Back issues of most of the issues are still available. Issues that are out of print are offered in photocopied form.

Issue no. 20 (January 1984) contained an index of the first nineteen issues of the newsletter; the spring 1987 issue (no. 28-29) brought the index up through issue no. 27. Issue no. 23 (October 1984) and the double issue that appeared in spring 1986 (nos. 28-29) were given entirely to book reviews and bibliographies.

■ *Of Prophets and Profits,* CANICCOR, An Interfaith Council on

Corporate Accountability, P.O. Box 6819, San Francisco, CA 94101. 12 issues/yr. Newsletter. 28 cm. 6pp. Individual and institutional subscriptions: $10/yr. News reports, network news, photographs.

Since its launching in 1974 this newsletter has reflected the local and regional concerns of its publisher, the Northern California (later California/Nevada) Interfaith Committee on Corporate Responsibility. In 1988 the publisher, an agency of the Northern California Ecumenical Council, adopted a new name to emphasize its broadened interest in corporate accountability—especially regarding financial institutions—on an international level: An Interfaith Council on Corporate Accountability (with California and Nevada tucked away in the acronym CANICCOR).

Of *Prophets and Profits* summarizes research reports compiled by CANICCOR staff members (on subjects such as the financing of South Africa's foreign trade or South Africa's gold and diamond trade), reports on activities in the "socially responsible investing" movement, and occasionally runs short articles on topics such as U.S. support for the mine workers' strike in South Africa.

The newsletter devotes a good deal of attention to South Africa; it focuses less on other Third World areas.

■ *Our Times,* 390 Dufferin St., Toronto, Ontario M6K 2A3, Canada. 10 issues/yr. Magazine. 28 cm. 42pp. Individual subscription: $18/yr. Institutional subscription: $30/yr. Add $3/year outside of Canada. Feature articles, advertisements, comment and analysis, illustrations, letters to the editor, network news, news reports, photographs, poetry, audiovisual reviews, book reviews.

The unionized cooperative—worker-owned and managed—that has been producing this "independent labour magazine" for seven years trumpets the fact that it publishes articles, not *about* labor, but *by* labor.

Although most articles pertain to the Canadian labor movement, many also have an international aspect. Articles in recent issues covered Canadian immigration policy, workers in South Africa, international newspaper empires, and a statement submitted by the National Council of Jesuits in Nicaragua to the U.S. Congress regarding U.S. aid to the contras.

Articles have also dealt with the effects of multinational corporations on workers—Canadians and others, the effects of the control and domination of U.S. corporations, and plant shutdowns and runaways: all topics of interest worldwide.

The magazine is well-designed and easy to read; the reviews and even the ads serve to keep the reader up-to-date on labor and related issues.

■ *Philippine Labor Alert,* Philippine Workers Support Committee, P.O. Box 11208, Moiliili Station, Honolulu, HI 96828. 4 issues/yr. Newsletter. 28 cm. 12pp. Individual and institutional subscriptions: $7/yr. News reports, comment and analysis, illustrations, photographs.

The PWSC publishes this newsletter to support the growth of "a genuine [organized] labor movement in the Philippines." The labor federation that the PWSC has in mind is the Kilusang Mayo Uno (KMU), which was founded in 1980 as an alternative to the Trade Union Congress of the Philippines, a right-wing organization that has been described as a "make-things-safe-for-the-multinationals" labor union. (The TUCP has the support of the AFL-CIO's conservative Asian-American Free Labor Institute.)

The *Labor Alert* carries news of KMU affairs in the Philippines and articles on other labor-related activities in the country. In addition the newsletter reports on "the efforts of workers in the United States and around the world to improve their working and living conditions."

■ *Plant Shutdowns Monitor,* DataCenter, 464 19 St., Oakland, CA 94612. 12 issues/yr. 28 cm. 56pp. Individual and institutional subscriptions: $200/yr. $300 for corporate and government subscriptions. News clippings.

This DataCenter publication has for more than seven years provided its professional readers with the best of the press on a variety of issues related to plant shutdowns—in the United States and elsewhere around the world. The publication contains full-text reproductions of newspaper and magazine articles on unemployment, international trade, industrial development, plant closings, layoffs, wage cutbacks and concessions, runaway shops (i.e., factories leaving one area or nation to open in another), labor negotiations, initiatives such as employee stock ownership plans, and actions by church, labor, and community activists to stop plant closings. The articles offer descriptions and analyses of economic affairs; they also weigh the negative personal and social impact of plant shutdowns.

DataCenter staff select the articles for the *Plant Shutdowns Monitor* from more than two hundred publications that they read and clip on a regular basis. Articles in a typical issue were chosen from *AFL-CIO News, Congressional Record, Economic Notes, Guardian, INC Magazine, Journal of Commerce, Los Angeles Times, Miami Herald, New York Times, OCAW Reporter, People's Daily World, San Francisco Chronicle, Washington Post,* and the *Wall Street Journal.*

A unique feature of the monthly publication is a computerized printout of all reported shutdowns, layoffs, and cutbacks. Information provided in the "Plant Shutdowns Directory" includes name of affiliate, parent company, location, Standard Industrial Classification (SIC) code, name of industry, number of employees affected, and a short description of the reported activity.

■ *Raw Materials Report,* P.O. Box 81519, S-10282 Stockholm, Sweden. 4 issues/yr. Magazine. 29.5 cm. 68pp. Individual subscription: 225 Swedish kroner/yr. Institutional subscription: 500 Swedish kroner/yr. Feature articles, documentation, editorial, figures, news reports, notes, photographs, references, statistical tables, book reviews, interviews.

Subtitled "A Quarterly Magazine on the Political Economy of Natural Resources," *Raw Materials Report* carries lengthy articles in a section entitled "Area Reports"; the articles treat subjects such as the impact of mining transnational corporations on developing countries in Africa, copper fabrication in Zambia, or the state of Canada's minerals and metals industry. The magazine also offers company reports (e.g., on CODELCO-Chile), special reports (e.g., on Chile's highly politicized and militant copper miners), the texts of significant documents, and lengthy book reviews. Reference notes and statistical tables and data are abundant.

The magazine, which entered its sixth year of publication in 1988, has correspondents in seven industrialized countries and information exchange arrangements with numerous documentation centers such as IBASE (Brazil), Tampere Peace Research Institute (Finland), Third World Studies Center (Philippines), Asia Monitor Resource Center (Hongkong), and the DataCenter (USA).

The detailed and often technical articles in *Raw Materials Report* will meet the information needs of serious students of transnational corporations, labor, and international development.

■ *Sugar World*, International Commission for the Co-ordination of Solidarity among Sugar Workers, ICCSASW, P.O. Box 66, Sta. B, Toronto M5T 2T2, Canada. 6 issues/yr. Newsletter. 28 cm. 6pp. Individual subscription: $8/yr. Institutional subscription: $15/yr. Feature articles, action suggestions, comment and analysis, editorial, illustrations, news reports, photographs, statistical tables, charts.

This newsletter of the ICCSASW covers the world of sugar: from Fiji and St. Kitts, to Spain, Brazil, and the Philippines. (The newsletter's annual index shows that events in fifteen individual nations and two "regions" [the European Economic Community and "international"] were covered in *Sugar World* in 1987.) Subjects treated include plant closures, layoffs, wage cuts, labor actions, the effects of herbicide use in sugar cane fields, attacks on sugar workers, and labor organizing efforts.

Published regularly since October 1977 this authoritative resource is essential reading for those interested in the story behind the commodity that is so much a part of our everyday lives and for those who care about the workers worldwide who labor to produce sugar and other commodities.

■ *TIE Report*, Transnationals Information Exchange, 20 Paulus Potterstraat, 1071 DA, Amsterdam, Netherlands. 4 issues/yr. Magazine. 75pp. Individual subscription: $15/yr. Institutional subscription: $25/yr. $50/yr. for organizations other than trade union branches, research groups, and libraries. Back issues available. Feature articles, editorial, network news, news reports, action suggestions, documentation, illustrations, notes, photographs, list of resources.

"Issues associated with the growth of transnational corporate power," write the editors of *TIE Report*, "concern many workers, action groups, trade unions, and researchers all over the world." Since its formation in 1978 the Transnationals Information Exchange has attempted to act as a forum for such groups and individuals. "TIE exists," they say, "to promote the exchange of information and experience [among] those working in this area, and, in particular, to make this information fully accessible to those that it most concerns—working people."

The organizational goals of TIE are reflected in its publication: articles deal with issues that affect workers directly (such as plant closures, hazardous chemicals, and industrial restructuring); the shop-floor experience of workers and the organizing experience of labor activists are woven throughout the articles; news reports and lists of resources aid working people in establishing links with co-workers throughout the world.

The magazine has carried reports on and analyses of women in the global textile industry, shop-floor internationalism and the auto industry, the churches and transnational corporations, industrial relations in Europe, Japan, and the United States, the agrochemicals industry, and the labor movement in Brazil. An issue of *TIE Report* is occasionally devoted to an in-depth examination of one transnational corporation such as Philips (no. 12) or the Ford Motor Company (no. 9).

■ *Who Owes Whom?* Project Abraço: North Americans in Solidarity with the People of Brazil, 515 Broadway, Santa Cruz, CA 95060. 4 issues/yr. Newsletter. 28 cm. 16pp. Donation requested. News reports, comment and analysis, illustrations.

Who Owes Whom? is unique among resources. It focuses on an important but neglected area of concern: the world system of finance, debt, and economic dependence. Further, the publication consistently points out the very real effects of high finance on the lives of ordinary people of both the Third and First Worlds as well as their own interrelatedness.

A typical issue contains one or two major articles (for example, "U.S. Farmers and the Third World," "The Dramatic Unfolding of the Debt Crisis: A View from Below," "The Youngest Pay the Most: Abandoned Children in Brazil," "The Effects of the Third World Debt Crisis on U.S. Workers"), short updates ("World Bank Campaign Continues"), excerpts from documents or books, a "What You Can Do" section, and a list of resources pertinent to the topic of the main article. The articles are popularly written and attractively interspersed with cartoons and drawings. Most of the issues dealt with pertain to Latin America, but even these bear a strong relationship to similar questions in other Third World regions.

Project Abraço, publisher of this quarterly, is a project of the Resource Center for Nonviolence. The group also publishes a bimonthly news update on events in Brazil called *Terra Nossa.*

■ *Work Ethics,* Plant Closures Project, 433 Jefferson, Oakland, CA 94607. 4 issues/yr. Newsletter. 28 cm. 10pp. Donation requested. News reports, action suggestions, calendar, comment and analysis, illustrations, network news.

Work Ethics is an excellent example of how the printed word can serve the organizing efforts of plant closures activists on a local or regional level. Published by the Oakland-based Plant Closures Project the newsletter reports on the progress of organizing campaigns, issues action alerts, calls attention to new resources (including funding sources), explains national and statewide legislative initiatives, and reproduces short articles from trade union publications.

Each issue offers at least one article or news report on the international dimensions of economic dislocation in the United States. The summer 1987 issue, for example, described the links between the proposed closing of the Delaval/Transamerica plant in Oakland and the repression of organized laborers in South Korea.

SUPPLEMENTARY LIST OF PERIODICALS

American Labor, American Labor Education Center, 1835 Kilbourne Pl., NW, Washington, DC 20010. 6 issues/yr. Newsletter. 28 cm. 8pp. Individual subscription: $9.95/yr. Institutional subscription: $40/yr. Single issue: $1.65.

Brazil Labor Report, 10 Roderick Rd., London NW3 2NL, England. 12 issues/yr. Individual and institutional subscriptions: $20/yr.

Canadian Dimension, Dimension Publishing, 44 Princess St., Suite 801, Winnipeg, Manitoba R3B 1K2, Canada. 8 issues/yr. Magazine. 27 cm. 64pp. Individual subscription: Canadian $25/yr. Institutional subscription: Canadian $18/yr. U.S. rate: add $4. Overseas: add $7. Single issue: Canadian $2.50.

Dollars and Sense, 1 Summer St., Somerville, MA 02143. 12 issues/yr. Magazine. 28 cm. Individual subscription: $18/yr. Institutional subscription: $32/yr.

ILR Report, New York State School of Industrial and Labor Relations, Ives Hall, Rm. 194, Cornell University, Ithaca, NY 14851-0952. 2 issues/yr. Magazine.

Industrial Worker, 3435 N. Sheffield, Suite 202, Chicago, IL 60657. 12 issues/yr. Newsletter. Individual subscription: $4/yr. Institutional subscription: $8/yr. Single issue: $.25.

International Labor and Working Class History, University of Illinois Press, 54 E. Gregory Dr., 608 S. Wright St., Urbana, IL 61820. 2 issues/yr. Magazine. 23 cm. 144pp. Individual subscription: $12/yr. Institutional subscription: $20/yr. Single issue: $10.50.

Labor Research Review, Midwest Center for Labor Research, 3411 W. Diversey Ave., Suite 14, Chicago, IL 60647. 2 issues/yr. Magazine. 21 cm. 102pp. Individual subscription: $12/yr. Institutional subscription: $18/yr. Single issue: $7.

Labor Studies Journal, Transaction Periodicals Consortium, Rutgers State University, Dept. 2000, New Brunswick, NJ 08903. 96pp. Individual subscription: $15/yr. Institutional subscription: $25/yr. Single issue: $10.

Labor Update, National Labor Law Center, c/o National Lawyers Guild, 2000 P St., NW, Suite 612, Washington, DC 20036. 5 issues/yr. Newsletter. 28 cm. Individual and institutional subscriptions: $12/yr.

Labour: Journal of Canadian Labor Studies/Le Travail: Revue d'études ouvrières canadiennes, Memorial University, Department of History, St. John's, Newfoundland A1C 5S7, Canada. 2 issues/yr. Magazine. 22.5 cm. 264pp. Individual subscription: Canadian $15/yr. Institutional subscription: Canadian $20/yr. Single issue: Canadian $10.

Left Business Observer, 250 W. 85 St., New York, NY 10024. 11 issues/yr. Newsletter. 28 cm. 8pp. Individual subscription: $18/yr. Institutional subscription: $45/yr.

Links, Third World First, 232 Cowley, Oxford OX4 1UH, England. 4 issues/yr. Individual subscription: £8/yr. Institutional subscription: £12/yr.

News from IRENE, International Restructuring Education Network Europe, c/o Centrum voor Ontwikkelingssamenwerking (COS), Korvelseweg 127, 5025 JC Tilburg, The Netherlands. Magazine. 21 cm. 40pp. Inquire.

South African Labour Bulletin, P.O. Box 31073, Braamfontein 2017, South Africa. 8 issues/yr. Magazine. Individual subscriptions: £25/$36/yr. Institutional subscriptions: £50/$75/yr. Companies: £100/$150/yr. Workers and students: £25/$20/yr.

Struggling for the Sharing of Wealth and Power, WCC Programme on Transnational Corporations, Commission on the Churches' Participation in Development, 150 route de Ferney, 1211 Geneva 20, Switzerland. 4 issues/yr. Magazine.

Trade Union Studies Journal, Workers' Educational Association, 9 Upper Berkeley St., London W1H 8BY, England. 2 issues/yr. Magazine. Individual and institutional subscriptions: £3/yr.

Workers World, Workers World Publishers, 46 W. 21 St., New York, NY 10010. 52 issues/yr. Newspaper. 44 cm. 12pp. Individual and institutional subscriptions: $10/yr. Trial subscriptions available.

INFORMATION SOURCES

The eleventh edition (1988) of *The Standard Periodical Directory* published by Oxbridge Communications (New York) provided six pages of periodicals under the general "labor" heading and seven more under "labor union." The latter category contains the names of official labor union newspapers and magazines. Other library reference guides, such as *The IMS Ayer Directory of Publications* and *Ulrich's International Periodicals Directory* should also be consulted.

The following three newsletters contain inserts that are devoted to news about transnational corporations and labor:

Asia Link, Center for the Progress of Peoples, 48 Princess Margaret Rd., Homantin, Kowloon, Hongkong. Four-page insert, "Labor Communications," with abstracts of labor news from around the Asia region.

Central America Update, P.O. Box 2207, Sta. P, Toronto, Ontario M5S 2T2, Canada. One-page insert, "Labour Briefs," with short news items and action suggestions regarding labor in Central America.

Listen Real Loud: News of Women's Liberation Worldwide, Nationwide Women's Program, American Friends Service Committee, 1501 Cherry St., Philadelphia, PA 19102. Eight-page insert, "Women and Global Corporations: Work, Roles, Resistance," with reports on "the expanding international network of individuals and groups involved in research, education, support, and direct organizing related to global industries where women are concentrated as workers or targets of consumer culture: electronics, agribusiness, textiles and the garment trades, tourism, media, and pharmaceuticals."

Write to the Social Investment Forum, 711 Atlantic Ave., Boston, MA 02111, for a list of periodicals dealing with "socially responsible" investments.

Newspapers such as *The Guardian* (33 W. 17 St., New York, NY 10011) regularly carry reports and progressive analyses regarding transnational corporations and labor. Magazines such as *Human Rights Internet Reporter* (Harvard Law School, Pound Hall, Rm. 401, Cambridge, MA 02138) report on attacks against trade union workers around the world.

See also the publications from **Third World Resources** described in the preface to this directory and the reference to the four-page guide to resources on transnational corporations and labor in the information sources section of chapter 1 above.

4

Pamphlets and Articles

The aim of this chapter is to present printed resource materials that are self-contained (usually an entire issue of a magazine on one topic), brief, inexpensive, and easily available, often at bulk rates.

The dividing line between a book and a pamphlet (or booklet) is a thin one at times. The rule of thumb we used to identify a pamphlet was: bound, printed materials that numbered less than one hundred pages, were priced at less than $5, or were one issue of a serial publication. Admittedly this dividing line is arbitrary, and it is hoped that no author will be offended that her/his work is classed as a pamphlet. Resources in this chapter are no less important because they are concise.

This chapter is divided into three parts: annotated entries, supplementary list of pamphlets and articles, and sources of additional information on pamphlets and articles.

Information in the **annotated entries** is given in the following order: author(s) or editor(s); title; publisher; periodical name; publication data (volume, number, date); number of pages; price; keyword description of format; and description of content.

Pamphlets and articles in the **supplementary list** (pp. 114–119) are grouped under these headings: general; Africa; Asia and Pacific; Latin America and Caribbean; and Middle East. Information in the entries in this section is given in the following order: author(s) or editor(s); title; publisher; name of periodical; publication data; number of pages; and price.

The **information sources** section (pp. 119–120) provides information on how readers can find out about other articles and pamphlets related to transnational corporations and labor in the Third World.

The titles of all the entries in this chapter are integrated into the titles index at the back of the directory. See the organizations index for addresses of publishers or distributors that appear in this chapter.

ANNOTATED ENTRIES

■ American Friends Service Committee, Nationwide Women's Program. *The Global Factory: An Organizing Guide for a New Economic Era.* Forthcoming, fall 1989. Photographs, charts, illustrations, statistical tables, notes, list of resources.

This guide is designed to be of use in planning educational and action-oriented programs on issues that fall under the broad heading of "the global factory." This term refers to the restructuring of the United States and other national economies into an integrated global economy whose productive power is dominated by transnational corporations. What impact has this restructuring had on workers in the industrialized nations? How has it affected working people in Third World nations?

The Global Factory demonstrates the interconnectedness of First and Third World workers by examining three case studies: plant closings in the United States, the situation in U.S.-owned factories (or *maquiladoras*) in Mexico, and labor issues in the Philippines. Problems are described and analyzed, but attempts to solve the problems are also dealt with through personal stories of educational and organizing efforts that stretch across national boundaries.

The authors of this guide have gone to great lengths to write in terms that lay people will understand and to explore ways that complex issues such as international debt, sex discrimination, national industrial policies, and corporate social responsibility can be examined fruitfully in educational settings.

■ Baylies, Carolyn, and Robin Cohen. *Workers, Unions and Popular Protest. Review of African Political Economy*, no. 39, September 1987. 128pp. £3.50/$6. Diagrams, notes, references, statistical tables.

This special issue of the highly regarded *Review of African Political Economy* brings together a number of articles and interviews and a range of documentation that make the point that these, indeed, are difficult times for labor movements throughout Africa. "They are confronted by a massive reduction in their bargaining power," write the editors, "as the reserve army of the unemployed grows larger and larger; the state is hostile—in South Africa, violently so; employers are using increasingly more impenetrable ideologies, strategies, and tactics, while democratic forces are making more claims on the labour movement."

At the same time, however, "workers have responded with great courage, even heroism." "But," Baylies and Cohen conclude, "the virtues of working class solidarity and resistance, necessary and commendable as they are, have now to be supplemented by more complex forms of political action and association." *Workers, Unions and Popular Protest* describes what these forms might be and analyzes the prospects for their creation.

Two articles cover labor in West Africa: "The Recession and Workers' Struggles in Vehicle Assembly Plants: Steyr-Nigeria" and "Agricultural Development in Nigeria: The Role of Market and Non-market Forces." One article covers South Africa ("The Two Faces of the Black Trade Union Movement in South Africa") and another discusses "Labour Movements or Popular Struggles" in Africa as a whole.

Nathan Godfried contributes a brief analysis of the way in which U.S. unions use conservative organizations such as the African-American Labor Center to influence the education of African trade unionists. His article is entitled "Spreading American Corporatism: Trade Union Education for Third World Labour."

■ Bell, John Donnelly, ed. *The Royal Dutch/Shell Group of Companies Alternative Corporate Report 1987.* National Labor Boycott Shell Committee. 1988. 22pp. Photographs, illustrations.

This glossy report, prepared for Shell shareholders and potential investors, explains (1) the reasons behind the current worldwide boycott of Shell products, (2) the concerns of some shareholders about company mismanagement, and (3) why an investment in Royal Dutch/Shell is considered to be "a bad risk" at this time.

The international boycott, which has involved a dozen industrialized countries on three continents, is being carried out because of Royal Dutch/Shell's activities in South Africa, particularly the company's role in supplying petroleum products to the South African military and police and its actions in suppressing the rights of its workforce. Chapters 1 and 2 describe the company's activities in South Africa and the growing strength of the boycott.

Chapter 3 directs attention to charges about company mismanagement. "In the face of the growing boycott and worldwide media attention," the report maintains, "chronic mismanagement at the top of Shell has become evident—ranging from the refusal to pull out of South Africa to oil price gouging and toxic chemical dumping in the United States costing the company hundreds of millions of dollars."

"There could hardly be a worse time to invest in the economy of the Republic of South Africa." This assessment, voiced at the opening of chapter 4, is echoed in numerous quotations from Wall Street investment advisers. South Africa, in the opinion of these advisers, is simply a bad investment risk. And so is Royal Dutch/Shell, say the authors of this booklet, as long as it maintains its $400 million subsidiary holdings in racist South Africa.

The inside back cover lists more than seventy U.S. national organizations (representing some 20 million Americans) that have endorsed the Shell boycott.

■ Bounds, Elizabeth, and James Winkler. *Closed: Control Data Korea. Wanted: A Future for Blacklisted Workers.* Interfaith Center on Corporate Responsibility. *ICCR Brief* 13, no. 2 (1984). 4pp. 60 cents.

In this *ICCR Brief* Bounds and Winkler recount the story of the closing of Control Data Corporation's computer assembly subsidiary in

Seoul, South Korea, in mid-1982 and the dismissal of the unit's 270 union employees—most of them women. But this is not simply a tale of yet another plant closing. This story has a special edge because not only were the workers dismissed but most of them have had difficulty finding other jobs because they have been blacklisted by the South Korean government for union activities during negotiations with Control Data and—the authors charge—"because Control Data has not given its promised assistance."

The authors give a brief account of the rise of the worldwide electronics industry—the global assembly line—and of relations between the United States and Korea in the post-World War II period. They describe how Korea's economic development since the 1960s has been based on foreign capital and export-oriented investment and how the government has clamped down on trade union activities to insure a stable investment climate for foreign investors.

Bounds and Winkler then turn their attention to the history of Control Data's operations in South Korea, focusing particularly on labor union activities regarding wages and "the lack of healthy working conditions" in Control Data Korea's assembly plant. They recount the negotiations that led up to the closing of the Seoul plant and the subsequent arrest and blacklisting of active union members.

Control Data, the authors note, is a company "acclaimed by many in the United States for its social responsibility." Under pressure from church and other activists worldwide Control Data made many promises of support for the dismissed workers, but—as one church-sponsored resolution declared—"the closing [of the CDK plant] and its consequences have raised questions internationally about the company's responsibilities towards its workers and damaged its public image."

■ Boyer, Sandy. *Black Workers under Siege: The Repression of Black Trade Unions in South Africa.* American Committee on Africa. 1984. 8pp. Maps, figures, photographs.

This short pamphlet, co-produced by the Africa Fund and District Council 37 of the American Federation of State, County, and Municipal Employees (AFSCME), documents the repression of trade unions in South Africa, demonstrating that the struggle for trade union rights and the struggle for freedom are the same. In the face of this repression black unions are still able to attract a wide and militant membership. The Federation of South African Trade Unions, the largest federation of black unions, has more than 100,000 members. Two other federations, the Council of Unions of South Africa and the South African Allied Workers Union, claim a total membership of around 140,000.

Directed to a labor union audience, *Black Workers under Siege* would be useful in other educational settings as well. Information is clearly and attractively presented.

■ *Brazil: The New Militancy. Trade Unions and Transnational Corporations.* Transnationals Information Exchange. *TIE Report*, no. 17. March 1984. 56pp.

The aim of this *TIE Report* is "to explain to workers in transnational companies in Europe, the United States, and elsewhere how their colleagues in Brazil are struggling against the same employers." "An understanding of the difficulties Brazilian workers are facing," the editors state, "is a first step in the development of international solidarity activities."

During 1982 and 1983 TIE staff members traveled to Brazil and spoke with workers in companies such as General Motors, Ford, Philips, Volkswagen, Mercedes, Unilever, Scania, and Massey Ferguson. In addition, they interviewed a number of trade union officials and other active trade unionists. "Because most of the interviews were carried out in the São Paulo area," the editors caution, "most of the emphasis [in this report] is given to industrial struggles, particularly in the auto industry. It is important to point out this emphasis," they say, "because we by no means wish to downplay struggles which have occurred in the rural and service sectors."

The report covers the development of the trade union movement in Brazil, conditions of employment in Brazilian subsidiaries of transnational corporations, the anti-labor strategies of transnational corporations, the establishment of the Central Workers' Organization (CUT in Portuguese), and the progress that Brazil's labor movement has made in forging links with trade unionists overseas.

■ Cantor, Daniel, and Juliet Schor. *Tunnel Vision: Labor, the World Economy, and Central America.* South End Press. 1987. 87pp. $5. Notes, figures, list of resources, tables.

This booklet was produced "for trade unionists and others who believe that a healthy labor movement is not only desirable but necessary," Cantor and Schor write. "Our purpose," they continue, "is to connect the debates on Central America, AFL-CIO foreign policies, and labor's economic problems."

In *Tunnel Vision* Cantor, a labor union organizer, and Schor, an economics professor at Harvard, discuss the reasons why so many trade unionists oppose U.S. government policies in Central America and "how that opposition challenges some of the fundamentals of the AFL-CIO's worldview of the last forty years." They show how changes in the structure of the international economy after World War II—especially those that have taken place since the early 1970s—have "ultimately weakened labor's position vis-à-vis management." They conclude by arguing that if the labor movement is to thrive again "it will have to change its view of the rest of the world, the actions it takes, and the policies it supports." In their final chapter they critically examine several arguments offered for continuation on the present course and then elaborate their own principles of a new foreign policy for labor.

■ *Challenging Transnationals: And How Transnationals React to Their Critics.* International Coalition for Development Action. March 1983. 53pp. Notes, illustrations.

This ICDA booklet holds up for examination three case studies of successful actions taken against transnational corporations by groups and individuals worldwide. The aim of all three actions was "to publicize and force changes in the policies adopted by transnational corporations which conflict with the interests of people whether they live in the North or the South." The three articles in this booklet analyze the history and strategies of each of the campaigns and describe the resistance they encountered from the transnational corporations.

The three articles are: (1) "The Genetics Supply Industry," a study by Pat Mooney of attempts by Royal Dutch/Shell and other transnational corporations to control the very first link in the food chain—the seed industry—and of how these efforts have met resistance from an international coalition of development activists and educators. (2) "Win a Battle... and Lose a War," Annelies Allain's account of the very successful infant formula campaign waged against Nestlé by the International Baby Food Action Network. (3) "The International Electrical Association—Another IEA," the story of Swedish journalist Gunnar Adler-Karlsson's attempts to expose the fact that the world's major electrical companies have operated within a cartel agreement for more than half a century.

In the final article, "Can Transnational Corporations Be Controlled?," Asbjorn Lovbraek sketches the historical development of the transnational corporations and of attempts by national, intergovernmental, and nongovernmental organizations to regulate their activities. He pays particular attention to the three case studies, looking for points of commonality both in the actions of the critics and the reactions by the transnational corporations.

■ Chaney, Elsa M. *Scenarios of Hunger in the Caribbean.* Women in International Development, Michigan State University. *Working Papers on Women in International Development,* no. 18, 1983. 31pp. $3. References, bibliography.

Concentrating particularly on the Jamaican situation, this paper searches for the root causes of hunger and malnutrition in the English-speaking Caribbean in these four areas: (1) high levels of "outmigration" from the rural areas to the cities, as well as "foreign" migration by thousands of West Indians to England, Canada, and the United States; (2) declining productivity in the small farm sector that raises the domestic foods that poor people eat; (3) the "feminization of farming," with women taking on more and more responsibility for both food and cash crops without receiving the supports they need; and (4) "overdependence on food purchased from abroad and scarcity of foreign exchange to buy it." Chaney's fourth point is of particular concern as far as transnational corporations are concerned.

Chaney, an associate of the Equity Policy Center (Washington, D.C.), cites the following statistics to illustrate how the dependence on food imports leaves Jamaica's poor in a very precarious situation: "The most important items in the diet of the Jamaican poor, after sugar, are flour and rice—95 percent of which are imported. Lower-income groups—calculated at about 70 percent of the population, who spend 80 percent of their income on food—depend upon sugar, flour and rice as their most important sources of energy, and on flour, rice and bread as their principal sources of protein."

Chaney's solutions to the problems she describes and analyzes are to strengthen national nutrition policy (linking food consumption and nutritional issues to agricultural policies) and to increase the emphasis on small-holder agriculture.

- Chetley, Andrew. *Cleared for Export: An Examination of the European Community's Pharmaceutical and Chemical Trade.* Coalition Against Dangerous Exports. August 1985. 75pp. Sources, bibliography, notes, references, statistical tables, tables.

European Community countries are responsible for 61.5 percent of worldwide pesticides exports and 50 percent of the world trade in pharmaceuticals. This significant position on the world market has led numerous nongovernmental organizations (NGOs) in Europe to press the European Community and its member states to develop coherent policies to control the export to developing countries of all pharmaceuticals and pesticides that are banned, severely restricted, withdrawn, or unregistered in EC countries. This oversized report, published by a coalition of European NGOs, provides the justification for the concerns of the Coalition Against Dangerous Exports.

Cleared for Export explains the dangers in current practices in the export of dangerous and inappropriate pesticides, drugs, and other products to the Third World. The report also examines related activities of the pharmaceutical and pesticide companies, including the storage and disposal of hazardous wastes and hazardous production processes, the marketing of artificial infant foods, the monopolization of the seeds industry, and deceptive advertising.

In his two final chapters Andrew Chetley describes the initiatives that have been taken—particularly in Europe—to curb the dangerous activities of the pesticide and pharmaceutical companies.

- Committee for Asian Women and Isis International. *Industrial Women Workers in Asia. Isis International Women's Journal,* no. 4. September 1985. 160pp. $4. Charts, bibliography, diagrams, illustrations, list of resources, notes, photographs, statistical tables.

This collection of twelve articles written by nine Asian women researchers and organizers is a major contribution to our understanding of the complex situation of industrial women workers in the capitalist countries of Asia. The impact of industrialization on women, strategies and prospects for organizing women workers, the role of women in trade unions, gender subordination and sexual discrimination at work—these and many other subjects are treated in well-documented fashion.

An annotated bibliography of print and audiovisual materials on working women completes this invaluable handbook.

- Crabtree, John, Gavan Duffy, and Jenny Pearce. *The Great Tin*

Crash: Bolivia and the World Tin Market. Latin America Bureau. April 1987. 104pp. $5. Statistical profile, bibliography, charts, maps, photographs. Available in North America from Monthly Review Press.

This Latin America Bureau publication examines the tin crisis from the point of view of those who suffer most from the changing fortunes in this commodity—the mineworkers of Bolivia and their families. The authors present a brief history of the mining and use of tin and then offer a clear, precise description of how the world commodity markets work in theory and in practice. They conclude by showing how the disastrous drop in sales of tin has become a national tragedy for Bolivia.

The Great Tin Crash is noteworthy for its clarity of presentation and effective use of graphics, tables, and charts. It takes a technical, highly specialized subject—the collapse of the world tin market—and explains it in a language and form that are easily accessible to the average reader.

Labor union activists—especially those in mineworkers' unions—will find this pamphlet illuminating. So, too, will anyone who believes that we need a new world economic order—one that protects working people from the capriciousness and volatility of commodity markets such as the one described by Crabtree, Duffy, and Pearce.

■ Danaher, Kevin. *Can the "Free Market" Solve Africa's Food Crisis?* International Union of Food and Allied Workers' Association (IUF). 1987. 36pp. £3, plus postage. Notes, statistical tables.

This paper is the text of a speech delivered by Kevin Danaher at an IUF-sponsored conference in Zambia in 1986. In it he critically examines the most popular explanations offered for Africa's food crisis, focusing most of his attention on "the position of those who argue that the 'free market' holds the solution to Africa's agricultural problems." This is far from an academic exercise, Danaher maintains, "because those promoting 'privatization' [of agriculture] happen to be organizations (e.g., the International Monetary Fund and the U.S. Agency for International Development) that control large amounts of capital that Africa desperately needs." "If we are to represent and defend the interests of African working people," Danaher states, "we must have a clear analysis of what the problem is, what are its causes, and whose proposed solutions are likely to be most effective."

After these introductory remarks, Danaher proceeds to an informative presentation on the historical roots of agricultural underdevelopment in Africa; the transnational "elite alliance" of Western governments, transnational corporations, African elites, and international agencies; conditionality and Western-backed reforms; and Africa's debt crisis.

Danaher's lengthy and persuasive conclusions reject pessimism about Africa's future. "Most African countries," he notes, "are in the youth of their independence and are beset by many of the same problems that have troubled other countries early in the nation-building process. We must keep in mind this continent's vast potential."

- Emmanuel, Jorge. *Monster in Morong: The Dreadful Tale of the Bataan-Westinghouse Nuclear Plant in the Philippines.* Friends of the Filipino People and Alliance for Philippine Concerns. June 1984. 4pp. 25 cents. Recommended readings, action suggestions, list of resources.

This is the incredible story of the construction of the Bataan Nuclear Power Plant (in Morong, Bataan, the Philippines) — reputed to be "one of the most expensive nuclear facilities of its size and one of the most dangerous in the world." "It is threatened," Emmanuel writes, "by possible volcanic eruptions, severe earthquakes, and plagued by faulty design problems."

Though it is now possible that the plant will not be put into operation under the Aquino government it is still eye-opening and instructive to read about the role that Westinghouse and the U.S. Export-Import Bank played in the promotion, design, and construction of the plant.

- *Focus on Labour.* Toronto Committee for the Liberation of Southern Africa. *Southern Africa Report* 2, no. 1 (June 1986). 34pp. $3.50. Maps, illustrations, photographs.

The major article in this special issue of *Southern Africa Report* describes the tremendous growth of the South African trade union movement and analyzes the reasons why the Canadian trade union movement has been unable to stand as one in support of organized labor in South Africa. The article, "South African Trade Unions: The Canadian Connection," describes the split that exists between the solidarity activities of the upper levels of the Canadian Labour Congress (especially its International Affairs Department) and those of a number of CLC affiliates. It also examines the differences in trade union strategies in South Africa and how these have led to divergent points of view among solidarity groups in Canada. A major question, for instance, is how much support to give to the South African Congress of Trade Unions (SACTU), which was the key trade union central of the 1950s and is closely linked to the African National Congress, and how much to give to the more recently created Congress of South African Trade Unions (COSATU).

The editors recognize that the controversies surrounding the Canadian labor movement's positions regarding South Africa must be dealt with sensitively and tentatively. They criticize the "ideologizing and institutional self-interest" that they see on all sides and call for a "flexible and open-minded approach" to the subject.

- *Focus on the Eastern Caribbean: Bananas, Bucks, and Boots.* Resource Center. Spring 1984. 72pp. $3.50. Bulk rates available. Maps, notes, photographs, statistical tables.

The alliterated nouns in the subtitle to this pamphlet signify the authors' interest in agriculture, foreign investment, and militarization as these relate to the islands in the lower eastern portion of the Caribbean archipelago: the English-speaking islands of the Leeward and the Windward groups.

Focus on the Eastern Caribbean examines (1) Geest Industries (U.K.) and its monopoly control of the banana industry in the region, (2) attempts by the U.S. Agency for International Development (USAID) to restructure the banana industry in the interest of U.S. investors, (3) the introduction of assembly plants that use only one local input—the labor of Caribbean workers—to produce not for the local or regional market but for the U.S. market, (4) Washington's plans for the "economic rescue" of Grenada, (5) the role the USAID-funded American Institute for Free Labor Development (AIFLD) has played in challenging progressive and radical unions in the area and in supporting U.S. foreign policy in the region, and (6) the "almost overnight" militarization of the islands by the Pentagon.

Country-by-country surveys and a comprehensive list of U.S. and other foreign corporations in the region complete this very informative booklet.

▪ Freiwald, Aaron. *Mexico: A Multinational Haven.* Essential Information. *Multinational Monitor* 6, no. 16 (November 1985). 7pp. $2.00. Tables.

"American corporations by the hundreds are picking Mexico over the Far East for assembly plants, or as they are called in Spanish, maquiladoras," states Aaron Freiwald. What takes these companies south of the border? "Abundant and dirt-cheap labor" originally, and now the system is vitally important to the economies of the countries on both sides of the Rio Grande. U.S. companies continue to seek cheap, nonunionized labor; Mexico needs "employment, industrial development, and U.S. dollars."

This article explores the changes that have taken place over the twenty years of the maquiladora industry, the effects of the industry on Mexican and U.S. workers (especially women workers), the attempts at local unionizing, the potential for industry-wide multinational unionization, and capital flight.

▪ Fuentes, Annette, and Barbara Ehrenreich. *Women in the Global Factory.* South End Press. 1983. 64pp. $4.75. Photographs, bibliography, illustrations, list of resources, notes, statistical tables.

Young Third World women are today's "factory girls," a "giant reserve army of labor at the disposal of globe-trotting multinationals," according to the authors of *Women in the Global Factory.* This powerful booklet examines the exploitative situations in which the "factory girls" find themselves and describes their strategic importance and their increasing militancy.

After an opening chapter on the history of the global factory and of women "on the global assembly line," the authors devote two chapters to studies of women workers in two areas of the Third World: East Asia and Mexico. Chapter 4 details the ways in which Third World governments team up with the U.S. government and with U.S. government-supported organizations like the Asian-American Free Labor Institute and the American Institute for Free Labor Development to promote the exploitation of Third World women workers. Chapter 5 brings the story home to the United States, describing the "twentieth century sweatshops" that can be found in many parts of the United States.

"The answer is global," the authors insist in the final chapter in the booklet. "The most difficult yet most important task in confronting multinational domination," they conclude, "is to create direct links between women workers around the world." "It may take years before international links are extensive and powerful enough to challenge successfully multinational corporations and the governments which support them," the authors realize, "but women's lives grow closer all the time." "We all have the same hard life," one woman worker told the authors. "We are bound together with one string."

■ Goodman, Amy, et al. *The Case Against Depo-Provera.* Essential Information. *Multinational Monitor* 6, no. 2 & 3 (February/March 1985). 20pp. $1.75. Photographs, action suggestions, documents, illustrations, list of resources.

How can a drug manufactured by a U.S.-based multinational and unapproved for use as a contraceptive in the United States be marketed and widely used on women in more than eighty other countries? These articles raise this question and many others surrounding the synthetic hormone depot medroxyprogesterone acetate, or as it is called by its manufacturer (the Upjohn Company), Depo-Provera.

The articles cover the origin and testing of the drug, its safety and side-effects (as noted by the FDA and by women who have used it), its history in the U.S. drug approval process, its accessibility in the Third World, and the apparent targeting of Third World and minority women by Upjohn's aggressive marketing techniques.

A two-page list of resources broadens the scope of the articles even further, setting the themes in the larger context of women's health rights, world population control, and world poverty. This issue of *Multinational Monitor* would be a useful tool for any person or group concerned with any of these issues.

■ Halliday, Fred, et al. *Migrant Workers in the Middle East.* Middle East Research and Information Project. *MERIP Reports* 14, no. 4 (May 1984). 32pp. $2.75. Photographs, maps, statistical tables.

This issue of *MERIP Reports* contains two major articles on migrant workers in the Middle East. The first, by Fred Halliday, covers the broad subject of labor migration in the Arab world. The second, by Robert LaTowsky, looks at Egyptian labor abroad. The subject of migration is also dealt with in the book review section.

"By 1980," Halliday writes, "over 3 million Arabs had migrated to other states of the Arab world, and an estimated 1.8 million non-Arabs had joined them as labour imported by the oil producers." These migratory flows in the Arab world, he notes, "have meant that in three states immigrants make up over half of the total population, while in five others, immigrants make up from 40 percent to 75 percent of the economically active population." "Moreover," he adds, "the financial flows from oil producers to labor-exporters have created a new pan-Arab economy, within which the states without oil have come to be more and more dependent on the income earned by their exiled citizens." Halliday analyzes the different types of Arab world migration and weighs the consequences of this migration on both the labor importing and labor exporting countries.

In his article Robert LaTowsky draws attention to the remarkable economic benefits that "Egypt's thirsty economy" has realized from massive transfers of wages and remittances by Egyptian migrant laborers in neighboring Arab countries. In one year alone — 1979 — LaTowsky notes that migrant labor-related income of $2 billion was equivalent "to the combined returns that year of Egypt's cotton exports, Suez Canal receipts, tourism, and the value added from the Aswan High Dam." But, he adds, while cumulatively impressive, "the sums diminish to more modest proportions when divided among their innumerable owners and measured against the frugality of [the migrant workers'] lives abroad." LaTowsky takes this paradox as the theme for his article: "Mass Participation and Modest Returns."

■ Harman, Inge Maria. *Women and Cooperative Labor in the Southern Bolivian Andes.* Women in International Development, Michigan State University. *Working Papers on Women in International Development,* no. 65, September 1984. 10pp. $2.25. Notes, references.

This paper by anthropologist Inge Maria Harman describes and analyzes the activities of women in communal labor among Quechua-speaking peasant farmers in the south central Bolivian Andes. Elements of equality, reciprocity, and hierarchy in the sexual division of labor in the area are discussed and their relationship to the collective agricultural work of women and men is explored.

Harman situates her study within the framework of the much-debated question about female subordination: Is it or is it not a universal element of human social organization that males are valued more highly than females? Harman finds that the Yura women that she studies in the Bolivian Andes have a "relatively" egalitarian relationship with men in the region, and she concludes that it is the equal involvement of women in communal, agricultural production — labor that makes a significant contribution "to the larger group" — that accounts for their elevated status.

■ Hobbelink, Henk. *New Hope or False Promise? Biotechnology and Third World Agriculture.* International Coalition for Development Action. September 1987. 72pp. $5. Resource guide, appendixes, graphs, illustrations, list of abbreviations, notes, photographs, tables.

"One can hardly open a popular scientific magazine these days," writes Henk Hobbelink, "without finding exciting articles on the potential blessings of the newly emerging biotechnologies for agricultural production. Some of these articles stress the potential of yield increases through genetic engineering. Others tell us about super-plants that could produce their own nitrogen-fertilizer and pesticides, thus reducing the need for costly and harmful agro-chemicals, or about plants that could be grown on poor soils on which agriculture is difficult if not impossible." Does this new technology offer new hope—especially to farmers in Third World countries—or is it a false promise?

ICDA, the publisher of this booklet, has long been concerned about the dangerous narrowing of the world's food base and the impact of monopolistic control of genetic resources in the hands of a few transnational corporations. It approaches this new subject of biotechnology with appropriate skepticism, asking not *whether* this new technology will reach the poor, but *how* and *with what consequences.*

This booklet describes the emerging technology in easy-to-understand terms. It critically weighs its potential impact on the world's poor and suggests ways that concerned nongovernmental organizations can and should be involved in shaping the development of biotechnology.

■ Hosmer, Ellen, et al. *Paradise Lost: The Ravaged Rainforest.* Essential Information. *Multinational Monitor* 8, no. 6 (June 1987). 14pp. $2.00. Maps, illustrations, list of resources, photographs.

Why the concern over the annual loss of 27 million acres of tropical rainforests, the loss of half the world's rainforests to date, and the likelihood that the rainforests may be completely gone in thirty to forty years? Destruction of the world's rainforests will mean not only the loss of natural beauty and timber resources, say the authors of these articles, but also the destruction of the earth's most diverse ecosystem, of plants used for medicinal purposes, of food and fuel for millions of people who live in the developing world, of tropical plants, of "a part of the planet's heritage that is crucial to our health, to our climate, to the very maintenance of our biosphere."

These articles explore the unique and significant meaning of the rainforests of Asia, South America, and Africa to humanity, the role of the World Bank in this environmental issue, the environmental groups' efforts in the conservation campaign, the particular cases of Madagascar and the Philippines, and the disastrous effects of deforestation on the entire continent of Africa.

■ Jagan, Larry, and John Cunnington. *Social Volcano: Sugar Workers in the Philippines.* W.O.W. Campaigns Ltd. July 1987. 35pp. £1.95. Maps, illustrations, photographs.

Ninety percent of the 1.8 million people on the island of Negros in the central Philippines are dependent on the island's sugar industry for their livelihood. The island, which has more than one-half of the country's sugar mills and produces 68 percent of nation's sugar crop, is so sugar-dependent that it has earned the name "Sugarlandia."

This booklet describes the impact that the sugar industry has had on the people of Sugarlandia. "Bitterness," the authors contend, "is the only legacy sugar has left the people of Negros." "Growing and refining sugar cane," they explain, "have virtually ceased on the island. Some 250,000 sugar workers were laid off after the 1984 milling season.

Two of Negros's eighteen mills have completely closed down. Unemployment [in 1987] exceeds 400,000, according to reliable estimates, while it is expected to reach 600,000 within the next year."

Social Volcano, which draws heavily from a similarly titled publication of the Association of Major Religious Superiors in the Philippines, describes the development of the sugar industry in Negros, the tragic condition of sugar workers and their families, the rise of the National Federation of Sugar Workers, political repression and murder, the failure of the Aquino government to bring about an economic and social revolution on a scale with its political revolution in February 1986, and efforts by displaced sugar workers and others to secure land for the production of much-needed food. (An estimated 80 percent of Negros's population is "virtually starving" as a result of the decline in the sugar industry.)

The gripping black-and-white photographs (more than fifty in all) in this oversized booklet tell the story as effectively as the well-documented text.

■ *Jamaica: Open for Business*. Resource Center. Spring 1984. 52pp. $3.50. Map, appendixes, notes, photographs, tables.

This study of the island-nation that the Reagan administration put forth as a showcase of Third World development covers the political situation under the government of Michael Manley's People's National Party (1972-1980) and during the first years of the government of Edward Seaga's Jamaica Labor Party (1980-1988).

"Open for Business" is the shingle that the Seaga government's economic policymakers hung for foreign investors and international financial institutions to see. Resource Center staff members examine the impact that the infusion of foreign dollars has had on agriculture, mining, industry—and on the people of Jamaica. They describe, as well, the programs that the Pentagon and the U.S. Agency for International Development have advanced for Jamaica. The pamphlet closes with a thirteen-page list of foreign corporations with operations in Jamaica.

■ *Japanese Industry Moves Out*. Pacific-Asia Resource Center. *AMPO: Japan-Asia Quarterly Review* 19, no. 1 (1987). 35pp. Available in North America from the Asia Resource Center (Washington, D.C.).

The fall 1985 decision by the leaders of the major industrialized nations to inflate the value of the Japanese yen against the U.S. dollar (in an effort to reduce the U.S. trade deficit) has brought about an unprecedented surge in Japanese investments abroad. Hampered in their ability to export products from Japan (because of soaring prices) Japanese manufacturers have established assembly operations in Europe and the United States and parts manufacturing facilities in Korea and Southeast Asia.

"The launching of overseas manufacturing operations is most remarkable in the automobile industry, the typical Japanese exporting industry," says Kitazawa Yoko in the lead article in *Japanese Industry Moves Out*. But foreign investments have taken place in other industries as well, including electrical appliances and home electronics, office equipment, telecommunications equipment, machine tools, and industrial machinery.

The cover story traces the history of the transnationalization of Japanese companies in the post-war period, paying special attention to the automobile, electronics, and service industries. Author Kitazawa Yoko next compares Japanese and U.S. transnational corporations and then describes the impact that the recent growth in Japanese foreign investments has had on the coal mining, iron and steel, shipbuilding, and other industries in Japan. She foresees "the coming of [a] massive unemployment era" and the "collapse of the Japanese lifetime employment system" as a result of these recent developments.

■ *Japan's Human Imports: As Capital Flows Out, Foreign Labor Flows In.* Pacific-Asia Resource Center. *AMPO: Japan-Asia Quarterly Review* 19, no. 4 (1988). 37pp. Available in North America from the Asia Resource Center (Washington, D.C.).

The rise in the value of the Japanese yen against other major currencies has led to increased Japanese investments abroad. At the same time it has drawn an estimated 50,000 to 100,000 men and women migrant laborers to Japan in search of higher paying employment. This new development has forced Japan's leaders—especially those with "a single-race vision"—to reassess the nation's present immigration and employment policies.

The cover story in this issue of *AMPO* describes the lines that this reassessment has taken in a variety of government departments, including the Foreign Ministry, Labor, Justice, and Police. The report describes the experiences of immigrant workers from Pakistan and Bangladesh, but devotes most of its coverage to the discrimination and exploitation encountered by short-term workers from the Philippines.

■ Kervyn, Bernard, et al. *The Textile Challenge and the Third World: NGO Views on the Multi-Fibre Arrangement.* International Coalition for Development Action and Frère des Hommes International/Mensenbroeders. October 1986. 64pp. Notes, charts, illustrations, photographs, tables.

The Textile Challenge is a clearly written introduction to a subject that the authors themselves admit is complicated and relatively unknown to activists in the United States. (Activists in Canadian and European nongovernmental organizations are by and large more conversant about international trade and aid issues than are their U.S. counterparts.)

This joint publication of ICDA and Frère des Hommes describes the importance of world trade for developing countries ("in volume [it is] much more important than aid") and identifies the ways in which developing nations are being discriminated against by the major trading powers. The Multi-Fibre Arrangement is one example.

The MFA, which is an "authorised departure" from the rules and principles that govern world trade (the General Agreement on Tariffs and Trade), permits the importing industrial countries "to impose discriminatory restrictions and quotas on imports of products in [the textile and clothing] sector from the Third World."

The authors situate the MFA in the context of a lucid explanation of the dynamics of world trade and explain how the present arrangements hurt workers and consumers in both the North and the South.

■ Lin, Vivian. *Health, Women's Work, and Industrialization: Women Workers in the Semiconductor Industry in Singapore and Malaysia.* Women in International Development, Michigan State University. *Working Papers on Women in International Development,* no. 130. October 1986. 76pp. $5.00. Notes, figures, statistical tables, references.

This study attempts to "go beyond anecdotes" about the condition of women employees in electronics factories in Southeast Asia in order to understand systematically "the phenomenon of large numbers of young women entering the formal sector work force for the first time in Asia's history." "Health is of specific interest in this research," Vivian Lin states, "not only as a necessary contributing factor to the stability and productivity of the labor force, but also as a reflection of industrial and social conditions." Taking a "political economy of health perspective," Lin's study seeks to understand "the relationship between the micro-level functions of workers' bodies and the macro-level dynamics of capital accumulation." Her report confirms "some of the anecdotal evidence of occupational health problems"—on both the psychological and physical levels. She describes these problems in great detail, setting them in their societal context in Singapore and Malaysia and in their industrial context in the electronics industry and pointing to differences she notes among Chinese, Malay, and Indian workers in the industry. Lin opens her report with a survey of the development of the electronics industry in Asia and a review of the literature on Asian women workers in that industry. The following sections present the findings from her study in five factories among nine hundred workers in Singapore and Malaysia.

Lin concludes that "in bringing about capitalist development and proletarianization of women, the new international division of labor has unleashed a process of social change that will be difficult to bring under control." "The long-term social consequences of economic development are likely to be more extensive than government planners ever anticipated," she writes.

■ Lo, Porise. *The Plight of Asian Workers in Electronics.* Christian Conference of Asia, Urban-Rural Mission. October 1982. 85pp. $2. Cartoon illustrations, photographs, statistical tables.

"This is the story of over 600,000 workers in Asia," this booklet begins. "Eighty percent of [them] are young women, mostly aged between 15 and 25. All of them are employed in the electronics industry—the technologically most advanced industry in the modern world."

In five chapters and in engaging cartoon style this pamphlet tells readers about these women workers, how they are being exploited, by whom, why Asian governments accommodate the electronics multinationals, and what actions have been and can be taken to transform present conditions.

- McAfee, Kathy. *Why Farmers Go Hungry. Food Exports from the Third World: Honduras.* Oxfam America. *Facts for Action,* no. 12. 8pp. 50 cents. Bulk rates available. Maps, action suggestions, list of resources, photographs.

"The conquest of territory by the coffee industry is alarming. . . . Although it is possible to prove mathematically that these changes make the country richer, in fact they mean death. . . . What good does it do to make money from the sale of coffee when it leaves so many in misery?" Alberto Masferrer wrote these words in *La Patria,* a Salvadoran newspaper, in 1929. "Today," writes Kathy McAfee, "Masferrer's vision has come true on a larger scale than even he imagined."

This *Facts for Action* pamphlet looks at the situation of farmers in Third World countries who raise food for export, though they go hungry themselves. Honduras is a case in point.

Throughout the twentieth century, McAfee shows, Honduras has increased the amount of land it devotes to producing export crops and, as a result, less arable land is available to Honduran peasants to produce crops to feed themselves. She analyzes the role played in this development by U.S.-based banana companies, which have been the largest owners of farmland in Honduras for most of this century. She explains how other export crops — coffee, cattle, and cotton — have become important over the past twenty years. Finally, McAfee considers the role of the U.S. government and U.S. development experts in Honduras.

Especially effective is the centerfold of this publication, which illustrates the major Third World suppliers of food to the United States and poses the question "Who's feeding whom?"

- McCarthy, Florence E., and Shelley Feldman. *Rural Women Discovered: New Sources of Capital and Labor in Bangladesh.* Women in International Development, Michigan State University. *Working Papers on Women in International Development,* no. 105, November 1985. 23pp. $2.75. Notes, references, statistical tables.

In analyzing the effects of capitalist penetration in Bangladesh the authors of this study advance and defend three theories that, in effect, challenge two current models of progressive thinking on development: the development-underdevelopment approach advanced by André Gunder Frank and the world-systems model popularized by Immanuel Wallerstein.

The theories are: (1) In current expressions of dependency theory the internal conditions of countries experiencing capitalist penetration are often overlooked. (2) In countries where commercial and industrial interests have only limited scope for investment and profit making, foreign assistance and aid become the main instruments of capitalist penetration. (3) Capitalist transformation necessitates the incorporation of all segments of the population and all aspects of production under its auspices. In developing this latter point, the authors illustrate how "the productive activities of women, and women themselves as potential sources of labor, are increasingly involved in development processes." They go on to explain how and why rural women, in particular, are becoming more integrated into economic development schemes.

The authors conclude by spelling out various policy interpretations that flow from their analysis of women's involvement in development processes in Third World nations.

■ *Meeting the Corporate Challenge: A Handbook on Corporate Campaigns.* Transnationals Information Exchange. *TIE Report* nos. 18 & 19, February 1985. 78pp. Charts, chronology, illustrations, list of resources, photographs, statistical tables.

The content of this special issue of *TIE Report* is drawn largely from the proceedings of a conference held in Washington, D.C., in June 1984. The conference, entitled "Meeting the Corporate Challenge," brought together about one hundred researchers and activists "to address the urgent need to evaluate past campaigns [against transnational corporations] and to discuss future responses to corporate power."

A major concern of the conference was to describe and understand the evolution and present-day forms of corporate power and to search out ways that unions, consumer groups, women's organizations, church groups, indigenous peoples' organizations, environmental groups and others could more effectively meet the challenge of corporate power. The aims of the conference organizers are reflected in this issue of *TIE Report,* with the first part devoted to "Corporate Strategies" and the second part covering "Counterstrategies." Part Three consists of detailed and self-critical case studies of eight corporate campaigns, including the Nestlé baby food campaign, anti-apartheid actions, the struggle at the Coca-Cola plant in Guatemala City, and actions to prevent union-busting at Control Data in South Korea.

Deborah Smith's eight-page guide to organizational resources on transnational corporations closes this informative, action-oriented booklet.

■ *Min-ju No-jo: South Korea's New Trade Unions.* Asia Monitor Resource Center. *Asia Labour Monitor,* 1987. 102pp. Maps, index, list of resources, notes, photographs, tables.

This booklet—the first in a new series being published by the Asia Monitor Resource Center—has its origins in "urgent requests from trade unionists in other countries and international unions for information on the surge in labor movement activity [in Korea] which saw extensive media coverage of the mid-1987 strikes, the demonstrations, and the pitched battles between workers and security forces."

The aim of this report is "to assist in providing a better understanding of the Korean workers movement [especially of Korea's democratic trade union organization, the Min-Ju No-Jo] and to provide a succinct account of some of Korea's labor history and the particular circumstances which help to explain the actions and developments which occurred during the summer of 1987."

Much of this report was compiled from interviews with workers, trade unionists, and labor support groups in South Korea, and also from written materials that are unattributable due to the political sensitivity of the situation in South Korea. It covers working conditions in the industrial and agricultural sectors of the South Korean economy, the country's labor history and law, and the recent growth of "genuine and democratic" unions. Chapters are devoted to the establishment of the "first genuine union" in the Hyundai group of companies and to case studies of the labor actions in Inchon in mid-1987.

The booklet closes with an analysis of the government-controlled FKTU (Federation of Korean Trade Unions) and an assessment of the potential for international trade union support for the organizing efforts of Korean workers.

■ Mokhiber, Russell. *Corporate Crime and Violence*. Essential Information. *Multinational Monitor* 8, no. 4 (April 1987). 22pp. $2.50. Photographs, illustrations.

Seven articles profile seven cases in which the products or actions of corporations caused the deaths or injury of thousands of people. Author Mokhiber examines these tragedies: the release of forty tons of deadly gas from a Union Carbide plant in the city of Bhopal, India; Dalkon-Shield-related injuries to women who used the A.H. Robins contraceptive device—the injured women were from at least eighty countries; the health effects on GI's who sprayed or patrolled the Vietnam forests sprayed with Agent Orange (its contaminant, dioxin, "the most poisonous small molecule known"); deformities caused in babies born to mothers who had taken thalidomide, touted by manufacturer Chemie Grunenthal in the 1950s and 1960s as a nontoxic tranquilizer despite early evidence of dangerous side-effects; mercury poisoning suffered by the inhabitants of Minamata because the Chisso Corporation ignored warnings and dumped chemical wastes in the Minamata waters; the industry's cover-up of the serious lung diseases caused by asbestos; the corporate effort to convince Third World mothers to substitute the less healthful (and, in certain circumstances, deadly) infant formula for the naturally nutritious breast milk.

The assembled facts are carefully documented, clearly presented, and sobering indeed. Russell Mokhiber has also written a book on corporate crime and violence (Sierra Club Books, 1988).

■ Moorsom, Richard. *Exploiting the Sea*. Catholic Institute for International Relations. *Future for Namibia Series*, no. 5, 1984. 100pp. $2.95.

Overfishing in Namibia's fishing grounds has destroyed thousands of jobs. The large profits from the fishing boom have gone to foreign companies, and the taxes to the illegitimate South African administration. This CIIR booklet substantiates these charges and suggests ways of reestablishing Namibia's fishing industry once the nation has gained its independence from South African rule.

■ Morsy, Soheir A. *Familial Adaptations to the Internationalization of Egyptian Labour.* Women in International Development, Michigan State University. *Working Papers on Women in International Development,* no. 94, August 1985. 28pp. $2.75. Notes, references.

An anthropologist whose research and writing have been mainly in the area of the political economy of health, peasantry and agrarian change, underdevelopment, and gender in cross-cultural perspective, the author of this paper here draws on previous studies of Egyptian labor migration and on her own research carried out in the village of Bahiya.

She first examines the general features and economic and political effects of the international labor movement within the Arab world. Over the past twenty years the oil industry has drawn a large number of (predominantly male) workers from Egypt's rural areas to Libya, Saudi Arabia, and Kuwait. Next familial adaptations, especially in regard to familial power relations, are considered, and finally, the many and varied ways of familial adaptation are placed in the context of agrarian transformation. The author's aim is to show "the differential impact of male migration on family-centered production and related authority patterns."

As is usual with the papers published by the Office of Women in International Development, the bibliographies are rich in related and additional resources.

■ Newland, Kathleen. *Women, Men, and the Division of Labor.* Worldwatch Institute. *Worldwatch Paper,* no. 37, May 1980. 44pp. $2.

The age-old division that places most men in paid labor and most women in unpaid work is breaking down, according to the author of this study. "Nearly half the world's adult women are in the labor force," Newland states, "a category that excludes women who do only unpaid work at home."

One issue is still untouched, says the author: "the sharing of unpaid household labor between women and men receives only a fraction of the attention given to equality in formal employment." "If women are to take full advantage of newly won access to the formal labor market," writes Newland, "men must increase their share of the essential work that goes on outside of it [i.e., in the home]. Otherwise, equal opportunity for women will turn out to be a recipe for overwork."

Newland, who is the author of *The Sisterhood of Man* (New York: W. W. Norton, 1979), examines the impact of reforms in this situation in Peru and describes actions that the government of Sweden has taken regarding the division of labor.

■ O'Brien, Patricia J. *Population Policy, Economic Development, and Multinational Corporations in Latin America.* Women in International Development, Michigan State University. *Working Papers on Women in International Development,* no. 32, 1983. 30pp. $3. Tables, references.

For many years, this study notes, social scientists have debated various ideological positions on the population-development issue. What has been absent from these discussions, however, is "the role played by multinational corporations in perpetuating both adverse population processes and economic underdevelopment in Third World countries."

The author, a university professor of sociology, first examines the impact of this neglected dimension as it relates to an understanding of the structural crisis of Latin American countries. Second, she analyzes the impact of multinational corporations on Latin American women and how the globalization of capital undermines some widely accepted propositions concerning the role of women in economic development. Finally, Professor O'Brien describes the impact of multinational corporations on internal migration pressures.

"There are structural tendencies inherent in the present global economy," this report concludes, "that perpetuate economic underdevelopment. To the extent that population policies aimed at containing population growth and directing population distribution are often adopted in response to such underdevelopment, it is not surprising that they are less than adequate as a national response to a global problem."

■ Plumb, Richard, et al. *"We Will Neither Go Nor Be Driven Out." A Special Report by the IUF Trade Union Delegation on the Occupation of the Coca-Cola Bottling Plant in Guatemala.* International Union of Food and Allied Workers Associations. 1984. 28pp. Notes, appendixes, chronology, photographs.

On February 18, 1984, 460 workers in a Coca-Cola bottling plant in Guatemala City decided to occupy their plant rather than suffer the loss of their jobs and the loss of their union as a result of the company's decision to close the plant. In March of that year a North American trade union delegation went to Guatemala on a solidarity and fact-finding mission "to lend support to the Guatemalan workers and their union." "The mission," the authors of this booklet write, "was based not only on a deep concern for the safety of the workers but also on the knowledge that the labor practices of a large multinational, like Coca-Cola, in foreign countries has significant ramifications for the trade union movement in the United States." "Corporate responsibility," they point out, "must be enforced not only within U.S. borders, but throughout the world."

This booklet gives the background to the conflict, describes the response from North American trade unions, and reports on the trade union delegation's meeting with Guatemalan government officials and on their findings at the Coca-Cola plant.

The appendixes include further documentation on the financial position of Coca-Cola's principal bottler in Guatemala, EGSA S.A., and on the dreadful social consequences that the workers and their families suffered because of their labor action.

■ Rakowski, Cathy A. *Women in Nontraditional Industry: The Case of Steel in Ciudad Guayana, Venezuela.* Women in International Development, Mich. State U. *Working Papers on Women in International Development,* no. 104, 1985. 23pp. $2.75. Notes, bibliography.

This paper describes the incorporation of women into heavy industry in and around Ciudad Guayana, site of the large-scale Venezuelan Guayana Development Program, during the employment boom of 1974-1979 and the decline in female employment in the years thereafter.

The first two sections of *Women in Nontraditional Industry* outline the features of the incorporation of women into the work force at a specialty steel plant and at the state-owned steel mill which, combined, account for over 70 percent of all manufacturing employment in the city.

The third section describes the discrimination that two groups of women, laborers and engineers, faced at the plant and the mill.

The final section analyzes the effects of discrimination on workers' behavior and suggests that both male discriminatory behavior and female coping mechanisms are not only the result of the structural factors of power, opportunity, and numbers identified in previous studies, but are also associated with factors of class, age, and culture. These latter factors are "important to the development or implementation of corrective programs designed to increase productivity and to overcome discrimination as a factor adversely affecting productivity in a particular organization or culture."

■ *Seeds and Food Security.* Sahabat Alam Malaysia (Friends of the Earth). 1984. 85pp. $4. Photographs, appendixes, illustrations, maps, notes, tables.

The Green Revolution, now more than two decades old, promised great results for Third World countries suffering food shortages when it was first launched. The "revolution" depended heavily on irrigation, chemical fertilizers and pesticides, high yield varieties of seeds (HYVs), and farm machinery. Third World governments saw it as a way of avoiding land reform and other changes in the status quo. Agribusiness interests in the First World cooperated with international development institutions such as the World Bank in implementing the Green Revolution as a supposed short-cut solution to the problem of rural poverty.

Seeds and Food Security concentrates on one small but critical component of the Green Revolution strategy: the seed industry. The booklet "sounds the alarm bell on the situation," pointing to the little known "story of how lopsided and rushed scientific and technological transfer in the area of seeds has spawned a series of localised and national ecological disasters and crop failure" and to the "possibility of the international seed industry being monopolised by a few transnational corporations more concerned about profits and the interests of their shareholders than the anguished cries of the hungry and unfed in the world."

The Friends of the Earth report analyzes the international seed industry and documents the way in which the farmers in Malaysia are responding to HYVs and to the problems associated with them.

Finally, the report recommends government action "to ensure protection of our seed heritage and to minimise the adverse effects of HYV introduction."

■ Shiva, Vandana. *Forestry Crisis and Forestry Myths. A Critical Review of "Tropical Forests: A Call for Action."* World Rainforest Movement. 1987. 56pp. Chart, photographs, references.

Tropical Forests: A Call for Action is a joint report of the World Bank, the United Nations Development Programme, and the U.S. Agency for International Development. This booklet is a critical review of that report.

The World Bank's $8 billion plan, Tropical Forests Action Plan (TFAP), to "save" tropical forests, according to the author of this study commissioned by the World Rainforest Movement, only "extends forestry activities in the same disastrous directions that the World Bank has initiated and encouraged in the past."

The study finds the TFAP biased against the poor, geared only toward healthy investment returns, and "indifferent to human and ecological concerns." Control is placed in the hands of industry and other forces outside the indigenous population.

The World Rainforest Movement is preparing a People's Action Plan that it will offer as an alternative to the World Bank proposal.

■ *Solidarity across Borders: U.S. Labor in a Global Economy.* The Midwest Center for Labor Research. *Labor Research Review* 8, no. 1 (spring 1989). 98pp. $7. Figures, illustrations, photographs, tables.

"International solidarity has long been an ideal of the labor movement," writes the managing editor of *Labor Research Review.* "Today it is a necessity." "What is needed," she continues, "are practical methods of achieving it, or at least building toward it. Also needed is a clear conceptual understanding of the *real* commonality of working people's interests worldwide." That is what this special issue of *Labor Research Review* provides.

The first of five articles in the main section of the magazine gives a lengthy description of a successful strike by textile workers at the Lunafil plant outside of Guatemala City and a resulting corporate campaign by international supporters. Other articles cover the organizing of immigrants in Los Angeles; using labor's trade secretariats; working women and the food secretariat; and, finally, women, solidarity, and the global factory.

■ Taylor, Elizabeth, et al. *Women and Labour Migration.* Middle East Research and Information Project. *MERIP Reports* 14, no. 5 (June 1984). 32pp. $2.75. Notes, maps, photographs.

This issue of *MERIP Reports* contains three articles on the effects of labor migration on women in the Middle East: two on women in Egypt ("Egyptian Migration and Peasant Wives" by Elizabeth Taylor and "One Village in Egypt" by Fatma Khafagy) and one on women in (North) Yemen: "Yemeni Workers Abroad: The Impact on Women."

The exodus of skilled and unskilled laborers from both Egypt and

Yemen to high-paying jobs in other parts of the Middle East has had a profound impact on the economies and social structures of the two countries. The authors of these three articles describe the scope of regional labor migration and its overall impact—with Khafagy focusing her attention on just one village south of Cairo, Egypt. Each author then analyzes the ways in which the temporary absence of male heads of households has altered the traditional roles of women in Middle Eastern societies.

■ Thomson, Robert, et al. *Green Gold: Bananas and Dependency in the Eastern Caribbean.* Latin America Bureau. 1987. 94pp. £3.95/$7.50. Map, bibliography, charts, figures, notes, photographs, statistical tables. Available in North America from Monthly Review Press (New York).

This high-quality LAB booklet offers an in-depth look at the growth and development of the banana industry in the four Windward Islands of the eastern Caribbean: Dominica, Grenada, St. Lucia, and St. Vincent. As subjects of the colonial powers (the French and the British at different times) and now as laborers for the transnational corporations that manage the economies of their politically independent nations, the small farmers of the eastern Caribbean find themselves with "little control over their futures and few options for improving their way of life." *Green Gold* explains why.

For all their dependence on the growing and exporting of bananas the Windward Islands actually play a very small role in the global banana trade, as the authors demonstrate in their opening chapter. A sign of their relative insignificance is the fact that the three U.S. transnational corporations that dominate the world banana trade (United Brands, Standard Fruit, and Del Monte) have no involvement whatsoever in the production or export of bananas from the Windward Islands. The sole buyer of Windward Islands bananas for export is Geest PLC, a public company that is Britain's largest importer and distributor or fruits and vegetables. *Green Gold* discusses Geest's role in the banana trade in the eastern Caribbean, pointing out the similarities and differences in its operations and those of the big three.

The booklet closes with case studies of three of the islands: St. Lucia, Dominica, and Grenada, and with a brief examination of alternatives that offer the people of the Windward Islands an escape from their poverty and dependency.

■ Tiano, Susan. *Maquiladoras, Women's Work, and Unemployment in Northern Mexico.* Women in International Development, Michigan State University. *Working Papers on Women in International Development,* no. 43, February 1984. 32pp. $3. Notes, references, statistical tables.

Although Mexico's Border Industrialization Program (BIP) was initiated to relieve unemployment in northern Mexican cities, critics claim that it has not served this end. Many analysts have charged that the main reason for this failure is that unemployment in northern Mexico, as in the nation as a whole, is a male problem, yet women constitute the bulk of the BIP work force.

In this WID research study, Susan Tiano, an assistant professor of sociology at the University of New Mexico, gathers aggregate data on men's and women's labor force participation to demonstrate that the analysts' criticism is based on several inaccurate assumptions. Average unemployment rates, for instance, are actually higher among women than men of comparable ages throughout the nation. Furthermore, joblessness is more pronounced among younger women, that is, among the very people from which the majority of BIP workers are recruited.

Dr. Tiano's conclusion is that the BIP does not appear to have enhanced women's labor-market situation relative to men's. Rather, she maintains, "the same conditions which weaken women's employment status in other parts of Mexico also operate in the North, despite any job opportunities the program might offer." The author draws upon propositions from Marxist-feminist theory to interpret these empirical trends.

- *The Tobacco Trap.* Essential Information. *Multinational Monitor* 8, nos. 7 & 8 (July/August 1987). 14pp. $2.00. Tables, illustrations, list of resources, photographs.

As the dangers of smoking become better known and as tobacco use becomes less acceptable in the developed world, cigarette consumption in the Third World grows and effects on the health of Third World people are largely ignored. The short articles in this collection take up several issues pertinent to this fact: U.S. tobacco companies in the Third World, the tobacco export industry in Zimbabwe, the top tobacco conglomerates and their diversification, tobacco advertising, smokeless tobacco, and the health effects of tobacco.

A one-page list of resources refers to other articles, books, and organizations that focus on the tobacco industry in general and tobacco production, promotion, and use in the Third World in particular.

- Trade Union International Research and Education Group. *Beggar My Neighbour.* NALGO Education. 1986. 70pp. £2.50. Maps, figures, illustrations, list of resources, photographs, statistical tables.

A publication of the British trade union NALGO's Education Department and originally written for NALGO's membership by the Trade Union International Research and Education Group (Ruskin College, Oxford), this booklet asks why world poverty exists in a world that has enough resources to provide for all its people. A further observation: most of this poverty is borne by the people of the Third World and as their condition worsens that of the people of the First World seems to become better.

The booklet first examines the historical backgrounds and the present-day crises of hunger, debt, and militarization. One chapter in this section compares poverty in the Third World with poverty in Britain. Possible solutions and appropriate responses for trade unions are then considered. Four appendixes suggest printed resources and pertinent

organizations. Each chapter concludes with suggestions for discussion.
The booklet is intended primarily for union education sessions but is appropriate for individuals or study group use. "Its purpose," write the authors, "is the traditional rallying call of the trade union movement: Educate, Agitate, Organise." A teacher's guide is in preparation.

■ *Transnational Corporations in the Caribbean: Strangers in Paradise.* Resource Center. Spring 1984. 50pp. $3.50. Bulk rates available. Map, notes, tables.

"Transnational corporations—firms that have business outside their home countries—have penetrated the Caribbean more than other regions of the world," state the authors of this booklet. After a brief introduction analyzing the effects foreign corporations have had in the region, the booklet lists the names of subsidiaries of British, French, Dutch, Canadian, and U.S. corporations active there. The listing is alphabetical by country and includes information about the lines of business each corporation operates.

■ Tsui, Elaine Yi-lan. *Are Married Daughters "Spilled Water"? A Study of Working Women in Urban Taiwan.* National Taiwan University, Population Studies Center, Women's Research Program. *Monograph,* no. 4, January 1987. 67pp. $6. Abstract, bibliography, chronology, figures, tables.

Based on the author's dissertation, this pamphlet studies women's changing roles in a patrilineal society, Taiwan. Taiwan has undergone significant changes in the past several years, as it moved from traditional agricultural economy to industrial economy. The author concentrated her study on working women who have been well educated, assuming that this group would show "the most marked change from the traditional situation."

The four sections of the study describe women's position in traditional Chinese society and in modern Taiwan; the theoretical framework for the study; intergenerational wealth flow and working women's management of their finances; and finally, the relationship between socio-economic development and women's status.

The study suggests that as women become more economically independent, they are treated and respond in a manner similar to the ways of sons in the past.

■ *Violence against Sugar Workers.* International Commission for the Co-ordination of Solidarity among Sugar Workers. July 1985. 12pp. 50 cents. Notes, chronology, illustrations, photographs.

This ICCSASW publication graphically illustrates the ways in which violence—both indiscriminate and targeted—is used against sugar workers "to weaken the organization of the workers and to destroy every attempt of the workers to defend themselves." It explains, too, how this violence is institutionalized in a repressive political and military system that those who exploit the sugar workers can use "legally" and with "technical efficiency" to further their own aims. Examples selected from three Third World countries—Brazil, the Philippines, and Haiti—substantiate ICCSASW's charges.

This pamphlet was published with sugar workers in mind. Its aim is to show sugar workers everywhere that "there are other groups which experience similar problems and situations, and that it is necessary to join together in order to solve their common problems."

■ Ward, Kathryn B. *Women and Transnational Corporation Employment: A World-System and Feminist Analysis.* Women in International Development, Michigan State University. *Working Papers on Women in International Development,* no. 120, July 1986. 19pp. $2.50. Notes, references.

Women of Southeast Asia and Latin America have become the prime labor force for transnational corporations located in those areas. Some see this as a positive step toward women's economic independence, others as exploitation. The author of this paper reviews the conflicting research, maintaining that it must be evaluated in light of "the effects of TNCs on both the underdevelopment of the country and the economic independence and empowerment of women relative to men."

She discusses the relation of the economic status of women to underdevelopment, the rise of the global assembly line and export processing, the relation of women's economic position to the global assembly line, and the long-range effects of TNC investment on underdevelopment, on women, and on the forces for change.

The extensive list of references furnishes the interested reader with ample related material.

■ Weinrub, Al, and William Bollinger. *The AFL-CIO in Central America: A Look at the American Institute for Free Labor Development (AIFLD).* Labor Network on Central America. September 1987. 40pp. $4.50. Resource guide, charts, illustrations, list of abbreviations, notes, photographs.

This attractive and well-documented booklet is an outgrowth of the five-part series on the American Institute for Free Labor Development (AIFLD) that appeared in the Labor Network's *Labor Report on Central America* in 1986.

The authors describe the shameful involvement of AIFLD in South and Central America: dividing, weakening, and destroying Latin America's trade union movement, as it "supports U.S. government and big business objectives." Chapter 1 identifies the roots of AFL-CIO Central American policy. Chapter 2 studies the funding of AIFLD. Chapter 3 analyzes AIFLD's attempts to undermine democracy in Latin America. Chapters 4 and 5 examine AIFLD's activities in two Central American nations: El Salvador and Nicaragua. (Guatemela and Honduras are covered in the booklet's appendixes.)

The final chapter describes the aggressive role that the normally secretive AIFLD has been forced to take in the United States to counteract increased exposure of its "dirty deeds" throughout Latin America.

The authors state their belief that "for the first time in decades, the possibility now exists of building a coalition in the United States that can not only alter U.S. Central America policy, but address the broader peace and justice issues of concern to U.S. workers as well." The Labor Network on Central America produced this booklet to provide progressive forces in the trade union movement with "readily accessible information and [a] clear analysis of the role played by the AFL-CIO in the [Central America] region."

- West Coast Trade Union Delegation to Nicaragua. *Nicaragua: Labor, Democracy, and the Struggle for Peace*. Labor Network on Central America. November 1984. 32pp. $2. Bulk rates available. Glossary, photographs.

This report presents the findings, conclusions, and recommendations of a delegation of national, state, and local trade union leaders that visited Nicaragua in September 1984. The delegation went to Nicaragua in search of the facts "that the members of our unions, and working people more generally, needed [about Nicaragua]."

The delegation came to two conclusions: (1) since 1979, as a result of the Sandinista revolution, the workers of Nicaragua have made unprecedented gains in their political, economic, social, and cultural wellbeing; and (2) the gains that have been made by Nicaraguan workers are being undermined by the U.S. government, which is waging a war of economic and military aggression against the people of Nicaragua.

In the light of their findings and the conclusions they reached, the delegation made three recommendations: "(1) that the U.S. government stop all interference in the affairs of Nicaragua, including all forms of U.S. military intervention, aid to the *contras*, and the U.S. economic blockade of the country; (2) that trade unions in the United States develop friendly relations with the labor movement of Nicaragua and support the efforts of Nicaraguan workers to rebuild and defend their country; and (3) that the AFL-CIO revise its position on Nicaragua to reflect more accurately the realities of that country and to oppose U.S. aid to the *contras* and all other U.S. military intervention in Nicaragua."

- Winkler, James E. *Losing Control: Towards an Understanding of Transnational Corporations in the Pacific Islands Context*. Pacific Conference of Churches. 1982. 82pp. $4. Notes, illustrations, maps, photographs, tables.

In this booklet James Winkler builds a case in support of his contention that the Pacific Ocean represents a frontier that "is increasingly being exploited for food, mineral resources, and oil by the industrial nations and transnational corporations." "Thus," he concludes, "the island nations [of the Pacific] and their resources are being used to fulfill the needs of people in the West, not the people who actually live [in the Pacific Ocean region]."

Winkler gives a general description of transnational corporations and then examines their activities in the Pacific, concentrating on the mining, fishing, forestry, and tourism industries. He concludes with an exploration of alternatives and a discussion of the churches' role in defense of those exploited by these powerful corporations.

■ *Women and Labour.* International Documentation and Communication Center (IDOC). *IDOC Internazionale* 18, no. 5 (October/November 1987). 42pp. Sources, bibliography, charts, illustrations, maps.

This issue of *IDOC Internazionale* contains reprints of articles from a variety of publications on the subject of women and labor in Third World settings. As the articles make clear over and over again women work in the most underpaid, unrecognized, and undervalued sectors of the global economy.

Subjects covered include the struggles of India's Self-Employed Women's Association; the organizing efforts of women garment workers in Mexico; the effects on women of male labor migration in India; the formation of a union of domestic workers in South Africa; women and trade unions in Asia (three articles reprinted from the *Asian Women Workers Newsletter*); working women in the Philippines; and women workers in Jamaica's Free Trade Zone.

This issue closes with a nine-page annotated bibliography of IDOC's library holdings on the subject of women and labor.

SUPPLEMENTARY LIST OF PAMPHLETS AND ARTICLES

GENERAL

Bluestone, Barry, Bennett Harrison, and Lawrence Baker. *Corporate Flight: The Causes and Consequences of Economic Dislocation.* Progressive Alliance. Published with the National Center for Policy Alternatives and Working Papers for a New Society. March 1981. 94pp.

Boyd, Rosalind, and Dipankar Gupta. *Internationalizing Labour: Modalities of Intervention through Labour Studies and Publications.* Centre for Developing-Area Studies, McGill University. 1987. 42pp. Canadian $3.
Cheru, Fantu. *Bitter Harvest for U.S. Banks: The Making of a Debtors Cartel.* Interfaith Center on Corporate Responsibility. *ICCR Brief* 13, no. 5 (1984). 4pp. 60 cents.
Conglomerates: Where the Product Is Profit. engage/social action, November 1984. 31pp. 75 cents.
Dixon-Mueller, Ruth, et al. *Women's Work in Third World Agriculture: Concepts and Indicators.* International Labour Office (Geneva). *Women, Work and Development,* no. 9.
Elson, Diane, and Ruth Pearson. *Subordination of Women and the Internationalization of Factory Production.* Women's International Resource Exchange. 1981. 12pp. $1.40.
Getting a Handle on Pesticides. Transnationals Information Exchange. *TIE-Europe,* no. 15, May 1983. 23pp.
Jaquette, Jane S. *Women Food Producers: Potential Power for Combating World Hunger.* OEF International. 1985. 28pp. $5.
Lall, Sanjaya. *The Indirect Employment Effects of Multinational Enterprises in Developing Countries.* International Labour Office (Geneva). *Working Paper,* no. 3. 15 Swiss francs.
Nunez, Osvaldo. *The Trade Union Movement and the Third World.* Centre for Developing-Area Studies, McGill University. 1984. 13pp. Canadian $3.
Oil, Politics and the Pursuit of Profits. Essential Information. *Multinational Monitor* 7, no. 8 (April 1986). 12pp. $2.
Pesticides Don't Know When to Stop Killing. Multinational Monitor 6, no. 13 (September 1985). 13pp. $2.
Short Circuit: Women on the Global Assembly Line. Participatory Research Group. Sept. 1985. 39pp.
Teh Poh Ai. *Ciba-Geigy's Cover-Up.* Essential Information. *Multinational Monitor* 6, no. 11 (August 1985). 7pp. $2.00.
Watanabe, S. *Multinational Enterprises and Employment Oriented "Appropriate" Technologies in Developing Countries.* International Labour Office (Geneva). *Working Paper,* no. 14. 15 Swiss francs.
Weir, David. *Global Pesticide Issues.* Interfaith Center on Corporate Responsibility. *ICCR Brief* 13, no. 3 (1984). 4pp. 60 cents.
Yachir, Faysal. *The World Steel Industry Today.* United Nations University/Third World Forum. *Studies in African Political Economy,* 1988. 85pp. $12.50. Available from Zed Books (London and New Jersey).
Zawad, Kazi. *The Fight to Ban Bogus Drugs.* Essential Information. *Multinational Monitor* 6, no. 9 (July 1985). 4pp. $2.00.

AFRICA

Bello, J. A., and O. Iyanda. *Appropriate Technology Choice and Employment Creation by Two Multinational Enterprises in Nigeria.*

International Labour Office (Geneva). *Working Paper,* no. 17. 15 Swiss francs.

Bhagavan, M. R. *Angola's Political Economy, 1975-1985.* Scandinavian Institute of African Studies. *Research Report,* no. 75, 1986. 89pp. 30 Swedish kroner.

Child Labour in South Africa. Anti-Slavery Society. No. 7 (1983). 88pp. $3.

Conrad, Thomas. *South Africa's Multinational Connections: Putting Apartheid on Computer. Multinational Monitor* 3, no. 4 (April 1982). 4pp.

Female White Collar Workers: A Case Study of Successful Development in Lusaka, Zambia. Women in International Development, Michigan State University. *Working Papers on Women in International Development,* no. 29, 1983. 31pp. $3.

Giacometti, A *The Labour Movement in Tropical Africa: Its Beginnings.* International Union of Food and Allied Workers' Association. September 1986. 38pp.

Hansen, Karen Tranberg. *The Work History: Disaggregating the Changing Terms of Poor Women's Entry into Lusaka's Labor Force.* Women in International Development, Michigan State University. *Working Papers on Women in International Development,* no. 134, January 1987. 33pp. $3.

Hector, Tim. *The Black Working Class in South Africa. Race Today* 17, no. 7 (July 1986). 4pp. 70 pence.

Iyanda, O., and J. A. Bello. *Employment Effects of Multinational Enterprises in Nigeria.* International Labour Office (Geneva). *Working Paper,* no. 10. 15 Swiss francs.

Jules-Rosette, Bennetta. *Women's Work in the Informal Sector: A Zambian Case Study.* Women in International Development, Michigan State University. *Working Papers on Women in International Development,* no. 3, January 1982. 24pp. $2.75.

Kaplinsky, R. *Employment Effects of Multinational Enterprises: A Case Study of Kenya.* International Labour Office (Geneva). *Working Paper,* no. 8. 15 Swiss francs.

Labor and South Africa. Economic Notes 53, nos. 7-8 (1985). 20pp. $1.

Leonard, Richard. *When You Bank with Citibank, You Bank in South Africa.* Interfaith Center on Corporate Responsibility. *ICCR Brief* 16, no. 1 (1987). 4pp. $1.25. Bulk rates available.

McAfee, Kathy. *Opening the Road to Hunger. Food Exports from the Third World: Senegal. Facts for Action,* no. 11, May 1984. 8pp. 50 cents.

Somplatsky-Jarman, Rev. Bill, ed. *Divestment for South Africa: An Investment in Hope. Corporate Examiner, ICCR Brief* 14, no. 1 (1985). 4pp. $1.

Van Hear, Nick. *Attracting Agribusiness in Nigeria. Multinational Monitor* 6, no. 12 (August 1985). 5pp. $2.

ASIA AND PACIFIC

Agarwal, Anil, Juliet Merrifield, and Rajesh Tandon. *No Place to Run: Local Realities and Global Issues of the Bhopal Disaster.* Highlander Center and the Society for Participatory Research in Asia. 1985. 40pp.

Cho, Uhn, and Hagen Koo. *Capital Accumulation, Women's Work, and Informal Economies in Korea.* Women in International Development, Michigan State University. *Working Papers on Women in International Development,* no. 21, 1983. 18pp. $2.50.

Committee for Asian Women. *Retrenchment! Asian Women Workers Newsletter* 4, no. 3 (December 1985). 12pp. $1.

Committee for Asian Women. *Tales of the Filipino Working Women.* Christian Conference of Asia, Urban-Rural Mission. June 1984. 68pp. $2.50.

Dar, U. *The Effects of Multinational Enterprises on Employment in India.* International Labour Office (Geneva). *Working Paper,* no. 9. 15 Swiss francs.

Gallin, Rita S. *Rural Industrialization and Chinese Women: A Case Study from Taiwan.* Women in International Development, Michigan State University. *Working Papers on Women in International Development,* no. 47, 1984. 21pp. $2.75.

Introductory Course for the Workers. Ecumenical Institute for Labor Education and Research. September 30, 1986. 66pp.

Kim, Young-ock. *Position of Women Workers in Manufacturing Industries in South Korea: A Marxist-Feminist Analysis.* Institute of Social Studies, Publications Office. *ISS Working Papers, Sub-Series on Women's History and Development,* no. 6, January 1988. 81 pp. Dfl. 5.

Kurian, Rachel, et. al. *Women Workers in the Sri Lanka Plantation Sector: An Historical and Contemporary Analysis.* International Labour Office (Geneva). *Women, Work and Development,* no. 5.

Kuwahara, Y. T. Harada, and Y. Mizuno. *Employment Effects of Foreign Direct Investments in ASEAN Countries.* International Labour Office (Geneva). *Working Paper,* no. 6. 15 Swiss francs.

Lim, L., and Pang Eng Fong. *Technology Choice and Employment Creation: A Case Study of Three Multinational Enterprises in Singapore.* International Labour Office (Geneva). *Working Paper,* no. 16. 15 Swiss francs.

Lind, John E. *Philippine Debt to Foreign Banks.* CANICCOR November 1984. 26 pp. $5.

Lives of Working Women in India. Manushi. Selected readings from *Manushi: A Journal about Women and Society, 1979-1980.* 21pp. $1.50. From WIRE.

Mies, Maria, et al. *Indian Women in Subsistence and Agricultural Labour.* International Labour Office (Geneva). *Women, Work and Development,* no. 12, 1986. 158pp. 20 Swiss francs.

Our Stories: Lives of Filipina Women. Synapses. February 1985. 8pp.

Pesticide Dilemma in the Third World: A Case Study of Malaysia. Sahabat Alam Malaysia (Friends of the Earth). 1984. 76pp.

Phongpaichit, Pasuk. *From Peasant Girls to Bangkok Masseuses.* International Labour Office (Geneva). *Women, Work and Development,* no. 2, 1982. 80pp. 15 Swiss francs.

Right Wing Vigilantes in Labor Repression in the Philippines. KMU International Department. October 1987. 24pp.

Sambamoorthi, Usha. *Labor Market Discrimination against Women in India.* Women in International Development, Michigan State University. *Working Papers on Women in International Development,* no. 58, 1984. 16pp. $2.50.

Sturdevant, Saundra. *On the Situation of Working Women in the Urban and Rural Areas of the Southern Part of Korea.* American Friends Service Committee (San Francisco). April 1987. 26pp. $2.50.

Tadem, Eduardo C. *Grains and Radicalism: The Political Economy of the Rice Industry in the Philippines, 1965-1985.* Third World Studies Center. *Commodity Series,* no. 5, September 1986. 84pp.

Tanchoco-Subido, C. *Employment Effects of Multinational Enterprises in the Philippines.* International Labour Office (Geneva). *Working Paper,* no. 11. 15 Swiss francs.

Vietnam's Quest for Foreign Investment: A Bold Move. Indochina Project. *Indochina Issues,* no. 80, March 1988. 8pp. $2.

Wong, Aline K., and Yiu-Chung Ko. *Women's Work and Family Life: The Case of Electronics Workers in Singapore.* Women in International Development, Michigan State University. *Working Papers on Women in International Development,* no. 64, 1984. 37pp. $3.

LATIN AMERICA AND CARIBBEAN

Bass, Emily, and Theodore Lieverman. *Trade Union Activity and Government Repression in El Salvador: A Report.* 1987. 25pp. $2. From authors: 1616 Walnut St., 2nd floor, Philadelphia, PA 19103.

Deere, Carmen Diana, and Magdalena Leon de Leal. *Women in Andean Agriculture: Peasant Production and Rural Wage Employment in Colombia and Peru.* International Labour Office (Geneva). *Women, Work and Development,* no. 4.

Furtado, Celso. *No to Recession and Unemployment: An Examination of the Brazilian Economic Crisis.* Third World Foundation for Social and Economic Studies. 1984. 78pp. £2.95/$5.

Keck, Mimi. *Brazil's New Labor Militancy: A Break from the Past.* Interfaith Center on Corporate Responsibility. *ICCR Brief* 12, nos. 8 & 9 (1983). 4pp. 60 cents. Bulk rates available.

Munck, Ronaldo. *Cycles of Class Struggle and the Making of the Working Class in Argentina.* Centre for Developing-Area Studies, McGill University. 1985. 24pp. Canadian $3.

Neither Pure Nor Simple: The AFL-CIO and Latin America. North Amer-

ican Congress on Latin America. *NACLA Report on the Americas* 12, no. 3 (May/June 1988). 40pp. $3.50.
Possas, M. L. *Employment Effects of Multinational Enterprises in Brazil.* International Labour Office (Geneva). *Working Paper,* no. 7. 15 Swiss francs.
Rosenberg, Terry Jean. *Women's Productive and Reproductive Roles in the Family Wage Economy: A Colombian Example.* Women in International Development, Michigan State University. *Working Papers on Women in International Development,* no. 68, 1984. 26pp. $2.75.
Smith, Sandy. *Labor in El Salvador.* Essential Information, Inc. *Multinational Monitor* 9, no. 5 (May 1988). 4pp. $2.50.
The Struggle in the U.S. Labor Movement over Central America. Labor Network on Central America. *Background Paper,* no. 2. November 1984. 8pp. 50 cents.
Taking Care of Business in Nicaragua. Essential Information, Inc. *Multinational Monitor* 6, no. 4 (April 1985). 13pp. $2.00.
Turner, Terisa. *Multinational Enterprises and Employment in the Caribbean with Special Reference to Trinidad and Tobago.* International Labour Office (Geneva). *Working Paper,* no. 20, 1982. 62pp. 15 Swiss francs.
Young, Gay. *Gender Identification and Working Class Solidarity among Maquila Workers in Ciudad Juarez.* Women in International Development, Michigan State University. *Working Papers on Women in International Development,* no. 124, September 1986. 24pp. $2.75.

MIDDLE EAST

Melrose, Dianna. *Great Health Robbery: Baby Milk and Medicines in Yemen.* Oxfam (U.K.). 1981. 50pp. $1.30.
Owen, Dr. Roger. *Migrant Workers in the Gulf.* Minority Rights Group. *MRG Report* 68, 1985. 24pp. $4.

INFORMATION SOURCES

For information on the release of new pamphlets and articles on transnational corporations and labor in the Third World we recommend that you request to be placed on the mailing list of the publishers mentioned in this directory, especially IDOC International, the Interfaith Center on Corporate Responsibility, the International Coalition for Development Action, the International Labour Organisation, and Women in International Development (Michigan State University).

Back issues of several of the periodicals that appear in this directory make excellent resource materials for group or individual study. Publications that are regularly devoted to one topic include *Asia Labour Monitor, Multinational Monitor, ICCR Brief,* and *TIE Report.* Check your library or write for a list of back issues.

The publishers of *International Labour Reports* (see periodicals chapter above) compile thirty-two page "education packs" for trade unionists. The packs include major articles from *ILR,* an introductory overview, suggestions for educational use, reviews of resources, and a file of contacts. The education packs have covered themes such as the auto industry, South Africa, hazardous industries, women and trade unions, Central America, and the Philippines. Inquire for bulk discounts and for the special prices available on combination orders.

Matty Klatter's bibliographies in the *Newsletter of International Labour Studies* are a regular source for updated references to pamphlets and articles. See the periodicals chapter above.

See also the publications from **Third World Resources** described in the preface to this directory and the reference to the four-page guide to resources on transnational corporations and labor in the information sources section of chapter 1 above.

5

Audiovisuals

This chapter is divided into two parts: **visual resources** (films, filmstrips, slideshows, and videotapes) and **audio resources** (records and tapes). The visual resources part is divided into three sections: annotated entries, supplementary list, and sources of additional information. The audio resources part contains only annotated entries.

It was impossible for us to preview all the audiovisuals included in this directory. In most cases we have reproduced the description of the audiovisual directly from the distributor's catalog. The source is given in small capital letters at the end of each annotation: either DIST to signify the principal distributor or the initials of the secondary distributor. (AFCA = *Access to Films on Central America*, edited by Wendy Tanowitz.) Annotations not within quotation marks are our own.

We have done our best to select audiovisuals that appear to be worthy of your consideration, but we caution you to arrange for previews of audiovisuals to determine their appropriateness in your setting.

All audiovisuals are integrated into the titles index at the back of this directory. See the organizations index for the addresses of distributors listed in this chapter.

(See p. 142 for the introduction to the audio resources.)

Visual Resources

Information in the **annotated entries** is given in the following order: title; producer(s); director(s); date; length (in minutes); format; principal distributor; rental and purchase price; secondary distributor(s); description of content; and source of annotation.

When an audiovisual is available from distributors other than the principal one, we have listed those as secondary distributors, but in deference to the rights of the principal distributor we have omitted the often lower rental rates of the secondary distributors. You are free, of course, to make your own inquiries. Rental/purchase information should be taken only as being indicative. We urge you to inquire about all fees and conditions before ordering an audiovisual. Some distributors have sliding price scales depending upon the nature of your organization and the intended use of the audiovisual, so it is advisable to ask about discounts when you make your inquiry.

Audiovisuals in the **supplementary list** (pp. 137–142) are grouped under these headings: general; Africa; Asia and Pacific; Latin America and Caribbean; and Middle East.

The **information sources** section (p. 142) provides information on guides and catalogs that contain the names of other audiovisuals related to transnational corporations and labor in the Third World.

ANNOTATED ENTRIES

■ *The ABC's of Philippine EPZ's.* Produced by Interim Media Productions. 1983. 28 minutes. Color slideshow with cassette tape. 142 slides with script. Distributor: Synapses Audiovisuals. Rental: $15 for ten days.

This slideshow describes—in a down-to-earth and entertaining manner—the complex social, political, and economic realities surrounding export processing zones (EPZs). The EPZs are special tax-exempt zones set aside for use by foreign corporations. In the words of one of the characters in this show: "EPZs are part of the Philippine government's open-door policy—an 'export promotion' program which invites foreign, giant corporations to take advantage of our cheap labor and many exemptions from taxes and custom duties on imported machinery, raw materials, and equipment."

EPZ workers discuss the exploitative working conditions at German, Australian, Japanese, and U.S. factories in the zones and describe the terrible living conditions around the zones.

"Even if workers were given slightly better wages or allowed to form genuine trade unions," says one worker, "the fact is that these foreign corporations do not answer either the physical or basic human needs of the Filipino people!" With the picture of a Mattel-brand Barbie doll on the screen, he concludes: "The creative energies, labor force, and natural resources of the Philippines should first serve to feed, house, and clothe the people instead of housing and clothing Barbie dolls."

■ *Address—Earth: Living in a Global Society.* Produced by Marjorie Kelly. 1985. 10 minutes. Color slideshow with cassette tape. 80 slides with script and teacher's guide. Distributor: Immaculate Heart College Center. Purchase: $60, plus $2.40 postage and handling.

Examining both imports and exports in terms of agriculture, industry, and consumer goods, this presentation introduces students at all levels (middle school to adult) to the realities of today's global economy.

The producers conclude that Americans are so globally interconnected that it is virtually impossible to differentiate between the foreign and the domestic and it therefore behooves us to be aware of our role in the world economy so as to participate in a more responsible and intelligent manner.

■ *AFL-CIO (AIFLD), Israel, and Central America.* Produced by Steve Zeltzer and Lee Heller. 1988. 60 minutes. Videocassette. Distributor: Labor Video Project. Rental: $20, plus $3 shipping and $20 deposit, for 15 days.

"Discussion as to U.S. labor's role and Israel's role in the labor movements of Central America with speakers from the Labor Network on Central America, Labor Committee on the Middle East, SEIU 250, and Faculty Committee for Human Rights in El Salvador and Central America and inserts of speeches by David Jessup of AIFLD and Daniel Cantor, author of *Tunnel Vision.*

"Also included on this tape is an interview with Rodrigo Duarte Clark, Director of Teatro de la Esperanza, concerning labor and Latino theater." DIST

■ *Agriculture's Vanishing Heritage.* Produced by International Genetic Resources Programme. 1984. 25 minutes. Color slideshow with cassette tape. Also slideshow on videotape. Distributor: Church World Service. Rental: free.

"This slideshow examines the causes of the extinction of crop and livestock genetic resources throughout the world, along with some possible solutions. Examples are shown of crop epidemics due to genetic uniformity. Also examined are seed storage banks, multinational corporate interests in the seed industry, and the seed/pesticide connection. *Agriculture's Vanishing Heritage* shows several organizations working throughout the world to preserve genetic diversity in crops." DIST

■ *Alpaca Breeders of Chimboya.* Produced by Marianne Eyde. 1983. 30 minutes. Color film and videocassette. Distributor: Icarus Films. Rental: $55 (film only). Purchase: $530 (film), $290 (video). Also from IDERA Films.

"This film from Peru depicts the life of a small peasant community high in the Andes mountains which depends on the marketing of Alpaca fleece for its survival. *Alpaca Breeders of Chimboya* traces the cycle of the Chimboyan economy, from raising and shearing of the alpacas, to market, to textile production, and export. The film looks at the structure of the Indian peasant communities which the alpaca industry supports: middlemen (buyers for the large textile companies) provide credit between marketing seasons; textile exporters ship 85 percent of the Peruvian alpaca each year, but when cash runs low peasants of different communities barter among themselves in order to survive. A warm, sensitive portrayal of a typical Andean community, the film combines a disciplined anthropological view with a cogent social and economic analysis." DIST

■ *The American Connection.* 1987. 27 minutes. Videocassette. Distributor: American Labor Education Center. Purchase: $40.

This program was produced to educate Americans about apartheid in South Africa, the international boycott of Shell, and the need to win human rights in other countries for the protection of workers both there and here.

The American Connection describes Shell boycott activity in Birmingham, Alabama. It includes rare footage of South African police violence and an interview with a representative of South Africa's largest union.

A ten-minute version of the program, which omits a panel discussion with church and labor leaders, is also available.

■ *Back to Coca-Cola.* Produced by the International Union of Food Workers. 1984. 35 minutes. Black and white film. Spanish and English with subtitles. Distributor: Guatemala News & Information Bureau. Rental: Inquire.

"Documents the ongoing struggle of Guatemalan Coca-Cola workers to preserve their union. Footage and interviews with the workers inside the occupied plant show their determination and strength in the face of potentially violent opposition. The support of other workers in Guatemala who are bringing food and supplies to the strikers highlights the importance of the Coca-Cola trade union for the rest of the labor movement in Guatemala." DIST

■ *Basta Ya! Women in Central America.* Produced by Resource Center. 1983. 25 minutes. Black and white film. Also in slideshow/tape format. Distributor: Resource Center. Purchase: $65 (individuals or groups), $100 (organizations). Also from Church World Service and American Friends Service Committee (Cambridge).

"A powerful portrayal of the daily life of rural and urban women in Central America. Examines the role of U.S. corporations in perpetuating underdevelopment and the effects of war on the women of Central America. Points out that women do have a feminist consciousness throughout Central America but argues that progress for women depends fundamentally on changes in the social, political, and economic structures in their countries. Describes the changes women are determinedly making in their lives. Good for use with solidarity organizations and women's groups, as well as in classrooms and for general audiences." AFSC

■ *Bread with Dignity: Voices of Nicaraguan Labor.* 1987. 20 minutes. Videocassette. Distributor: Seattle Labor Committee on Central America. Purchase: $30.

"*Bread with Dignity* is a twenty-minute video about the working people of Nicaragua. Addressing U.S. workers directly, Nicaraguan men and women talk about what the Sandinista revolution has meant to them and about the impact of the U.S.-sponsored contra war and economic blockade on their struggle for a better life.

Shot in Nicaragua in spring 1986, *Bread With Dignity* is addressed to union audiences in the United States." DIST

■ *Bringing It All Back Home.* Produced by Sheffield Film Co-op. 1987.

48 minutes. Videocassette. Distributor: Sheffield Film Co-op. Also from Committee for Asian Women.

"The video depicts the situation of women workers in the Third World free trade zones as well as in Britain. It underlines the link between them in the global context of capital internationalization and the failure of the trade union movement to acknowledge the challenge." CAW

- *The Business of America.* Produced by California Newsreel. 1984. 42 minutes. Color film. Distributor: California Newsreel. Also from IDERA Films. IDERA also distributes a 58-minute videocassette of this film.

"*The Business of America* . . . confronts a critical issue of the 1980s: Can the traditional American business system reverse the current industrial decline and provide for the economic and social needs of all Americans? This film, following California Newsreel's earlier release, *Controlling Interest,* looks at the pressing economic issue of 'industrial policy' in both a broad historical perspective and in terms of the impact on the lives of ordinary people.

"*The Business of America* . . . contrasts two typical Pittsburgh steelworkers' faith in private enterprise with the actual priorities and plans of a giant corporation, U.S. Steel. By comparing the views of steelworkers, community leaders, business executives and economists, the film tracks down the underlying reason companies like U.S. Steel no longer are providing Americans with the economic opportunities they've come to expect. The film scrutinizes the arguments of business that government taxes and regulations have robbed corporations of the profits needed to modernize. And it evaluates the actual impact of Reaganomics on the investment strategies of basic industries.

"Wall Street stock analysts and corporate managers, as well as Harvard Business School Professor Robert Hayes, reveal how pressure on mature industries to move into more immediately profitable ventures has discouraged long-term investment in manufacturing technology and research. U.S. Steel chairman David Roderick declares: 'The duty of management is to make money. Our primary objective is not to make steel.' In response, steelworkers are demanding a new, more active role in the economy. They are exploring self-reliant alternatives to corporate control over investment-worker ownership, targeted pension fund investment, and regional economic planning. An unemployed steelworker concludes: 'I think we've been too complacent. We've got to become totally involved in the running of companies. It's going to take a long time – but now's the time to start.' " IDERA

- *The Business of Hunger.* Produced by Robert Richter. 1985. 28 minutes. Color film and videocassette. Distributor: Maryknoll World. Rental: $25. Purchase: $325 (film only). Also from AFSC (Cambridge), EcuFilm, and Mennonite Central Committee (Akron and Manitoba).

"Presents a useful and clear analysis of the relationship between agribusiness and hunger in the Third World. Focusing on the Philippines, Senegal, Brazil, and the Dominican Republic, the film shows how multinational corporations acquire land and grow cash crops for export while the local population goes hungry. Small farmers lose their land, becoming migrant workers on plantations or slum dwellers in the cities. The film offers some hopeful alternatives, examining situations where farmers have been able to reclaim their land and return it to production of crops for local consumption. Also shows U.S. citizens trying to change the situation via education in consumer cooperatives and the lobbying of Congress members." CWS

■ *Child Labour in Thailand: The Dark Side of Thai Children.* Produced by Foundation for Children. n.d. 20 minutes. Color slideshow with cassette tape. Script and tape in Thai and English. Distributor: Thai-American Project.

This slideshow depicts the plight of millions of school-age Thai children who are forced into the child labor market where they are exploited and abused. *Child Labour in Thailand* shows the factories where the children work and the conditions under which the children are forced into prostitution.

■ *Commodities.* Produced by Sue Clayton and Jonathan Curling. 1986. 7 parts. Videocassettes. Distributor: First Run/Icarus Films. Fifteen percent discount for all episodes. Inquire for other discounts. Note: Each episode of *Commodities* can be used separately to focus on particular issues, countries, or time periods.

"The series of seven videos looks at the many ways that banks, corporations, governments, workers, and consumers are affected by such ordinary items as the coffee and tea we drink every day and the sugar we put in them. *Commodities* traces the history of production and trading around the world: it looks at the nature of exchange between the people who produce commodities in the Third World and those who control the processing, financing, and marketing of them.

"The series shows how producers try to get more profit from their crops; it considers the place of cartels, financiers, and multinationals; and it looks at the historical shifts in control from Amsterdam to London, then to the United States and the Pacific Basin.

"Filmed in Zimbabwe, Colombia, Brazil, Hongkong, China, Amsterdam, and the United Kingdom, with additional footage from Sri Lanka, the United States, and the Caribbean, *Commodities* ends with the present world debt crisis, mountains of commodity stockpiles, financial speculation, the decline of Western industry, and food riots in indebted countries." DIST

The episodes in the *Commodities* series are listed here according to the order in which the subjects covered occurred in history:

■ *Commodities: White Gold.* 1986. 26 minutes. Rental: $50. Purchase: $220.

"In the 1530s Portuguese settlers in Brazil began planting sugar cane using native labor, later importing slave labor from Africa. By 1630, the area around Recife in Northeast Brazil was producing more raw sugar than all the rest of the world. Much of it was sent to Amsterdam, the financial center and principal marketplace of the developing capitalist world; when the Dutch West India Company seized control of the sugar trade, many Dutchmen sailed for Brazil to cash in on the boom.

"White Gold is set during the 1630s and tells of the initial rise of sugar through the dramatized story of one Dutch merchant who takes over a Portuguese sugar plantation in Brazil. Obsessed with the development of a profitable sugar plantation, the Dutchman also becomes the master of African slaves.

"After 1654 the Dutch withdrew from Brazil and encouraged British planters in Barbados to grow sugar. Thus sugar, along with slavery, spread to the Caribbean." DIST

■ *Commodities: Black Market.* 1986. 26 minutes. Rental: $50. Purchase: $220.

"From 1650 onwards the British seized control of the seas and wrested the international trade advantage away from the Dutch. London became the next great financial and industrial center, exerting its influence through monopoly companies such as the British East India Company, which by 1830 had conquered most of India and dominated trade with China.

"During this time opium exports from India to China helped finance the company's administration of India and paid for the imports of porcelain, silk, and, most importantly, tea, to which the British were by now heavily addicted.

"When the Chinese Emperor tried to stop the illegal import of opium into his country, the British answered with the Opium War of 1840-42, one of the most one-sided wars in history.

"*Black Market* is a fictionalized story focusing on events leading up to the Opium War, as the company sends an agent to Canton to investigate the situation of British traders who are smuggling opium into China. It illuminates the relationships between the monopoly trading companies and the British Crown and their determination to impose their will on China and control its markets." DIST

■ *Commodities: Leaving Home for Sugar.* 1986. 52 minutes. Rental: $75. Purchase: $400.

"*Leaving Home for Sugar* continues the history of sugar [from *White Gold,* see above], focusing on later developments in the West Indies and in Zimbabwe.

"Following the withdrawal of the Dutch in 1654 from the Brazilian sugar cane industry, the Caribbean became the center of world sugar production. With an ever-increasing demand for sugar in Europe, and as many as 15 million slaves transported from Africa, the West Indian sugar industry was for 200 years one of the most profitable enterprises of all time.

"Following abolition, the plantations of the West Indies declined and the market favored European sugar beet production and newer ventures in the Pacific and Africa.

"Besides looking at the rise and fall of sugar in the West Indies, the film contrasts two sides of the history of sugar in Zimbabwe: the companies' story of turning semi-desert into model plantations, and the story told by local farmworkers who were dispossessed or brought in as forced labor.

"Today in Europe and North America the demand for cane sugar is falling as a result of protectionist policies, health concerns, and the use of new artificial sweeteners. The film ends with the multinational agricultural companies looking for new markets for cane sugar—ironically in the producing countries themselves." DIST

■ *Commodities: Tea Fortunes.* 1986. 52 minutes. Rental: $75. Purchase: $400.

"Following their victory in the 1840-42 Opium War [see *Black Market*, above], the British obtained the secrets of tea cultivation and set up their own massive tea plantations, first in Assam, India.

"*Tea Fortunes* documents the history of the tea industry from China to India, to Sri Lanka and East Africa, and back to China. It profiles the efforts of British grocers, in particular Sir Thomas Lipton, who first brought Tamil workers from Southern India to Sri Lanka as indentured laborers to work on his new plantations. Lipton and his imitators controlled every stage of the tea process, from planting to blending, from packaging to retailing.

"Today India controls its exports of tea; Sri Lanka has nationalized its tea estates; Zimbabwe's state-run plantations generate some cash in rural areas; but three British companies still dominate international trade in tea. In China, the original home of green teas, the film concludes by showing the situation of young women who work for some of the lowest factory wages in the world, producing black tea 'dust' as filler for Western blends to generate foreign exchange." DIST

■ *Commodities: Coffee Is the Gold of the Future.* 1986. 52 minutes. Rental: $75. Purchase: $400.

"Two-thirds of the world's coffee comes from Latin America, which has dominated world production since the nineteenth century. With an annual value of $15 billion, coffee is the second most valuable commodity after oil, providing ten countries, including Colombia, with over 50 percent of their foreign exchange.

"*Coffee Is the Gold of the Future* tells the history of coffee in Colombia, and a history of Colombia as seen through the story of coffee.

"Moving between small coffee growing communities, the world of big planters organized in the Colombia National Coffee Growers Federation, and the international arena of agribusiness and the control system of the International Coffee Agreement, *Coffee Is the Gold of the Future* explores the problems of land ownership, market control by middlemen, agrarian reform programs, and massive price fluctuations.

"Touching on aspects of Colombian political history such as the violent civil war 'La Violencia' as well as the development of its most important economic product, *Coffee Is the Gold of the Future* asks whether there is any future for small-scale peasant production in this era of agribusiness, modernized production methods, and international controls." DIST

■ *Commodities: Free Markets for Free Men.* 1986. 52 minutes. Rental: $75. Purchase: $400.

"In the eighteenth century the City of London was the financial center of the world economy, and merchants crowded the coffee houses to plan their global operations. Speculation was rampant, as it still is. Today, however, it has one positive function: to provide liquidity to the commodity futures markets such as the London Coffee Terminal Market, used by coffee merchants to hedge their financial risks and guard against adverse price fluctuations.

"But futures markets do not protect producer countries, like Brazil, against long-term falls in commodity prices. *Free Markets for Free Men* shows how constant deterioration of the terms of trade over 150 years has ensured that Brazil has gotten ever deeper into debt, despite its participation in international accords such as the International Coffee Agreement, designed to regulate trade and help to protect the position of the producer countries.

"*Free Markets for Free Men* looks at both the microeconomic workings of the futures markets, explaining how they work, and the macroeconomic realities of trade in a deregulated world economy which confront commodity producing countries like Brazil today." DIST

■ *Commodities: Grow or Die.* 1986. 52 minutes. Rental: $75. Purchase: $400.

"In the developed world there is a vast choice of consumer goods, but most markets are controlled by two or three companies that have bought out their competition and diversified into hundreds of fields to produce literally thousands of different items.

"*Grow or Die* shows how the consumer goods multinationals are today players on a complex world scale. These giant corporations, such as Unilever, the world's largest, need to ensure a constant supply of cheap raw materials, and will often switch suppliers, even though their actions disrupt producer economies. And with expanding consumer markets now to be found outside Europe and North America, the film shows how companies are shifting their focus from the Atlantic to the Pacific Basin.

"The United States and Europe may thus face a crisis in employment, and traditional producers of raw commodities also suffer as prices fall and their terms of trade worsen. The film concludes by showing how some countries, caught on the treadmill of rising debt and higher payments, lower prices and stunted growth—results of the world history which *Commodities* has surveyed—have attempted to overcome this situation by adopting policies of self-sufficiency, through commodity agreements, or through producer-country cartels like OPEC." DIST

- *Commodities: Time Is Money.* 1986. 56 minutes. Rental: $75. Purchase: $400.

"Minute by minute the prices of the most significant raw materials are determined on the international commodity exchanges of London, Tokyo, and New York. The vast majority of transactions comprise a paper trade of futures contracts. Eighty percent of the parties to these contracts are not traders, but speculators. *Time Is Money,* shot in New York, London, Ghana, and the Netherlands, looks at three commodities—silver, tin, and cocoa. It tells the story of the Hunt brothers, Texan billionaires who bought up all the silver they could and then actually started to have it delivered. They created a shortage on the world market, inflating the price 500 percent—before the market crashed and the Hunts went broke.

"*Time Is Money* contrasts the interest of traders and speculators—who candidly describe the tricks of their trade—with those of the producing countries. An example is Ghana, with two-thirds of its export income from one crop, cocoa, whose price fluctuations create havoc for the country's budget.

"Finally, *Time Is Money* looks at the story of one failed attempt to stabilize commodity prices: the International Tin Agreement. On October 24, 1985, the Tin Agreement collapsed and tin prices are once again subject to the whims of the free market.

"*Time Is Money* provides a lucid picture of the mechanisms of commodity trading." DIST

- *The Corporate Connection.* Produced by Committee for a New Korea Policy. 1984. 17 minutes. Color slideshow with cassette tape. Distributor: Committee for a New Korea Policy. Postage extra on rental.

"*Corporate Connection* examines: (1) corporations that leave American cities in search of low-paid labor; (2) grain companies that work to change Korean dietary habits; (3) computer firms that make South Korea's pass card system possible; (4) the relationship between U.S. support for a repressive government in South Korea and that government's help to U.S. multinationals; (5) U.S. policies that encouraged corporations to set up overseas.

"This slideshow is recommended for church and community groups, as well as college and high school classes." DIST

- *The Double Shift.* Produced by Trade Union Information Research and Education Group. 1986. 15 minutes. Videocassette. Also in slide/tape format. Distributor: TUIREG.

This audiovisual analyzes "the role of women as workers and housewives" in an international context. The slideshow portrays two women, one British, the other from Zambia, as they face discrimination daily in the work place and at home. *The Double Shift* also takes a critical look at the trade unions that have failed to accept the grievances of women workers as "legitimate" trade union issues.

- *Fruits of Toil.* 1985. 25 minutes. Color slideshow with cassette tape.

130 slides with script. English and Visayan. Distributor: Interim Media Productions. Purchase: $95, plus postage.

"A well-researched documentary on the Philippine Packing Corporation (Del Monte), Bukidnon, Mindanao, Philippines. The story of a pineapple plantation and the plight of its workers." DIST

■ *The Garment Workers in Bangladesh.* Produced by Commission for Justice and Peace, Bangladesh. n.d. 10 minutes. Color slideshow with cassette tape. Distributor: Committee for Asian Women.

"The slideshow depicts the exploitative working conditions of garment women workers in Dhaka." DIST

■ *Gentle Winds or Typhoon.* 1985. 35 minutes. Videocassette. U-matic, Beta, NTSC, and PAL formats. Distributor: Interim Media Productions. Purchase: $50.

"*Gentle Winds or Typhoon* is a thirty-five-minute documentary describing the Negros situation through the eyes of the sugar workers and their allies. Although filmed in 1985 it is as relevant today as it was then. The structures, both national and international, which are portrayed in the video, remain the same." DIST

■ *The Global Assembly Line.* Produced by Lorraine Gray. 1986. 58 minutes. Color film. Distributor: New Day Films. Also from EcuFilm, Church World Service, and AFSC (Cambridge).

"Filmed in the garment, textile, and electronics factories of Mexico, the Philippines, and the United States, as well as the corporate offices of several multinational corporations. Exposes the working conditions and the social, political, and economic environment that are shaping the lives of millions of women industrial workers. Background information is combined with interviews of workers, union organizers, and corporate officials. The explanations by corporate officials contrast sharply with the state violence, harassment, and intimidation used to enforce their policies and maintain their tight control." DIST

■ *Inside Haiti.* Produced by Resource Center. 1984. 20 minutes. Color slideshow with cassette tape. Distributor: Resource Center. Rental: $25 per week. Purchase: $50 (individuals or groups), $75 (institutions). Also from One Sky.

"*Inside Haiti* is a startling visual presentation of the contrasts in the poorest nation in the Western Hemisphere. This slideshow takes a penetrating look at the life and work of the six million Haitian people and gives the reasons why so many Haitians are fleeing their country.

"Through eighty slides and a taped narration, *Inside Haiti* gives viewers a close-up look at the repression and poverty that pervade the country, as well as a behind-the-scenes examination of U.S. corporations and the U.S. government in Haiti." DIST

■ *Is There Justice at Irryo?* Produced by Advance Media for Education and Development. 1986. 20 minutes. Color slideshow with script. Distributor: Committee for Asian Women.

"The slideshow documents the struggle of the women workers at Thai Irryo Garment to fight for their job security. The Thai Irryo workers held a strike in 1986 to demand permanent employment status." DIST

■ *Labor and Anti-Intervention.* Produced by Steve Zeltzer and Lee Heller. 1987. 60 minutes. Videocassette. Distributor: Labor Video Project. Rental: $20, plus $3 shipping and $20 deposit, for 15 days.

"An interview with San Francisco Bay Area trade union leaders on U.S. intervention in Central America." DIST

■ *The Long March.* Produced by Bonnie Donahue and Maure Aronson. 1986. 26 minutes. Videocassette. Distributor: AFSC (Cambridge). Rental: $20.

"An inside view of the struggle for trade union recognition by the working people of Mphopomeni, a small black township in Natal, South Africa. Interviews with residents provide overview of efforts over twenty-five years by the employees of the British multinational firm SARMCOL to obtain their rights. Focuses on the battle for union recognition starting in 1985. Gives the chronology of events month by month as workers first sitdown in the plant, then strike. When the company locks them out they respond with a boycott. To survive and continue their efforts the workers set up cooperatives. Each phase of the story is depicted through interviews and statistics followed by portions of a play produced by the workers that re-enacts each phase. Very low key and 'non-slick' in style. Presents a microcosm of apartheid." DIST

■ *The Midas Touch.* Produced by British Broadcasting Corp. 1987. 30 minutes. Videocassette. Distributor: One Sky. Rental: $10.

"A moving documentary which exposes British-owned Consolidated Goldfield's exploitative operation in the South African mining industry. It documents the union-busting activities of the corporation and its special private police force which is accused by the National Union of Mineworkers of brutalizing black mine workers." DIST

■ *Migrante.* Produced by Lito Tiongson. Produced also by Asia-Visions Media Foundation Production. 1987. Videocassette. U-matic and other video formats. Distributor: AsiaVisions.

"Brawn drain, a recent Philippine phenomenon, takes a pathetic turn when it comes to the case of the Filipino migrant workers in Hongkong. Employed in the host country as domestic helpers a great number of these Filipinas are degree holders or professionals in their country of origin. (The pathetic turns ironic when one considers the fact that the host country—Hongkong—was once a source of 'amahs,' Chinese domestic helpers, for elite Filipino families.) Like the past government under Ferdinand Marcos which greatly promoted and exploited labor migration to earn foreign exchange, the present Aquino administration is exerting very little effort, if any at all, to alleviate the plight of these thousands of Filipinas. It is only through the pressure exerted by nongovernmental institutions that any attention at all has been given to this issue.

"Often lost in the heap of discussions that concern such phenomena are the profound effects that migration brings to the minds of the migrant workers themselves. More a rule than an exception, the psychological and the physical effects are waived in favor of the more pressing but mundane matters of economics. This is not to place the latter on a lower shelf of concern. It is in fact the major point from which one should proceed, if one were to draw a detailed map of the problem of migration. The paths and alleys of cultural cross currents, however, take a longer time to plot. And it is from here that one gets lost as soon as she decides to take the course.

"*Migrante* documents the travails of the Filipina domestic helpers in Hongkong. It reflects on the phenomenon of labor migration and how it came about, placing the different factors in a social dimension. It comments on the labor migration policies of both the source country and the receiver country, and brings to the fore the interplay of geographical, political, economic, and cultural factors that have contributed in the rise of such phenomenon. It sheds light on issues rendered subjective by racial bias and attempts to place lingering questions in a proper perspective.

"*Migrante* interweaves the various stories of the migrant workers and creates a mosaic tale of woe." DIST

■ *People of No Interest.* Produced by Religious Television Associates/ Danchurchaid. Directed by Peter Flemington. July 1983. 28 minutes. Color film and videocassette. Distributor: Icarus Films. Rental: $55 (film only). Purchase: $515 (film), $290 (video).

"This film on Brazil looks at the struggle of poor farmers to keep their land. Filmed in the northern Brazilian state of Marnhão, it takes a critical look at a number of megaprojects and their impact on the lives of people there. A land takeover by a multinational corporation and by absentee landlords graphically illustrates the tension and upheaval that is part of many Third World people's daily lives. You'll 'experience' the process of underdevelopment in action, and the people's response." DIST

■ *Plunder in Paradise.* 1984. 25 minutes. Color slideshow with cassette tape. Distributor: Resource Center. Rental: $25 per week. Purchase: $65 (individuals or groups), $100 (institutions).

"Brings the diverse Caribbean nations sharply into focus. Through exceptional slides and thought-provoking narrative, examines the Caribbean's colonial past and its present-day conflicts. Takes a special look at how U.S. business and U.S. government and military have affected the region that stretches across the Caribbean Sea from the Bahamas and Cuba to Trinidad and Guyana." AFCA

■ *Que Viva! Labor in El Salvador.* Produced by Seattle Labor Committee on Central America. 1986. 20 minutes. Videocassette. Distributor: Seattle Labor Committee on Central America. Rental: $10. Also from One Sky.

"An eyewitness view of the current struggles of the Salvadoran labour movement is provided. Through interviews and live footage, the dynamism of El Salvador's labour movement is conveyed." ONE SKY

■ *The Real Thing.* Directed by Steven de Winter. Produced by Real to Reel Productions. 1984. 36 minutes. Color film. English and Spanish with English subtitles. Distributor: Icarus Films. Rental: $65 (film only). Purchase: $585 (film), $360 (video).

"*The Real Thing* documents a struggle between one of the largest corporations in the world and several hundred Guatemalan workers fighting for their jobs, their union, and all too often for their lives. In Guatemala, where less than 5 percent of the work force is unionized, workers who dare to organize are assassinated or disappear.

"This film chronicles the peaceful occupation of a Coca-Cola bottling plant in Guatemala City by its four hundred workers. It is a story of financial mismanagement at the local level and gross neglect of foreign responsibilities by Coca-Cola International. The use of corporate bankruptcy as a means of shutting down plants and busting unions, a practice familiar to unions in North America and Europe, is examined.

"The outcome of this conflict is being closely monitored not only by Guatemalan workers, but by trade unionists around the world. International support from labour and religious organizations grew from the time the occupation began. The International Union of Food and Allied Workers (IUF) in Geneva called a world-wide boycott of Coca-Cola International and its products. During April of 1984, workers in Europe, Mexico, Australia, and the Philippines halted production and distribution of Coca-Cola products. The Coca-Cola struggle...symbolizes the fate of the entire labour movement in Guatemala. From historical footage of the union's bloody battles in the late 1970s, to the present day occupations, *The Real Thing* is a story of courage and determination." DIST

■ *Rich Chips, Poor Chips.* Produced by Scottish Education and Action for Development. n.d. 30 minutes. Videocassette. Distributor: Scottish Education and Action for Development. Also from Committee for Asian Women.

"The video attempts to compare the situation of women workers in the electronics industry in two different worlds, one in Malaysia and the other in Scotland. It interviews workers on their working conditions, problems of health, organizing, etc." CAW

■ *Social Volcano.* 1985. 29 minutes. Color slideshow with cassette tape. 139 slides with script. English and Visayan. Distributor: Interim Media Productions. Purchase: $65, plus postage.

"Traces the colonial history of Negros, Central Philippines, from the destruction by British colonizers of an already flourishing weaving industry which pushes the farmers and workers of Negros to the verge of explosion." DIST

■ *Soil and Turmoil.* Produced by Brothers of All Men and the Philippine Peasant Institute. 1985. 30 minutes. Color film. Distributor: AsiaVisions.

"A documentary on the dislocation of peasants in Mindanao whose lands were expropriated in favor of a multinational palm oil plantation, the NDC-Guthrie." DIST

■ *Struggle in El Salvador: A Labor Viewpoint.* Produced by Labor Committee on El Salvador and Central America. 1984. 30 minutes. Color slideshow with cassette tape. Distributor: Labor Network on Central America. Rental: $25. Purchase: $80.

"Produced specifically for labor audiences, this slideshow describes conditions in El Salvador which have led to the current conflict. It gives the history of efforts to effect change through established political processes and the government's violent response, leading to the unification of union federations with other organizations into the FDR (Revolutionary Democratic Front). Elaborates on FDR's program for change. Shows how bad conditions for workers in El Salvador affect U.S. workers—i.e., runaway shops and foreign competition—and how the ultimate use of U.S. military force to protect multinational corporations harms workers in both countries. Describes the work of U.S. and international labor organizations to end U.S. intervention in El Salvador and urges others to join. This fast-paced slideshow requires time afterwards to address the many issues raised." DIST

■ *The Tea Garden.* Produced by Commission for Justice and Peace, Bangladesh. n.d. 20 minutes. Color slideshow with cassette tape. Distributor: Committee for Asian Women.

"The slideshow depicts the life and working conditions of the bonded workers on a tea estate in Bangladesh; many of the workers are women workers." DIST

■ *Thai Labour: The Next Step.* Produced by Meadow Group. 25 minutes. Color slideshow with cassette tape. Thai and English scripts and tapes. Distributor: Thai-American Project.

"This show relates the history of the labour movement in Thailand, from the time when labour unions were established, through their development in the period from 1973-76 until the October 6th coup." DIST

■ *A Typical Life Story of a Young Factory Woman in Korea.* Produced by Korean Women Workers Association. 1987. 60 minutes. Color slideshow with script. Distributor: Committee for Asian Women.

"The slideshow consists of two parts. Part I depicts the vulnerable position of women workers in Korea. It draws attention to the sexual exploitation women workers face. Part II analyzes the root causes of the oppression of women workers in Korea." DIST

■ *U.S. Labor and the CIA Connection.* Produced by Steve Zeltzer and Lee Heller. 1987. 60 minutes. Videocassette. Distributor: Labor Video Project. Rental: $20, plus $3 shipping and $20 deposit, for 15 days.

"The connection between the AFL-CIO's International Affairs Department and the CIA. An interview with South African labor expert and member of the CWA who went to El Salvador." DIST

■ *The Vanishing Earth.* Produced by Interim Media Productions.

1985. 30 minutes. Videocassette. Distributor: Mennonite Central Committee (Akron, Saskatchewan).

"*The Vanishing Earth* raises concerns for our environment through the example of the colorful T'Boli tribe in the hills of Southern Mindanao, Philippines. Describes how settlers, logging operations, the entry of multinational products and dam-building projects have eroded the T'Boli culture." DIST

- *Wahyuningsih: Woman Worker Seeking Justice.* 1987. 6 minutes. Videocassette. Distributor: Committee for Asian Women.

"Made by an Indonesian workers' group this short documentary introduces Wahyuningsih, a textile woman worker who describes her life and the struggle she has gone through with her fellow workers in asserting their rights to establish a union in their factory." DIST

- *With These Hands.* Produced by Chris Sheppard and Claude Sauvageot. 1986. 33 minutes. Color film and videocassette. Distributor: Filmakers Library. Rental: $55. Purchase: $525 (film), $350 (video). One-hour video version, *Man-Made Famine*, presented by Glenda Jackson: $75 (rental), $350 (purchase).

"In *With These Hands* three women—from Burkina Faso, Kenya, and Zimbabwe—tell in their own words of their struggle to feed their families, and how their efforts are often frustrated—by lack of support from men, by machines, and by big companies. The film reveals through several interspersed graphics that women grow 75 percent of Africa's food, a fact that should have far-reaching implications for development policies across the continent. In 1982, of all United Nations' spending on agriculture, less than 1 percent was going to projects for women." DIST

- *Workers and Unions in the New Nicaragua.* 1984. 15 minutes. Color slideshow with cassette tape. 106 slides. Distributor: Labor Network on Central America. Rental: $20, plus $3 postage. Purchase: $65, plus $3 postage.

"Through outstanding photography and a moving sound track, the viewer gains intimate exposure to the lives and thinking of Nicaragua's workers. The film discusses the changes that have taken place since the 1979 overthrow of Somoza—with emphasis on the growth of unions, democratic expression, and the impact of the U.S.-backed war.

"Based on the findings of the West Coast Trade Union Delegation to Nicaragua." DIST

- *The Workers Are Coming.* Produced by Afravision. 1986. 16 minutes. Videocassette. Distributor: One Sky. Rental: $10.

"Thirty-three unions met in late 1985 to launch the Congress of South African Trade Unions—COSATU. Through COSATU, South Africa's largest federation, two major trends of trade union resistance—one class-oriented and the other linked to national liberation—have come together. As one leading trade unionist describes it: 'The ANC is us. The UDF is us. And the community organizations are us; because we are fighting one battle.'" DIST

■ *The Workers' Struggle in South Africa.* Produced by Trade Union Information Research and Education Group and Catholic Institute for International Relations. 1983. 22 minutes. Color slideshow with cassette tape. Distributor: TUIREG. Purchase: £20.

This program focuses on the development of the black and nonracial trade unions in South Africa, set against the background of apartheid. Designed as an introduction to the workers' struggle in South Africa, the slideshow provides a brief history of the trade unions in South Africa, a who's who of the major unions, and interviews with labor movement representatives, who describe union achievements in gaining recognition, in improving pay and working conditions, and above all in raising the state and self-esteem of black workers.

■ *The Wrong End of the Rope.* Produced by Carla Rissieuw and Amara Amarasinghe. 1985. 120 minutes. Videocassette. Distributor: Committee for Asian Women.

"*The Wrong End of the Rope* is a documentary film about the lives of women workers in the rope-making industry in a village in Southern Sri Lanka. It portrays their daily activities, how they perceive their work, their future, and their relationship with their husbands. It also shows how these women workers organize themselves into cooperatives and learn to work among themselves." DIST

SUPPLEMENTARY LIST OF VISUAL RESOURCES

GENERAL

Bread, Justice & Multinational Corporations. Produced by Paulist Productions. 1980. 15 minutes. Color filmstrip with script. Distributor: Church World Service.

Christians in Corporations. Produced by Lutheran World Ministries. 1982. 32 minutes. Videocassette. Distributor: Villon Films. Rental: $20.

Controlling Interest: The World of the Multinational Corporation. Produced by California Newsreel. 1978. 45 minutes. Color film. Distributor: California Newsreel.

Fit as a Fiddle. Produced by Trade Union International Research and Education Group. 35 minutes. Videocassette. Distributor: TUIREG. Rental: £5. Purchase: £50.

For Export Only: Pesticides and Pills. Produced by Robert Richter. 1981. 56 minutes. Color film and videocassette. Two films (*Pesticides, Pills*), each 56 minutes. Distributor: Icarus Films. Rental: $100 (film only). Purchase: $885 (film), $560 (video). Prices are for each film.

Healthy Business: The Pharamaceutical Multinationals in the Third World. Produced by Belbo Film Productions. 1981. 55 minutes. Videocassette. Distributor: Asia Resource Center. Rental: $25.

Hungry for Profit. Produced by Robert Richter. 1985. 85 minutes. Color film and videocassette. Distributor: Richter Productions. Rental: $120 (film), $75 (video). Purchase: $1,195 (film), $695 (video).

Merchants of Grain. Produced by Canadian Broadcasting Corporation. 1983. 57 minutes. Videocassette. Distributor: Filmakers Library. Rental: $75. Purchase: $445.

Multinationals: For Better or Worse? Produced by Trade Union Information Research and Education Group. n.d. 20 minutes. Color slideshow with cassette tape. 80 slides. Also available in video. Distributor: TUIREG. Purchase: £20.

Nowhere to Run. Produced by Jon Alpert et al. 1982. 25 minutes. Videocassette. Distributor: Oxfam America and Downtown Community TV. Rental: $15 (Oxfam), $40 (DCTV). Purchase: $45 (Oxfam), $125 (DCTV).

Only Difference between Men and Boys Is the Price of Their Toys. Directed by Steven de Winter. Produced by Belbo/Novib. 1984. 50 minutes. Videocassette. Distributor: IDERA. Two parts, each 50 min.

Roots of Hunger, Roots of Change. Produced by Church World Service. 1985. 27 minutes. Color film. Distributor: Church World Service. Rental: Free.

Seeds of Revolution. Produced by Howard Enders. 1979. 28 minutes. Color film and videocassette. Distributor: Icarus Films. Rental: $55 (film only). Purchase: $500 (film), $315 (video). Produced for ABC News.

Sharing Global Resources. Produced by NARMIC. 1978. 35 minutes. Color slideshow with cassette tape. Distributor: NARMIC.

Weapons Bazaar. Produced by Arthur Kanegis. 1985. 28 minutes. Videocassette. Also in filmstrip and slideshow formats. Distributor: Center for Defense Information. Rental: $25. Purchase: $50.

AFRICA

Asante Market Women. Produced by Granada Television International. 1983. 52 minutes. Videocassette. Distributor: Filmakers Library. Rental: $75. Purchase: $445.

Labor and the South Africa COSATU Congress. Produced by Steve Zeltzer and Lee Heller. 1987. 60 minutes. Videocassette. Distributor: Labor Video Project. Rental: $20, plus $3 shipping and $20 deposit, for 15 days.

Moving On: The Hunger for Land in Zimbabwe. Produced by Peter Entell. 1982. 52 minutes. Color film. Distributor: Southern Africa Media Center, California Newsreel. Rental: $75. Also from IDERA Films.

Passing the Message. Produced by Cliff Bestall and Michael Gavshon. 1981. 47 minutes. Color film and videocassette. Distributor: First Run/Icarus Films. Rental: $50 (film). Purchase: $450 (film). Inquire for video rates.

Weaving Our Lives. Produced by David MacDougall and Judith MacDougall. Produced also by Participatory Research Group. 1982. 27 minutes. Color slideshow with cassette tape. Distributor: Mennonite Central Committee. Rental: Free.

ASIA AND PACIFIC

After the Difficulties. Produced by Souad Sharibane and Helen Kodawsky. 1982. 18 minutes. Color slideshow with cassette tape. Distributor: Development Education Centre. Rental: $510.

Agribusiness Goes Bananas. 1978. 18 minutes. Color slideshow with cassette tape. 140 slides with carousel and script. Distributor: Institute for Food and Development Policy. Purchase: $65.

The Buddha Is Smiling: Nuclear Proliferation in Asia. Produced by Michael Bedford. 1983. 23 minutes. Color slideshow with cassette tape. Distributor: AFSC (Cambridge).

Dole in Thailand: The Bitter Fruit. Produced by Catholic Council for Development in Thailand. 20 minutes. Color slideshow with cassette tape. Thai and English scripts and tapes. Distributor: Thai-American Project.

Dollars and Dictators. Produced by Resource Center. 1982. 28 minutes. Color slideshow with cassette tape. English or Spanish. Distributor: Resource Center. Rental: $25 per week. Purchase: $65 (individuals or groups), $100 (institutions). Also from IDERA Films, American Friends Service Committee, and Clergy and Laity Concerned.

From Rags to Riches. Produced by Thai-American Project. 1982. 30 minutes. Videocassette. Distributor: Thai-American Project. Rental: apply.

Giungad. Produced by Interim Media Productions. 1982. 20 minutes. Color slideshow with cassette tape. 112 slides with script. English or Visayan. Distributor: Interim Media Productions. Purchase: $90.

India's Working Women. Produced by Geraldine Forbes. 15 minutes. Color filmstrip with cassette tape. Includes teacher's guide. Distributor: Education Resources Center, State Education Department. Rental: $20.

A Matter of Taste. Produced by Belbo Film Productions. 1981. 60 minutes. Videocassette. 3/4-inch only. Distributor: IDERA. Rental: $60.

No Promise for Tomorrow: Communities Respond to the Bhopal Tragedy. 1985. Videocassette. Distributor: Highlander Center. Also from the Society for Participatory Research in Asia.

Nuclear Power and Martial Law. Produced by Mike Bedford. 1983. 54 minutes. Color slideshow with script. Distributor: Friends of the Filipino People.

People of the Field. Produced by Dorothy Friesen. 1982. 20 minutes. Color slideshow with script. Distributor: Mennonite Central Committee (Akron, Ontario).

Perhaps Women Are More Economical. Produced by Saskia Wieringa and Elsje Plantema. 1983. 27 minutes. Color film. Distributor: Institute of Social Studies, Women and Development Programme.

Philippine Labor. 1982. 20 minutes. Videocassette. Distributor: Philippine Resource Center. Rental: $25.

The Philippine Labor Movement. Produced by Steve Zeltzer and Lee Heller. 1985. 30 minutes. Videocassette. Distributor: Labor Video Project. Rental: $20, plus $3 shipping and $20 deposit, for 15 days.

Promised Land Lost. Produced by Mennonite Central Committee and Eastern Mennonite Board of Missions and Charities. 1980. 20 minutes. Color filmstrip with script. Distributor: Mennonite Central Committee (all except Akron, Saskatchewan, West Coast U.S.A.).

Stand Tall and Straight. Produced by Center for Women's Resources. 1983. 25 minutes. Color slideshow with cassette tape and script. Also in Tagalog version. Distributor: Committee for Asian Women.

Tenants in Our Own Land. Produced by Dorothy Friesen and Gene Stoltzfus. 1978. 16 minutes. Color slideshow with cassette tape and script. Distributor: Interim Media Productions. Purchase: $47.

The Time Is Now. 20 minutes. Color slideshow with cassette tape. Distributor: Philippine Resource Center. Rental: $25.

To Sing Our Own Song. Produced by Films Incorporated. 1984. 50 minutes. Color film.

Who Owns the Plains? 40 minutes. Color slideshow with cassette tape and script. Distributor: Interim Media Productions. Purchase: $75.

Who Owns the Sky? 1978. 23 minutes. Color slideshow with cassette tape. Distributor: American Friends Service Committee (Cambridge). Rental: $15.

LATIN AMERICA AND CARIBBEAN

Banana Company. Produced by Ramiro Lacayo. Produced also by Nicaraguan Film Institute (INCINE). 1982. 15 minutes. Color film and videocassette. Distributor: Icarus Films. Rental: $40. Purchase: $295 (film), $160 (video).

The Bitter Fruits (Dole Thai). n.d. Color slideshow with cassette tape. 80 slides. Distributor: Asia Resource Center. Rental: $20. Also from the Mennonite Central Committee (Central States only).

Chilean and Turkish Labor Struggles. Produced by Steve Zeltzer and

Lee Heller. 1985. 60 minutes. Videocassette. Distributor: Labor Video Project. Rental: $20, plus $3 shipping and $20 deposit, for 15 days.

CLUW Forum on Labor and Central America. Produced by Steve Zeltzer and Lee Heller. 1987. 90 minutes. Videocassette. Distributor: Labor Video Project. Rental: $20, plus $3 shipping and $20 deposit, for 15 days.

The Cost of Cotton. Directed by Luis Argueta. 1979. 30 minutes. Color film and videocassette. Spanish dialog with English subtitles. Distributor: Cinema Guild. Rental: $55. Purchase: $450 (film), $295 (video). Also from Church World Service (Indiana).

Guatemala Vencera. Produced by Central American Solidarity Committee. 1983. 16 minutes. Color slideshow with cassette tape. Distributor: IDERA.

Guatemala's Nightmare. Produced by Bev Burke and Rick Arnold. 1983. 12 minutes. Color slideshow with cassette tape. Distributor: IDERA. Rental: $20-30.

Obligations-Part I: International Banking, the Third World and Chile. Produced by Belbo Film Productions (Holland). 1980. 55 minutes. Videocassette. Distributor: IDERA.

Obligations-Part II: The International Monetary Fund, Britain and Jamaica. Produced by Belbo Film Productions (Holland). 1980. 55 minutes. Videocassette. Distributor: IDERA.

Sweet Sugar Rage. Directed by Honor Ford-Smith and Harclyde Walcott. 1985. 50 minutes. Color film and videocassette. In Jamaican dialect with English subtitles. Distributor: Sistren Theatre Collective. Also from Third World Newsreel and One Sky.

U.S. Construction Workers Brigade to Nicaragua. Produced by Steve Zeltzer and Lee Heller. 1985. 60 minutes. Videocassette. Distributor: Labor Video Project. Rental: $20, plus $3 shipping and $20 deposit, for 15 days.

Women and Work in Rosehall (St. Vincent, Caribbean). Produced by Beryl Carasco and Wendy Rodney. 1985. 12 minutes. Color slideshow with cassette tape. 40 slides. Distributor: Institute of Social Studies, Women and Development Programme. Rental: inquire.

Work and Workers. Produced by John Mraz. 1985. Color slideshow with script. 80 slides. Distributor: Third World Teaching Resource Center, University of California, Santa Cruz.

Working People of Central America. Produced by Bev Burke and Rick Arnold. 1983. 26 minutes. Color slideshow with cassette tape. Distributor: IDERA.

MIDDLE EAST

Chilean and Turkish Labor Struggles. Produced by Steve Zeltzer and Lee Heller. 1985. 60 minutes. Videocassette. Distributor: Labor

Video Project. Rental: $20, plus $3 shipping and $20 deposit, for 15 days.

Factories for the Third World: Tunisia. Produced by Gordian Troeller and Marie Claude Deffarge. 1981. 43 minutes. Color film and videocassette. Distributor: Icarus Films. Rental: $85. Purchase: $695 (film), $420 (video). Also from Church World Service and University of Illinois Film Center.

Israel, South Africa, and U.S. Labor. Produced by Steve Zeltzer and Lee Heller. 1988. 60 minutes. Videocassette. Distributor: Labor Video Project. Rental: $20, plus $3 shipping and $20 deposit, for 15 days.

The Price of Change. Produced by Elizabeth Fernea and Marilyn Gaunt. 1982. 26 minutes. Color film and videocassette. Distributor: Icarus Films. Rental: $55 (film only). Purchase: $470 (film), $260 (video). Also from IDERA.

INFORMATION SOURCES

For information on additional audiovisual resources on transnational corporations and labor in the Third World consult the section on directories and reference books in the books chapter, above. Catalogs from the distributors mentioned in this audiovisuals chapter would also be useful.

See the "JUST Resources" column in the fall 1986 issue of *New Pages* (4426 S. Belsay Rd., Grand Blanc, MI 48439) or the "Feature Insert" in the winter 1986 issue of *Third World Resources* for a lengthy description of sources of information regarding Third World-related audiovisuals and of free or inexpensive outlets for visual resources.

In 1979 *Film Library Quarterly* (vol. 12, no. 2/3) published a 112-page directory of "American Labor Films." The directory contains 250 entries, forty full-length movie reviews, and five essay reviews that analyze seventy-five films on working women; work; political education; occupational health and safety; and Hollywood and the working class. Also included are articles on the use of films in labor education and as organizing tools, and a list of labor-related films in Spanish. Major public and university libraries are likely to have back issues of this magazine.

See also the publications from **Third World Resources** described in the preface to this directory and the reference to the four-page guide to resources on transnational corporations and labor in the information sources section of chapter 1, above.

AUDIO RESOURCES

Information in the **annotated entries** is given in the following order: title; artist(s) or producer(s); date; length; format (record or tape); distributor; ordering number; price; and description of content.

AUDIOVISUALS 143

As with the visual resources the DIST code at the end of the annotation indicates that the description of the record or tape is the distributor's.

ANNOTATED ENTRIES

■ *American Involvement in South Korea.* 1980. Cassette tape. Distributor: Great Atlantic Radio Conspiracy. Order no.: 22-980-297. $5 (individuals), $8.50 (institutions).

"To protect corporate investments and maintain its military bases, the United States has supported a series of repressive dictatorships in South Korea. David Easter, an independent researcher for the American Friends Service Committee, and Wayne Brittenden, Southeast Asia correspondent for New Zealand Broadcasting, explore the reasons behind the continuing U.S. presence in South Korea today." DIST

■ *The Annals of Corporate Crime: Dow Chemical Co.* 1985. Cassette tape. Distributor: Great Atlantic Radio Conspiracy. Order no.: 32-185-428. $5 (individuals), $8.50 (institutions).

"Dow Chemical has a long history of producing herbicides and pesticides that cause cancer, birth defects, and other health hazards. While Dow may be best known to consumers for its Saran Wrap, Ziploc Bags, and bathroom cleaner, its criminal products have included napalm, TRIS, DBCP, and Agent Orange." DIST

■ *The Annals of Corporate Crime: Litton.* 1984. Cassette tape. Distributor: Great Atlantic Radio Conspiracy. Order no.: 30-684-412. $5 (individuals), $8.50 (institutions).

"Litton Industries, Inc., was one of the first giant conglomerates. It has ranked high as a military contractor and high among those corporations involved in military contracting frauds. Litton has a history of profiting from programs designed for the poor and a history of more labor grievances than any other business." DIST

■ *The Annals of Corporate Crime: Union Carbide.* 1986. Cassette tape. Distributor: Great Atlantic Radio Conspiracy. Order no.: 34-486-461. $5 (individuals), $8.50 (institutions).

"Glad Wrap, Eveready, Prestone, Simonize—familiar names to most consumers. So are Bhopal, India, and Institute, West Virginia. The same company, Union Carbide, has made all these names familiar. It produces dangerous chemicals, and in a dangerous manner. This is a history of Union Carbide's disregard for its workers, not to mention the rest of us." DIST

■ *Beware of the Generals.* 1986. Cassette tape. Distributor: Great Atlantic Radio Conspiracy. Order no.: 34-886-469. $5 (individuals), $8.50 (institutions).

"Like all generals, General Motors, General Dynamics, and General Electric control the livelihoods of thousands of people. They support the U.S. military build-up and the resulting war-time economy. They have bolstered apartheid in South Africa and capitalist exploitation around the world. Learn about the power and influence of these generals and why they and all generals must be stopped." DIST

■ *Bitter Fruit: Guatemala, 1954.* Produced by David Barsamian. 1983. Cassette tape. Distributor: Pacifica Radio Archive. Order no.: SZ0212. $13.

"In 1954 the United Fruit Co. and the CIA were involved in the overthrow of Guatemala's democratically elected government. In this interview Stephen Schlesinger, co-author of *Bitter Fruit,* talks about the status of United Fruit in Guatemala, how the coup was set up, the long-term influences of this coup, and the changes that happened within Guatemala as a result of the coup." DIST

■ *Divestment: The Offensive against Apartheid and Nuclear Weapons.* 1985. Cassette tape. Distributor: Great Atlantic Radio Conspiracy. Order no.: 32-385-432. $5 (individuals), $8.50 (institutions).

"Two direct action tactics, divestment of corporate stocks and consumer boycotts, are used to fight apartheid in South Africa and nuclear weapons production in the United States. We discuss the political meaning of these actions with Max Obuszewski of Nuclear Free America." DIST

■ *Don't Desert the Rain Forests.* 1987. Cassette tape. Distributor: Great Atlantic Radio Conspiracy. Order no.: 35687-488. $5 (individuals), $8.50 (institutions).

"Every half hour, two square miles of rain forest are wiped out. Social ecologist Steven Bunker describes who is responsible for doing this, what the ecological implications are, and how to fight this destruction of our environment." DIST

■ *Global Management.* Produced by Fernando Velazquez and Andrew Lanset. 1983. Cassette tape. Distributor: Pacifica Radio Archive. Order no.: KZ1321. $13.

"This documentary focuses on how trilateralism, the International Monetary Fund, the World Bank, and private banks influence the economies and policies of various Third World countries and the global economy. Heard are analysts, economists, and bankers." DIST

■ *Let's Have Another Cup of Coffee.* 1982. Cassette tape. Distributor: Great Atlantic Radio Conspiracy. Order no.: 27982-365. $5 (individuals), $8.50 (institutions).

"Coffee's origins are lost in the mists of time, but the economics of the industry are not. We look at coffee's history; at the exploitation of coffee pickers and the power of coffee cartels; at the confusing evidence on caffeine and the clear dangers of the chemical decaffeination process." DIST

■ *The Pesticide Plague.* 1987. Cassette tape. Distributor: Great Atlantic Radio Conspiracy. Order no.: 35-287-482. $5 (individuals), $8.50 (institutions).

"Every year, one pound of pesticide is produced for every person on earth and every minute one person is poisoned by pesticides. Sandra Marquardt of the National Coalition Against the Misuse of Pesticides describes the dangers of these compounds and explores alternatives to their use." DIST

■ *South African Trade Union Worker Choirs.* Long-playing record or cassette tape. Distributor: Rounder Records. Order no.: 5020. $8.98.

"An anthology of exciting worker choir vocal music—challenging and energetic. Songs that reflect the struggle in South Africa. Featuring textile workers, miners, etc." DIST

■ *The Sugar Connection.* Cassette tape. Distributor: Great Atlantic Radio Conspiracy. Order no.: 22-380-288. $5 (individuals), $8.50 (institutions).

"If you eat a typical American diet, every week you consume close to two pounds of sugar. How did we acquire our sweet tooth? Who grows and processes sugar cane and sugar beets? What about the people who profit and the people who go hungry so we can have our weekly ration?" DIST

■ *Tobacco Madness.* 1981. Cassette tape. Distributor: Great Atlantic Radio Conspiracy. Order no.: 25-881-327. $5 (individuals), $8.50 (institutions).

"Over 600 billion cigarettes are smoked each year in the United States. We look at the history and politics of tobacco; the industry and its marketing techniques; the health effects of smoking; and the tactics of the anti-smoking movement. Included are skits, anti-smoking poetry, interviews, and music." DIST

■ *U.S. Involvement in the Philippines.* 1985. Cassette tape. Distributor: Great Atlantic Radio Conspiracy. Order no.: 32285-430. $5 (individuals), $8.50 (institutions).

"Since 1898, the United States has been involved militarily and economically in the fate of the Philippine people. Delia Aguilar, whose sister is a political prisoner, and Eric Guyot, of the Philippine Support

Committee, help explain the role of the United States and the character of repression and resistance in the Philippines." DIST

■ *Women on the Global Assembly Line.* Produced by Maggie Geddes and Mary Sinclair at KPFA, Berkeley, Calif. Cassette tape. 1981. 28 minutes. Distributor: Pacifica Radio Archive. Order no.: AZ0585. $11.

"This documentary looks at the reasons multinational corporations hire mainly women assembly workers in the Third World and in the United States, the conditions under which these women work, why unionization is difficult, and how they respond to the stress." DIST

Indexes

ORGANIZATIONS

This index contains the names of all organizations associated with the production and/or distribution of resources included in this directory. See the Subjects Index below for references to organizations not directly connected to those resources. Addresses are provided whenever they were judged to be necessary for the acquisition of resources in this directory. Page numbers in bold face signify that the organization's address will be found in the text.

ABC News, 138
Addison-Wesley, 55
Advance Media for Education and Development, 131
Afravision, 136
Africa World Press, 63
Allen & Unwin, 65
Alliance for Philippine Concerns, North America National Office, P.O. Box 170219, San Francisco, CA 94117, 94
Alternative News and Features, **14**
Altinform, **16**
American Committee on Africa, 198 Broadway, Rm. 401, New York, NY 10038, 89
American Friends Service Committee, National Office, **85**, 87, 139
American Friends Service Committee, 2161 Massachusetts Ave., Cambridge, MA 02140, 125, 131, 132, 139, 140
American Friends Service Committee, 2160 Lake St., San Francisco, CA 94121, 118
American Labor Education Center, **18**, 83, 123
Anti-Slavery Society, 180 Brixton Rd., London SW9 6AT, England, 116
Arbetarorslsens Internationella Centrum (AIC), **16**
Asia Monitor Resource Center (AMRC), **2**, 53, 54, 68, 103
Asia Resource Center, P.O. Box 15275, Washington, DC 20003, 68, 100, 138, 140
Asian Bureau Australia, **14**
Asian Regional Exchange for New Alternatives, 29
Asian Women Workers' Center, **15**
AsiaVisions Media Foundation, 132, 134
Australia-Asia Worker Links, **2**
Australian Consumers' Association, **15**
Basic Books, 60
BASTA!, **16**
Belbo Film Productions, 138, 139, 141
Bergin & Garvey Publishers, 32, 40
Bern Declaration, **16**
Between the Lines, 27, 43, 62
Bhopal Action Research Center, 63
Birmingham Trade Union Group for World Development, **16**
Black Rose Books, 31
British Broadcasting Corp., 132
Brookings Institution, 33
Brothers of All Men, 134

148 INDEXES

CAITS (Centre for Alternative Industrial and Technological Systems), **16**
California Newsreel, 125, 137
California/Nevada Interfaith Committee on Corporate Responsibility, **78,** 117
Cambridge University Press, 60, 62, 63, 64, 65
Campaign against Arms Trade, **16**
Campaign against Foreign Control in New Zealand, **15**
Canadian Broadcasting Corporation, 138
CANICCOR (An Interfaith Council on Corporate Accountability), **78,** 117
CAPPS (Centro de Assessoria Pesquisas e Publicacoes Sindicais), **15**
Catholic Council for Development in Thailand, 139
Catholic Institute for International Relations, 22 Coleman Fields, London N1 7AF, England, 52, 53, 104, 137
CCA, URM. See Christian Conference of Asia, Urban-Rural Mission.
CEDAL, **18**
CEDETIM, **16**
Center for Alternative Mining Development Policy, **18**
Center for Defense Information, 303 Capitol Gallery West, 600 Maryland Ave., SW, Washington, DC 20024, 138
Center for Ethics and Corporate Policy, The, **18**
Center for Labor Studies, **15**
Center for Studies in Social Sciences, **15**
Center for the Progress of Peoples, **15,** 63, 85
Center for Women's Resources, 43 A. Roces Ave., Mar Santos Bldg., Rm. 314, Baguio City 2600, Philippines, 140
Center of Concern, 3700 13th St., NE, Washington, DC 20017, 54
Center on Transnational Culture, **18**
Central American Solidarity Committee, 141
Centre d'Information Organisation Internationale Catholique, **16**
Centre for Developing-Area Studies, McGill University, **76,** 115, 118
Centre for Research on Multinational Corporations (SOMO), **3**
Centre for Society and Religion, **15**
Centre on Transnational Economy, **3,** 66
Centre Tricontinental (CETRI), **16**
CEREM (Centre d'Etudes et de Recherches sur l'Enterprise Multinationale), **16**
CETIM, **16**
Christian Conference of Asia, Urban-Rural Mission, **15,** 27, 101, 117
Church World Service, P.O. Box 968, 28606 Phillips St., Elkhart, IN 46515, 123, 131, 137, 138, 141, 142
CIDOB (Centre d'Informacio i Documentacio Internacional), **16**
Cinema Guild, 141
Citizen's Alliance for Consumer Protection, **15**
Clergy and Laity Concerned, 198 Broadway, Rm. 302, New York, NY 10038, 139
Coalition Against Dangerous Exports, c/o International Coalition for Development Action (see below), 92
Columbia University Press, 34, 60, 62, 63, 64, 65
Commission for Justice and Peace, Bangladesh, 131, 135
Committee for a New Korea Policy, 130
Committee for Asian Women, **69,** 92, 117, 125, 131, 134, 135, 136, 137, 140
Cornell University Press, 30, 35
Council on Economic Priorities, **4,** 55, 69
Council on International and Public Affairs, **61**
Counter Information Services, **4**
Coventry Workshop, **16**
Croom Helm, 60, 61, 62, 65
DataCenter, **4,** 70, 80
DESCO, **18**
Development Education Centre, 394 Euclid Ave., Toronto, Ontario M6G 2S9, Canada, 139
Dias, **16**
DIEESE (Inter-Union Department for Statistics and Socio-Economic Research), **18**
Dimension Publishing, **83**
Downtown Community TV, 138
Earth Resources Research, 258 Pentonville Rd., London N1 9JY, England, 30
East-West Centre, Project on Women and Transnational Corporations, **18**
Eastern Mennonite Board of Missions and Charities, 140

INDEXES 149

EcuFilm, 125, 131
Ecumenical Development Week, **16**
Education Resources Center, 139
EILER (Ecumenical Institute for Labor Education and Research), **15,** 117
ELTSA (End Loans to Southern Africa), **16**
ESCAP/UNCTC Joint Unit on Transnational Corporations, **15**
Essential Information, 95, 96, 98, 104, 110, 115, 119. See *Multinational Monitor.*
European Centre for Study and Information on Multinational Corporations, 52
European Environmental Bureau, **16**
European Trade Union Institute (ETUI), **16**
Faber and Faber, 41
Fairleigh Dickinson University Press, 63
Filmakers Library, 136, 138
Films Incorporated, 140
First Run/Icarus Films, 126, 139
Foundation for Children, 126
Frère des Hommes International/Mensenbroeders, 100
Friends of the Filipino People, P.O. Box 2125, Durham, NC 27702, 94, 140
GATT-Fly, **5**
George Allen & Unwin, 62
Gewekschaftliche Einheit Alternative, **17**
Gower Publishing Co., 29, 62
Granada Television International, 138
Great Atlantic Radio Conspiracy, 143, 144, 145
Greenwood Press, 32, 46, 51
GRESEA-Oxfam Group, **17**
Grove Press, 22
Guatemala News & Information Bureau, P.O. Box 28594, Oakland, CA 94604, 124
Harper & Row, 56, 60
Health Action International (HAI), **17**
Highlander Center, Route 3, Box 370, New Market, TN 37820, 117, 140
Holmes & Meier, 61
Humanities Press, 61, 62
IBASE (Instituto Brasileiro de Análises Sociais e Econômicas), **5**
IBON Documentation Center, **15**
Icarus Films, 123, 133, 134, 138, 140, 142
ICAS (International Workers Solidarity Center), **17**
IDERA Films, 123, 125, 138, 139, 141, 142
IDOC International, **6,** 114, 119
IEPALA, **17**
ILET (Instituto Latinoamericano de Estudios Transnacionales), 51
ILO Publications, **66,** 73
ILR Press, 66
Immaculate Heart College Center, 10951 W. Pico Blvd., Suite 2021, Los Angeles, CA 90064, 122
Indian Institute of Public Administration, **15**
Indian Law Institute, 29
Indiana University Press, 45
INDOC, **17**
Indochina Project, 236 Massachusetts Ave., NE, Suite 510, Washington, DC 20002, 118
Industrial Restructuring Education Network Europe, **17,** 84
INFACT, **18**
Informationsdienst Dritte Welt, **17**
Institute for Food and Development Policy, 145 Ninth St., San Francisco, CA 94103, 139
Institute for International Economics, 61
Institute for Labor Education and Research, **18**
Institute for Policy Studies, **18,** 26, 60
Institute of Social Studies, **66**
Institute of Social Studies, Publications Office, 117
Institute of Social Studies, Women and Development Programme, 140, 141
Instituto Latinoamericano de Estudios Transnacionales. See ILET.
Interfaith Action for Economic Justice, **18**
Interfaith Center on Corporate Responsibility, **6,** 70, 88, 115, 116, 118, 119
Interim Media Productions, 122, 131, 134, 135, 139, 140

International Baby Food Action Network (IBFAN), 17
International Coalition for Development Action (ICDA), 22, Rue des Bollandistes, 1040 Brussels, Belgium, 90, 97, 100, 119
International Coalition of Consumers Unions (IOCU), 7
International Commission for the Co-ordination of Solidarity among Sugar Workers (ICCSASW), **8**, 81, 111
International Confederation of Free Trade Unions (ICFTU), **20**, 55
International Documentation and Communication Center. See IDOC.
International Foundation for Development Alternatives (IFDA), **17**
International Genetic Resources Programme, 123
International Labor Rights, Education and Research Fund, viii
International Labour Education Research and Information Foundation, 62
International Labour Office, **66**, 115, 116, 117, 118, 119
International Organization of Consumers Unions, Regional Office for Asia and the Pacific, 39
International Organization of Consumers Unions, **19**
International Union of Food and Allied Workers Associations (IUF), 93, 106, 116
International Union of Food Workers, 124
Interreligious Economic Crisis Organizing Network, **73**
Investor Responsibility Research Center, **8**, 55, 57
IPAL (Instituto para America Latina), **18**
Isis International, **92**
IWGIA (International Work Group for Indigenous Affairs), **17**
JAI Press, 65
John Wiley & Sons, 61
Johns Hopkins University Press, 60, 64
Kammer fur Arbeiter und Angestellte fur Wien, **17**
KMU International Department, 510 M. Earnshaw St., Jopson Bldg., 3rd floor, Sampaloc, Manila, Philippines, 11, 80, 118
KOGAI, **15**
Korean Women Workers Association, 135
KPFA (Berkeley, Calif.), 146
Labor Campaign for Unions in El Salvador, **18**
Labor Committee on El Salvador and Central America, P.O. Box 28014, Oakland, CA 94604, 135
Labor Committee on the Middle East, **18**, 76
Labor Education and Research Project, **74**
Labor Network on Central America, **9**, 112, 113, 119, 136
Labor Research Association, **9**, 71
Labor Video Project, P.O. Box 5584, San Francisco, CA 94101, 123, 132, 135, 139, 140, 141, 142
Latin America Bureau, 1 Amwell St., London EC1R 1UL, England, 64, 65, 93, 109
Latin American Working Group, **19**
Lexington Books, 61
Longman Group, 55
Lutheran World Ministries, 137
Lynne Rienner Publishers, 25, 63
Macmillan, 55, 56, 62, 63, 64
Manchester Employment Research Group, 17
Manushi, C1/202 Lajpat Nagar, New Delhi 110024, India, 117
Maryknoll World, 125
Mayday Publications, **73**
Meadow Group, 135
Memorial University, Department of History, **84**
Mennonite Central Committee, 21 South 12 St., Akron, PA 17501, 125, 136, 139, 140
Methuen, 38
Middle East Research and Information Project (MERIP), 475 Riverside Dr., Rm. 518, New York, NY 10115, 96, 108
Midwest Center for Labor Research, **19**, 84, 108
Minority Rights Group, 29 Craven St., London WC2, England, 119
MIT Press, 62, 65
Monthly Review Press, 28, 36, 61, 62, 65, 93
NACLA, **19**, 118
NALGO Education, 1 Mabledon Pl., London WC1H 9AJ, England, 110

INDEXES 151

NARMIC (National Action/Research on the Military Industrial Complex), **9,** 138
National Center for Policy Alternatives, 114
National Center for Trade Union Action and Democracy, **75**
National Institute for Occupational Safety and Health, 61
National Labor Boycott Shell Committee, c/o United Mine Workers of America, 900 15 St., NW, Washington, DC 20005, 88
National Labor Law Center, c/o National Lawyers Guild, **84**
National Taiwan University, Population Studies Center, Women's Research Program, Roosevelt Rd., Section 4, No. 1, Taipei, Taiwan, 111
Nationwide Women's Program, Project on Women and Global Corporations, **19,** 85, 89
New Day Films, 131
New Horizons Press, 29, 61
New York State School of Industrial and Labor Relations, **83**
Nicaraguan Film Institute (INCINE), 140
North River Press, 61
Northwest Transnationals Project (NWTP), **17**
Novib, 138
OEF International, 2101 L St., NW, Suite 916, Washington, DC 20037, 115
One Sky, 131, 132, 136, 141
OSACI, **17**
Oxbridge Communications, 84
Oxfam, **10,** 60, 61, 64, 65, 119
Oxfam America, 115 Broadway, Boston, MA 02116, 102, 138
Pacific Conference of Churches, 113
Pacific Studies Center, **19,** 72
Pacific-Asia Resource Center (PARC), **16,** 67, 99, 100
Pacifica Radio Archive, 144, 146
Pan African Women Trade Unionists, **14**
Pantheon Books, 48, 61
Participatory Research Group, 115, 139
Partizans, **17**
Paulist Productions, 137
Penguin, 65
Peninsula Watchdog, **16**
Pergamon Press, 61, 62
Pesticide Action Network International, **10**
Philippine Resource Center, P.O. Box 40090, Berkeley, CA 94704, 140
Philippine Workers Support Committee, **11,** 79
Pilgrim Press, 33
Plant Closures Project, **19,** 82
Pluto Press, 61
Praeger Publishers, 24, 32, 59, 60, 66
Princeton University Press, 60, 62, 64, 65
Progressive Alliance, 114
Project Abraço: North Americans in Solidarity with the People of Brazil, **82**
Random House, 32
Raw Materials Group, **17**
Real to Reel Productions, 134
Regional Economic Research and Documentation Center, **74**
Religious Television Association/Danchurchaid, 133
Research Group MOL, **17**
Research Policy Institute, **17**
Resource Center, The, **19,** 94, 99, 111, 124, 131, 133, 139
Richter Productions, 138
Riverdale Company, 63
Rodo Joho, **16**
Rounder Records, 145
Routledge & Kegan Paul, 37, 44
Sage Publications, 50, 60
Sahabat Alam Malaysia (Friends of the Earth), 37 Lorong Birch, 10250 Penang, Malaysia, 63, 107, 118
St. Martin's Press, 22, 39, 53, 60, 62, 65
Save Aramoana Campaign, **16**
Saxon House, 65

Scalabrini Migration Center, 68
Scandinavian Institute of African Studies, Dragarbrunnsgatan 24, Box 1703, S-751 47 Uppsala, Sweden, 52, 116
Scottish Education and Action for Development, 134
Seattle Labor Committee on Central America, P.O. Box 28090, Seattle, WA 98118-1090, 124, 133
Seeds Action Network, **17**
Sheffield Film Co-op, 124
Sistren Theatre Collective, 20 Kensington Crescent, Kingston 5, Jamaica, 141
SOBE, **17**
Social Audit Limited, **17**
Social Investment Forum, **19,** 85
Society for Participatory Research in Asia, 117, 140
SOLAGRAL, **17**
South End Press, 40, 90, 95
Southern Africa Media Center, California Newsreel, 139
Stanford University Press, 23
State University of New York Press, 43
Synapses, 1821 W. Cullerton, Chicago, IL 60608, 118
Synapses Audiovisuals, 122
Syracuse University Press, 66
Taskforce on the Churches and Corporate Responsibility, **11**
Temple University Press, 26
Thai-American Project, 6565 Green Valley Circle, No. 306, Culver City, CA 90230, 126, 135, 139
Third World Action Group, **17**
Third World First, **84**
Third World Foundation for Social and Economic Studies, New Zealand House, 80 Haymarket, London SW1Y 4TS, England, 118
Third World Newsreel, 141
Third World Studies Center, **12,** 118
Third World Teaching Resource Center, University of California, Santa Cruz, 141
Toronto Committee for the Liberation of Southern Africa, 427 Bloor St. W, Toronto, Ontario M5S 1X7, Canada, 94
Trade Union International Research and Education Group (TUIREG), **12,** 130, 137, 138
Transaction Periodicals Consortium, **84**
Transaction Publishers, 65
Transnational Co-operative Ltd. (TNC Workers Research), **16**
Transnational Corporations Research Project, **13,** 35, 62, 63, 64
Transnational Institute, c/o Institute for Policy Studies, **18**
Transnationals Information Exchange, **13,** 81, 89, 103, 115
United Nations, 57, 58, 59, 62, 66
United Nations Centre on Transnational Corporations, **14,** 52, 58, 62, 66, 71
United Nations Publications, **71**
United Nations University/Third World Forum, 115
University of British Columbia Press, 63
University of California Press, 46, 61
University of Illinois Film Center, 142
University of Illinois Press, **84**
University of Michigan, Center for South and Southeast Asian Studies, 63
University of New Mexico Press, 65
University of North Carolina Press, 49
University of Notre Dame Press, 48, 65
University of Ottawa Press, 47
University of Pittsburgh Press, 37, 47, 64
University of Sydney, Transnational Corporations Research Project, **13,** 35, 62, 63, 64
University of Texas Press, 61
University of Wisconsin Press, 64
University Press of America, 63
Verso/New Left Books, 60
Viking Press, 62
Villon Films, 137
Voedings Bond FNV, **17**
W.O.W. Campaigns Ltd., 98. See War on Want

INDEXES 153

W.W. Norton, 105
Walter de Gruyter, 61
War on Want, **17**
War on Want International, Women's Group, **17**
WCC Programme on Transnational Corporations, Commission on the Churches' Participation in Development, **84**
Wereldsolidariteit Group, V.Z.W., **18**
West Coast Trade Union Delegation to Nicaragua, 113
Westview Press, 61
Women and Work Hazards Group, **18**
Women in International Development, Michigan State University, 202 Center for International Programs, East Lansing, MI 48824-1035, 91, 97, 101, 102, 105, 106, 109, 112, 116, 117, 118, 119
Women Working Worldwide, **18**
Women's International Resource Exchange, 475 Riverside Dr., New York, NY 10115, 115
Workers World Publishers, **84**
Workers' Educational Association, **84**
Working Papers for a New Society, 114
World Confederation of Labor (WCL), **20**, 55
World Federation of Trade Unions (WFTU), **20**, 55
World Rainforest Movement, 108
Worldwatch Institute, 105
Zed Books, 24, 41, 42, 44, 47, 60, 61, 62, 63, 64, 65, 115

INDIVIDUALS

This index contains the names of all individuals associated with the production of resources included in this directory. See the Subjects Index below for references to individuals not directly connected to those resources.

Agarwal, Anil, 117
Aguilar, Delia, 145
Alpert, Jon, 138
Alschuler, Lawrence R., 22
Amarasinghe, Amara, 137
Angel Reyes, Miguel, 64
Argueta, Luis, 141
Arnold, Rick, 141
Aronson, Maure, 132
Baker, Lawrence, 114
Barry, Tom, 22
Barsamian, David, 144
Bass, Emily, 118
Bayat, Assef, 65
Baylies, Carolyn, 87
Bedford, Michael, 139
Bedford, Mike, 140
Bell, John Donnelly, 88
Bello, J. A., 115, 116
Bennett, Douglas, 64
Bennholdt-Thomsen, Veronika, 41
Berberogher, Berch, 59
Bergquist, C., 60
Bergquist, Charles, 23
Bestall, Cliff, 139
Bhagavan, M. R., 116
Biersteker, Thomas J., 62
Björkman, James Warner, 63
Blanchard, Peter, 64
Bluestone, Barry, 60, 114
Bollinger, William, 112
Bolton, Dianne, 62

Bornschier, Volker, 60
Bounds, Elizabeth, 88
Boyd, Rosalind E., 115
Boyer, Sandy, 89
Branford, Sue, 24
Brazier, Phyllis, 28
Brittenden, Wayne, 143
Bull, David, 60
Bunker, Steven, 144
Bunster, Ximena, 24
Burawoy, Michael, 60
Burke, Bev, 141
Butler, Nick, 60
Cantor, Daniel, 90
Caporaso, James A., 25
Carasco, Beryl, 141
Castro, Mary Garcia, 26
Cavanagh, John, 60, 63
Chaney, Elsa M., 24, 26, 91
Chaney, Elsa M., 26
Chapkis, Wendy, 26
Chase-Dunn, Christopher, 60
Cheru, Fantu, 115
Chetley, Andrew, 92
Cho, Uhn, 117
Clairmonte, Frederick, 60, 63
Clancey, Jack, 63
Clarke, Ian M., 60
Clarke, Robert, 27
Clayton, Sue, 126
Cohen, Robin, 28, 87
Collins, Jane L., 64

Conrad, Thomas, 116
Coote, Berlinda, 64
Cox, Robert W., 60
Crabtree, John, 92
Cunnington, John, 97
Curling, Jonathan, 126
Danaher, Kevin, 93
Dar, U., 117
de Shazo, Peter, 64
de Winter, Steven, 134, 138
Deere, Carmen Diana, 118
Deffarge, Marie Claude, 142
Dembo, David, 29
Deyo, Frederic C., 30
Dinham, Barbara, 30
Dixon-Mueller, Ruth, 115
Donahue, Bonnie, 132
Duffy, Gavan, 92
Dunning, John H., 53
Easter, David, 143
Eden, L., 62
Edquist, Charles, 64
Ehrenreich, Barbara, 95
Elson, Diane, 115
Emmanuel, Jorge, 94
Enders, Howard, 138
Enderwick, P., 60
Enloe, Cynthia, 26
Entell, Peter, 139
Evans, Peter, 64
Eyde, Marianne, 123
Falcon, Ricardo, 65
Feldman, Shelley, 102
Fernandez-Kelly, Maria P., 43
Fernea, Elizabeth, 142
Finch, H., 61
Finch, Ron, 31
First, Ruth, 62
Flamm, Kenneth, 33
Flemington, Peter, 133
Foner, Philip S., 32
Fong, Pang Eng, 117
Forbes, Geraldine, 139
Ford-Smith, Honor, 141
Frank, I., 60
Freiwald, Aaron, 95
Frieden, Jeffry A., 60
Friesen, Dorothy, 140
Frobel, Folker, 60
Frundt, Henry J., 32
Fuentes, Annette, 95
Furtado, Celso, 118
Galitelli, Bernardo, 65
Gallin, Rita S., 117
Garver, Paul, 51
Gassert, Thomas, 54
Gatehouse, Mike, 64
Gaunt, Marilyn, 142
Gavshon, Michael, 139
Geddes, Maggie, 146
Gerardi, R. E., 64
Gereffi, Gary, 60
Ghosh, Pradip K., 51
Giacometti, A., 116

Goodman, Amy, 96
Graham, Ronald, 60
Gray, Lorraine, 131
Green, Mark, 33
Greenaway, David, 60
Grunwald, Joseph, 33
Gupta, Dipanker, 115
Gutkind, Peter C. W., 28
Guyot, Eric, 145
Gwynne, Robert N., 64
Halliday, Fred, 96
Hansen, Karen Tranberg, 116
Hansen, Lynn, 54
Harman, Inge Maria, 97
Harper, F. John, 54
Harrison, Bennett, 60, 114
Harrod, Jeffrey, 34
Hawes, Gary, 35
Hector, Tim, 116
Heller, Lee, 123, 132, 135, 138, 140, 141, 142
Hines, Colin, 30
Hirota, Filo, 63
Hobbelink, Henk, 97
Hoffman, J., 60
Holloway, Steven Kendall, 60
Holmstrom, Mark, 63
Hosmer, Ellen, 97
Howard, Michael C., 35
Humphrey, J., 64
Innes, Duncan, 36
Ives, Jane H., 37, 60
Iyanda, O., 115, 116
Jagan, Larry, 97
Jaquette, Jane S., 115
Jenkins, R., 64
Jenkins, Rhys, 37, 38
Jones, Tara, 63
Jules-Rosette, Bennetta, 116
Kanegis, Arthur, 138
Kaplinsky, R., 116
Kapoor, Kabita, 50
Katz, Michael, 56
Keck, Mimi, 118
Kelly, Marjorie, 122
Kervyn, Bernard, 100
Kim, Young-ock, 117
Klare, Michael T., 61
Klatter, Matty, 66, 120
Ko, Yiu-Chung, 118
Kodawsky, Helen, 139
Kolko, Joyce, 61
Koo, Hagen, 117
Kronish, R., 64
Kucinski, Bernardo, 24
Kumar, Krishna, 61
Kurian, Rachel, 117
Kuwahara, Y., 117
Lacayo, Ramiro, 140
Ladjevardi, Habib, 66
Lal-Sanabary, Nagut M., 61
Lall, Sanjaya, 61, 115
Langdon, S., 62
Lanset, Andrew, 144
Lee, Philip R., 46

Leon de Leal, Magdalena, 118
Leonard, Richard, 116
Lernoux, Penny, 65
Leslie, Winsome J., 63
Lessard, Donald R., 61
Levering, Robert, 56
Lewin-Epstein, Noah, 66
Lieverman, Theodore, 118
Lifschitz, Edgardo, 51
Lim, L., 117
Lin, Vivian, 101
Lind, John E., 117
Lo, Porise, 101
Lydecker, Mia, 46
Lydenberg, Steven D., 55
McAfee, Kathy, 102, 116
McCarthy, Florence E., 102
McDonnell, Kathleen, 39
MacDougall, David, 139
MacDougall, Judith, 139
McLeod, Maxwell G., 61
MacShane, Denis, 40
Marcussen, Henrick Secher, 61
Marlin, Alice Tepper, 55
Marquardt, Sandra, 145
Mattelart, Armand, 40, 61
Maxcy, G., 65
Mekeirle, Joseph O., 52
Melrose, Dianna, 61, 65, 119
Mericle, K., 64
Merrifield, Juliet, 117
Mezger, Dorothea, 61
Mhone, Guy C. Z., 63
Mies, Maria, 41, 117
Mikkelsen, Britha, 52
Mitter, Swasti, 61
Mizuno, Y., 117
Mokhiber, Russell, 104
Montavon, R., 65
Moorsom, Richard, 104
Morehouse, Ward, 63
Morsy, Soheir A., 104
Moskowitz, Milton, 56
Mraz, John, 141
Muller, Mike, 41
Munck, Ronaldo, 42, 65, 118
Munslow, B., 61
Murphy, Denis, 63
Nash, June, 43, 65
Nemetz, Peter N., 63
Newfarmer, Richard S., 65
Newland, Kathleen, 104
Niosi, Jorge, 43
Nore, Petter, 61
Norris, Ruth, 61
Nunez, Osvaldo, 115
Nyangoni, Wellington, 63
O'Brien, Patricia J., 104
Odle, Maurice A., 61
Owen, Norman G., 63
Owen, Roger, 119
Pearce, Jenny, 92
Pearce, Robert D., 53
Pearson, Ruth, 115

Perrucci, Carolyn C., 61
Phizacklea, Annie, 44
Phongpaichit, Pasuk, 118
Plant, Roger, 44
Plantema, Elsje, 140
Plaut, Martin, 40
Plumb, Richard, 104
Possas, M. L., 119
Preusch, Deb, 22
Quamina, Odida T., 63
Rakowski, Cathy A., 104
Ramsaran, Ramesh F., 65
Rao, S.V. Ramani, 50
Richter, Robert, 125, 138
Riley, Maria, 54
Rissieuw, Carla, 137
Robinson, J., 62
Rodney, Wendy, 141
Room, Robin, 63
Rosenberg, Terry Jean, 119
Roxborough, I., 65
Ruggie, J. G., 62
Rugman, A., 62
Ruiz, Vicki L., 65
Rush, R., 60
Salaff, Janet W., 45
Sambamoorthi, Usha, 118
Sampson, Anthony, 62
Sassen Aashia, 62
Sauvageot, Claude, 136
Schor, Juliet, 90
Scott, Rebecca J., 65
Seidman, Ann, 63
Semyonov, Moshe, 66
Sharibane, Souad, 139
Sharpe, Kenneth, 64
Sheppard, Chris, 136
Sheridan, Mary, 45
Shiva, Vandana, 108
Silverman, Milton, 46
Sinclair, Mary, 146
Smith, Deborah, 1
Smith, Sandy, 119
Soldon, Norbert C., 46
Somplatsky-Jarman, Rev. Bill, 116
Southall, Roger, 47, 63
Stauffer, Robert B., 62, 64
Stoltzfus, Gene, 140
Strub, Sean O'Brien, 55
Sturdevant, Saundra, 118
Subramaniam, M. Arun, 63
Swift, Richard, 27
Tadem, Eduardo C., 118
Tamarin, David, 65
Tanchoco-Subido, C., 118
Tandon, Rajesh, 117
Tanzer, Michael, 62
Tavis, Lee A., 48
Taylor, Elizabeth, 108
Taylor, June H., 62
Taylor, Peter, 48
Teh Poh Ai, 115
Thomson, Robert, 109
Thorbek, Susanne, 64

Thorup, Cathryn L., 65
Tiano, Susan, 65, 109
Tiongson, Lito, 132
Torp, Jens Erik, 61
Torrie, Jill, 62
Troeller, Gordian, 142
Tsui, Elaine Yi-lan, 111
Turner, H. A., 64
Turner, L., 62
Turner, Terisa, 61, 119
Utrecht, Ernst, 64
Van Hear, Nick, 116
Velazquez, Fernando, 144
Villamil, Jose J., 62
Von Werlhof, Claudia, 41
Walcott, Harclyde, 141
Ward, David, 40
Ward, Kathryn B., 112
Watanabe, S., 115

Waterman, Peter, 62, 66
Weinrub, Al, 115
Weir, David, 115
Well, Louis T., Jr., 62
Wieringa, Saskia, 140
Williams, Robert G., 49
Williamson, John, 61
Winkler, James, 88
Winkler, James E., 113
Wong, Aline K., 118
Wood, Beth, 22
Woodward, Peter N., 66
Yachir, Faysal, 115
Yoffie, David B., 64
Yokell, Michael D., 62
Young, Gay, 119
Zawad, Kazi, 115
Zeltzer, Steve, 123, 132, 135, 138, 140, 141, 142

TITLES

This index contains the names of all the print and audiovisual resources included in this directory. Alphabetization follows the logic of the computer. Search for entries in this order: Israel / Israel's / Israel- / Israel: /. The distributor's address appears either in the text or in the Organizations Index when we have judged that the resource would not easily be available through a library or bookstore.

ABC's of Philippine EPZ's, The, 122
Address—Earth: Living in a Global Society, 122
Adverse Effects: Women and the Pharmaceutical Industry, 39
AFL-CIO (AIFLD), Israel, and Central America, 123
AFL-CIO in Central America: A Look at the American Institute for Free Labor Development (AIFLD), The, 112
After the Difficulties, 139
Agribusiness in Africa, 30
Agriculture's Vanishing Heritage, 123
Alpaca Breeders of Chimboya, 123
Aluminium Industry and the Third World: Multinational Corporations and Underdevelopment, The, 60
Aluminium Multinationals and the Bauxite Cartel, The, 60
American Arms Supermarket, 61
American Connection, The, 123
American Involvement in South Korea, 143
American Labor, 83
American Labor Films, 142
AMPO: Japan-Asia Quarterly Review, 67
Anglo American and the Rise of Modern South Africa, 36
Angola's Political Economy, 1975-1985, 116
Annals of Corporate Crime: Dow Chemical Co., 143
Annals of Corporate Crime: Litton, 143
Annals of Corporate Crime: Union Carbide, The, 144

Antinomies of Interdependence: National Welfare and the International Division of Labor, 62
Appropriate Technology Choice and Employment Creation by Two Multinational Enterprises in Nigeria, 115
Are Married Daughters "Spilled Water"? A Study of Working Women in Urban Taiwan, 111
Argentina from Anarchism to Peronism: Workers, Unions and Politics, 1855-1985, 65
Argentine Labor Movement, 1930-1945: A Study in the Origins of Peronism, The, 65
Asante Market Women, 138
Asia Labour Monitor, 68, 119
Asia Link, 85
Asian Migrant, 68
Asian Women's Workers Newsletter, 69
Attracting Agribusiness in Nigeria, 116
Australia, Argentina and World Capitalism, 1930-1945, 64
Back to Coca-Cola, 124
Banana Company, 140
Banking on Poverty: The Global Impact of the IMF and World Bank, 62
Banking on the World: The Politics of American International Finance, 60
Basta Ya! Women in Central America, 124
Beggar My Neighbour, 110
Beware of the Generals, 144
Bhopal Tragedy: One Year After, The, 63
Bhopal Tragedy: What Really Happened and

INDEXES 157

What It Means for American Workers and Communities at Risk, 63
Bibliografía Analítica Sobre Empresas Transnacionales/Analytical Bibliography on Transnational Corporporations, 51
Bibliography on the AFL-CIO's Foreign Policy, 51
Bibliography on Transnational Corporations, 52
Big Business Reader: On Corporate America, The, 33
Bitter Fruit: Guatemala, 1954, 144
Bitter Fruits (Dole Thai), The, 140
Bitter Harvest for U.S. Banks: The Making of a Debtors Cartel, 115
Bitter Pills: Medicines and the Third World Poor, 61, 65
Black Gold: The Mozambican Miner, Proletarian and Peasant, 62
Black Workers under Siege: The Repression of Black Trade Unions in South Africa, 89
Black Working Class in South Africa, The, 116
Brazil Labor Report, 83
Brazil's New Labor Militancy: A Break from the Past, 118
Brazil: The New Militancy. Trade Unions and Transnational Corporations, 89
Bread with Dignity: Voices of Nicaraguan Labor, 124
Bread, Justice & Multinational Corporations, 137
Bringing It All Back Home, 124
British Companies Operating in the Philippines, 52
Buddha Is Smiling: Nuclear Proliferation in Asia, The, 139
Business of America, The, 125
Business of Hunger, The, 125
Can the "Free Market" Solve Africa's Food Crisis?, 93
Canadian Dimension, 83
Canadian Multinationals, 43
Capital Accumulation, Women's Work, and Informal Economies in Korea, 117
Capital Flight and Third World Debt, 61
Capitalism, Socialism and Technology: A Comparative Study of Cuba and Jamaica, 64
Capitalist Control and Workers' Struggle in the Brazilian Auto Industry, 64
Case Against Depo-Provera, The, 96
Central America Update, 85
CEP Research Report, 69
Challenging Transnationals: And How Transnationals React to Their Critics, 90
Changing Division of Labor in South Asia: Women and Men in India's Society, Economy, and Politics, The, 63
Changing International Division of Labor, A, 25
Child Labour in South Africa, 116
Child Labour in Thailand: The Dark Side of Thai Children, 126

Chilean and Turkish Labor Struggles, 140
Christians in Corporations, 137
Ciba-Geigy's Cover-Up, 115
Cleared for Export: An Examination of the European Community's Pharmaceutical and Chemical Trade, 92
Closed: Control Data Korea. Wanted: A Future for Blacklisted Workers, 88
CLUW Forum on Labor and Central America, 141
Commodities, 126
Commodities: Black Market, 127
Commodities: Coffee Is the Gold of the Future, 128
Commodities: Free Markets for Free Men, 129
Commodities: Grow or Die, 129
Commodities: Leaving Home for Sugar, 127
Commodities: Tea Fortunes, 128
Commodities: Time is Money, 130
Commodities: White Gold, 126
Common Fate, Common Bond: Women in the Global Economy, 61
Conglomerates: Where the Product Is Profit, 115
Controlling Interest: The World of the Multinational Corporation, 125, 137
Copper in the World Economy, 61
Corporate Activity Catalogue: 1986, 53
Corporate Connection, The, 130
Corporate Crime and Violence, 104
Corporate Examiner, 70
Corporate Flight: The Causes and Consequences of Economic Dislocation, 114
Corporate Killings: Bhopals Will Happen, 63
Corporate Responsibility Monitor, 70
Cost of Cotton, The, 141
CTC Reporter, The, 71
Cycles of Class Struggle and the Making of the Working Class in Argentina, 118
Debt Squads: The U.S., the Banks, and Latin America, 24
Deindustrialization of America, 60
Dependent Development: The Alliance of Multinational, State and Local Capital in Brazil, 64
Divestment for South Africa: An Investment in Hope, 116
Divestment: The Offensive against Apartheid and Nuclear Weapons, 144
Dole in Thailand: The Bitter Fruit, 139
Dollars and Dictators, 139
Dollars and Sense, 83
Don't Desert the Rain Forests, 144
Double Shift, The, 130
Economic Development and International Trade, 60
Economic Notes, 71
Effects of Multinational Enterprises on Employment in India, The, 117
Employment Effects of Foreign Direct Investments in ASEAN Countries, 117
Employment Effects of Multinational Enterprises in Brazil, 119
Employment Effects of Multinational Enter-

prises: A Case Study of Kenya, 116
Employment Effects of Multinational Enterprises in Nigeria, 116
Employment Effects of Multinational Enterprises in the Philippines, 118
European Companies in the Philippines, 53
Everybody's Business: An Almanac. The Irreverent Guide to Corporate America, 56
Exploiting the Sea, 104
Export Agriculture and the Crisis in Central America, 49
Export of Hazard: Transnational Corporations and Environmental Control Issues, The, 37
Exportation of Hazardous Industries to Developing Countries, The, 60
Exporting Danger: A History of the Canadian Nuclear Energy Export Programme, 31
Factories for the Third World: Tunisia, 142
Familial Adaptations to the Internationalization of Egyptian Labour, 105
Female White Collar Workers: A Case Study of Successful Development in Lusaka, Zambia, 116
Fight to Ban Bogus Drugs, The, 115
Film Library Quarterly, 142
Fit as a Fiddle, 138
Focus on Labour, 94
Focus on the Eastern Caribbean: Bananas, Bucks, and Boots, 94
For a New Labour Internationalism: A Set of Reprints and Working Papers, 62
For Export Only: Pesticides and Pills, 138
Foreign Enterprise in Developing Countries, 60
Forestry Crisis and Forestry Myths. A Critical Review of "Tropical Forests: A Call for Action," 108
From Peasant Girls to Bangkok Masseuses, 118
From Rags to Riches, 139
Fruits of Toil, 130
Future for Namibia Series, 104
Garment Workers in Bangladesh, The, 131
Gender Identification and Working Class Solidarity among Maquila Workers in Ciudad Juarez, 119
Gentle Winds or Typhoon, 131
Getting a Handle on Pesticides, 115
Giungad, 139
Global Assembly Line, The, 131
Global Electronics, 72
Global Factory: An Organizing Guide for a New Economic Era, The, 87
Global Factory: Foreign Assembly in International Trade, The, 33
Global Management, 144
Global Marketplace: 102 of the Most Influential Companies Outside America, The, 56
Global Pesticide Issues, 115
Grains and Radicalism: The Political Economy of the Rice Industry in the Philippines, 1965-1985, 118

Great Health Robbery: Baby Milk and Medicines in Yemen, 119
Great Tin Crash: Bolivia and the World Tin Market, The, 92
Green Gold: Bananas and Dependency in the Eastern Caribbean, 109
Growing Problem: Pesticides and the Third World, A, 60
Guardian, The, 85
Guatemala Vencera, 141
Guatemala's Nightmare, 141
Health Hazards in Electronics: A Handbook, 54
Health of Nations: A North-South Investigation, The, 41
Health, Women's Work, and Industrialization: Women Workers in the Semiconductor Industry in Singapore and Malaysia, 101
Healthy Business: The Pharmaceutical Multinationals in the Third World, 138
Hewers of Wood and Drawers of Water: Noncitizen Arabs in the Israeli Labor Market, 66
Human Rights Internet Reporter, 85
Hunger Crop: Poverty and the Sugar Industry, The, 64
Hungry for Profit, 138
ICCR Brief, 119
IECON Newsletter, 73
ILR Report, 83
Impact of the International Mining Industry on Native Peoples, The, 35
IMS Ayer Directory of Publications, The, 85
In Banks We Trust, 65
India's Working Women, 139
Indian Women in Subsistence and Agricultural Labour, 117
Indirect Employment Effects of Multinational Enterprises in Developing Countries, The, 115
Industrial Labour in Africa: A Partially Annotated Bibliography, 52
Industrial Women Workers in Asia, 92
Industrial Worker, 83
Industrialization and Urbanization in Latin America, 64
Industry and Inequality: The Social Anthropology of Indian Labour, 63
Inside Haiti, 131
International Business in South Africa 1988, 55
International Grain Trade: Problems and Prospects, The, 60
International Labor and Working Class History, 84
International Labour Reports, 73, 119
International Labour Review, 73
International Labour Studies: A Third World and Labour-Oriented Bibliography, 66
Internationalization of Capital: Imperialism and Capitalist Development on a World Scale, The, 59
Internationalization of Capital: Prospects for the Third World, The, 61

Internationalizing Labour: Modalities of Intervention through Labour Studies and Publications, 115
Introductory Course for the Workers, 117
Is There Justice at Irryo?, 131
Israel, South Africa, and U.S. Labor, 142
Jamaica: Open for Business, 99
Japan's Human Imports: As Capital Flows Out, Foreign Labor Flows In, 100
Japanese Industry Moves Out, 99
JUST Resources, 142
Labor and Anti-Intervention, 132
Labor and Development: A Monthly Review of African Socio-Economic Events of Interest to Trade Union Leaders, 74
Labor and South Africa, 116
Labor and the Church in Asia, 63
Labor and the South Africa COSATU Congress, 138
Labor and Unions in Asia and Africa: Contemporary Issues, 63
Labor in El Salvador, 119
Labor in Latin America: Comparative Essays on Chile, Argentina, Venezuela, and Colombia, 23
Labor Market Discrimination against Women in India, 118
Labor Notes, 74
Labor Report on Central America, 75
Labor Research Review, 84
Labor Studies Journal, 84
Labor Today: The Rank and File in Action, 75
Labor Unions and Autocracy in Iran, 66
Labor Update, 84
Labour Movement in Tropical Africa: Its Beginnings, The, 116
Labour, Capital and Society, 76
Labour: Journal of Canadian Labor Studies/ Le Travail: Revue d'etudes ouvries canadiennes, 84
Last Colony: But Whose? A Study of the Labour Movement, Labour Market and Labour Relations in Hong Kong, 64
Left Business Observer, 84
Let's Have Another Cup of Coffee, 145
Links, 84
Listen Real Loud: News of Women's Liberation Worldwide, 85
Lives of Working Women in India., 117
Lives: Chinese Working Women, 45
Long March, The, 132
Losing Control: Towards an Understanding of Transnational Corporations in the Pacific Islands Contex, 113
Maquiladoras, Women's Work, and Unemployment in Northern Mexico, 109
Matter of Taste, A, 139
Meeting the Corporate Challenge: A Handbook on Corporate Campaigns, 103
Merchants of Drink, The, 60
Merchants of Grain, 138
Mexico: A Multinational Haven, 95
Microelectronics and Clothing: The Impact of Technical Change on a Global Industry, 60
Midas Touch, The, 132
Middle East Labor Bulletin, 76
Migrant Workers in the Gulf, 119
Migrant Workers in the Middle East, 96
Migrante, 132
Min-ju No-jo: South Korea's New Trade Unions, 103
Minangkabau: Story of People vs. TNCs in Asia, 27
Mineworkers of Guyana: The Making of a Working Class, 63
Mobility of Labor and Capital, The, 62
Money Lenders: Bankers and a World in Turmoil, The, 62
Monster in Morong: The Dreadful Tale of the Bataan-Westinghouse Nuclear Plant in the Philippines, 94
Moving On: The Hunger for Land in Zimbabwe, 139
Muchachas No More: Household Workers in Latin America and the Caribbean, 26
Multi-National Corporations and Third World Development, 51
Multinational Banks and Underdevelopment, 61
Multinational Business and Labour, 60
Multinational Corporations and the Control of Culture, 61
Multinational Corporations in the Political Economy of Kenya, 62
Multinational Corporations: The E.C.S.I.M. Guide to Information Sources, 52
Multinational Enterprises and Employment in the Caribbean with Special Reference to Trinidad and Tobago, 119
Multinational Enterprises and Employment-Oriented "Appropriate" Technologies in Developing Countries, 115
Multinational Managers and Poverty in the Third World, 48
Multinational Monitor, 77, 119
Multinational Motor Industry, The, 65
Multinationals and Maldevelopment: Alternative Development Strategies in Argentina, the Ivory Coast, 22
Multinationals and Political Control, 62
Multinationals and Transfer Pricing, 62
Multinationals for Developing Countries, 61
Multinationals of the South: New Actors in the International Economy, 39
Multinationals, the State, and Control of the Nigerian Economy, 62
Multinationals: For Better or Worse?, 138
National Boycott News, 77
Nationalization: A Road to Socialism? The Case of Tanzania, 62
Neither Pure Nor Simple: The AFL-CIO and Latin America, 118
New Hope or False Promise? Biotechnology and Third World Agriculture, 97
*New International Division of Labour: Struc-

tural Unemployment in Industrialised Countries and Industry, 60
New International Labour Studies: An Introduction, The, 42
New Multinationals: The Spread of Third World Enterprise, The, 61
New Pages, 142
News from IRENE, 84
Newsletter of International Labour Studies, 66, 78, 119
Nicaragua: Labor, Democracy, and the Struggle for Peace, 113
No Place to Run: Local Realities and Global Issues of the Bhopal Disaster, 117
No Promise for Tomorrow: Communities Respond to the Bhopal Tragedy, 140
No to Recession and Unemployment: An Examination of the Brazilian Economic Crisis, 118
Nothing to Lose But Our Lives: Empowerment to Oppose Hazards in a Transnational World, 29
Nowhere to Run, 138
Nuclear Power and Martial Law, 140
Obligations-Part I: International Banking, the Third World and Chile, 141
Obligations-Part II: The International Monetary Fund, Britain and Jamaica, 141
OECD and Western Mining Multinational Corporations in the Republic of South Africa, 63
Of Common Cloth: Women in the Global Textile Industry, 26
Of Prophets and Profits, 78
Oil and Class Struggle, 61
Oil and Labor in the Middle East, 66
Oil Companies in the International System, 62
Oil, Politics and the Pursuit of Profits, 115
On the Situation of Working Women in the Urban and Rural Areas of the Southern Part of Korea, 118
One Way Ticket: Migration and Female Labour, 44
Only Difference Between Men and Boys Is the Price of Their Toys, 138
Opening the Road to Hunger. Food Exports from the Third World: Senegal, 116
Origins of the Peruvian Labour Movement, 1883-1919, The, 64
Other Side of Paradise: Foreign Control in the Caribbean, The, 22
Our Stories: Lives of Filipina Women, 118
Our Times, 79
Pacific Rim: Investment, Development and Trade, The, 63
Paradise Lost: The Ravaged Rainforest, 98
Passing the Message, 139
Peasants and Proletarians: The Struggles of Third World Workers, 28
People of No Interest, 133
People of the Field, 140
Perhaps Women Are More Economical, 140
Pesticide Dilemma in the Third World: A Case Study of Malaysia, 118

Pesticide Plague, The, 145
Pesticides Don't Know When to Stop Killing, 115
Pharmaceutical Industry and Dependency in the Third World, 60
Philippine Debt to Foreign Banks, 117
Philippine Economy and the United States: Studies in Past and Present Interactions, The, 63
Philippine Labor, 140
Philippine Labor Alert, 79
Philippine Labor Movement, The, 140
Philippine State and the Marcos Regime: The Politics of Export, The, 35
Pills, Pesticides and Profits: The International Trade in Toxic Substances, 61
Plant Closings: International Context and Social Costs, 61
Plant Shutdowns Monitor, 80
Plight of Asian Workers in Electronics, The, 101
Plunder in Paradise, 133
Political Economy of a Dual Labor Market in Africa: The Copper Industry and Dependency in Zambia, 1929-1969, 63
Political Economy of the Latin American Motor Vehicle Industry, 64
Political Economy of the New Asian Industrialism, The, 30
Political Economy of the World-System Annuals: Vol. 7. Labor in the Capitalist World Economy, 60
Politics of Production, Factory Regimes under Capitalism and Socialism, 60
Population Policy, Economic Development, and Multinational Corporations in Latin America, 105
Position of Women Workers in Manufacturing Industries in South Korea: A Marxist-Feminist Analysis, 117
Poverty Brokers: The IMF and Latin America, 65
Power & Protectionism: Strategies of the Newly Industrializing Countries, 64
Power, Production, and the Unprotected Worker, 34
Power: Black Workers, Their Unions, and the Struggle for Freedom in South Africa, 40
Prescriptions for Death: The Drugging of the Third World, 46
Price of Change, The, 142
Production, Power, and World Order: Social Forces in the Making of History, 60
Profits, Progress and Poverty: Case Studies of International Industries in Latin America, 65
Proletarianisation in the Third World, 61
Promised Land Lost, 140
Que Viva! Labor in El Salvador, 133
Race for Resources, The, 62
Raw Materials Report, 80
Real Thing, The, 134
Refreshing Pauses, Coca Cola and Human Rights in Guatemala, 32

INDEXES 161

Restructuring the World Economy, 61
Retrenchment!, 117
Rich Chips, Poor Chips, 134
Right Wing Vigilantes in Labor Repression in the Philippines, 118
Role of Multinational Companies in Latin America: A Case Study in Mexico, The, 65
Roots of Crisis in Southern Africa, The, 63
Roots of Hunger, Roots of Change, 138
Royal Dutch/Shell Group of Companies Alternative Corporate Report 1987, The, 88
Rural Industrialization and Chinese Women: A Case Study from Taiwan, 117
Rural Women Discovered: New Sources of Capital and Labor in Bangladesh, 102
Scenarios of Hunger in the Caribbean, 91
Seeds and Food Security, 107
Seeds of Revolution, 138
Sellers and Servants: Working Women in Lima, Peru, 24
Sharing Global Resources, 138
Short Circuit: Women on the Global Assembly Line, 115
Slave Emancipation in Cuba: The Transition to Free Labor, 65
Smoke Ring: Tobacco, Money, & Multinational Politics, The, 48
Social Volcano, 134
Social Volcano: Sugar Workers in the Philippines, 98
Soft Drink, Hard Labour: Guatemalan Workers Take on Coca-Cola, 64
Soil and Turmoil, 134
Solidarity across Borders: U.S. Labor in a Global Economy, 108
South Africa's Multinational Connections: Putting Apartheid on Computer, 116
South African Labour Bulletin, 84
South African Trade Union Worker Choirs, 145
Spatial Organisation of Multinational Corporations, The, 60
Stand Tall and Straight, 140
Standard Periodical Directory, The, 84
Struggle in El Salvador: A Labor Viewpoint, 135
Struggle in the U.S. Labor Movement over Central America, The, 119
Struggling for the Sharing of Wealth and Power, 84
Struggling to Survive: Women Workers in Asia, 27
Subordination of Women and the Internationalization of Factory Production, 115
Sugar and Modern Slavery: A Tale of Two Countries, 44
Sugar Connection, The, 145
Sugar World, 81
Sweet Sugar Rage, 141
Taking Care of Business in Nicaragua, 119
Tales of the Filipino Working Women, 117
Tea Garden, The, 135
Technology and Development Perspectives of the Pharmaceutical Sector in Ethiopia, 59

Technology Choice and Employment Creation: A Case Study of Three Multinational Enterprises in Singapore, 117
Tenants in Our Own Land, 140
Textile Challenge and the Third World: NG0 Views on the Multi-Fibre Arrangement, The, 100
Thai Labour: The Next Step, 135
Third World Multinationals: The Rise of Foreign Investment from Developing Countries, 62
TIE Report, 81, 119
Ties That Bind: Canada and the Third World, 27
Time Is Now, The, 140
To Sing Our Own Song, 140
Tobacco Madness, 145
Tobacco Trap, The, 110
Trade Union Activity and Government Repression in El Salvador: A Report, 118
Trade Union Movement and the Third World, The, 115
Trade Union Studies Journal, 84
Trade Unions and the New Industrialization of the Third World, 47
Trade Unions of the World, 54
Transnational Capitalism and National Development: New Perspectives on Dependence, 62
Transnational Conglomerates and the Economics of Dependent Development, 65
Transnational Corporations and Industrial Transformation in Latin America, 64
Transnational Corporations and the Latin American Automobile Industry, 37
Transnational Corporations and the Political Economy of Development: The Continuing Philippine Debate, 64
Transnational Corporations and the State, 62
Transnational Corporations and Underdevelopment, 60
Transnational Corporations and Uneven Development: The Internationalization of Capital and the Third, 38
Transnational Corporations in International Tourism, 59
Transnational Corporations in South Africa and Namibia: United Nations Public Hearings, 57
Transnational Corporations in South East Asia and the Pacific, 64
Transnational Corporations in the Agricultural Machinery and Equipment Industry, 58
Transnational Corporations in the Caribbean: Strangers in Paradise, 111
Transnational Corporations in the Fertilizer Industry, 58
Transnational Corporations in the International Semiconductor Industry, 58
Transnational Corporations in the International Auto Industry, 58
Transnational Corporations in the Man-made Fibre, Textile and Clothing Industries, 58
Transnational Corporations in the Pharma-

ceutical Industry of Developing Countries, 58
Transnational Corporations in World Development: Third Survey, 62
Transnational Corporations vs. the State: The Political Economy of the Mexican Automobile Industry, 64
Transnational Enterprises: Their Impact on Third World Societies and Cultures, 61
Transnationals and the Third World: The Struggle for Culture, 40
Tunnel Vision: Labor, the World Economy, and Central America, 90
Typical Life Story of a Young Factory Woman in Korea, A, 135
U.S. and Canadian Business in South Africa 1987, 57
U.S. Construction Workers Brigade to Nicaragua, 141
U.S. Investment in Latin America and the Caribbean, 65
U.S. Involvement in the Philippines, 145
U.S. Labor and the CIA Connection, 135
U.S. Labor Movement and Latin America. Vol. 1: 1846-1919, 32
Ulrich's International Periodicals Directory, 85
Unions and Politics in Mexico: The Case of the Automobile Industry, 65
United States and Mexico: Face to Face with New Technology, The, 65
Unseasonal Migrations: The Effects of Rural Labor Scarcity in Peru, 64
Urban Workers and Labor Unions in Chile, 1902-1927, 64
Vanishing Earth, The, 135
Vietnam's Quest for Foreign Investment: A Bold Move, 118
Violence against Sugar Workers, 111
Voices from the City: Women of Bangkok, 64
Wahyuningsih: Woman Worker Seeking Justice, 136
We Eat the Mines, The Mines Eat Us: Dependency and Exploitation in Bolivian Tin Mines, 65
We Will Neither Go Nor Be Driven Out, 106
Weapons Bazaar, 138
Weaving Our Lives, 139
When You Bank with Citibank, You Bank in South Africa, 116
Who Owes Whom?, 82
Who Owns the Plains?, 140
Who Owns the Sky?, 140
Why Farmers Go Hungry. Food Exports from the Third World: Honduras, 102
With These Hands, 136
Women and Cooperative Labor in the Southern Bolivian Andes, 97
Women and Labour, 114
Women and Labour Migration, 108
Women and Transnational Corporation Employment: A World-System and Feminist Analysis, 112
Women and Work in Rosehall (St. Vincent, Caribbean), 141

Women and Work in the Third World: The Impact of Industrialisation and Global Economic Interdependence, 61
Women at Work in India: A Bibliography, 50
Women Food Producers: Potential Power for Combating World Hunger, 115
Women in Andean Agriculture: Peasant Production and Rural Wage Employment in Colombia and Peru, 118
Women in Nontraditional Industry: The Case of Steel in Ciudad Guayana, Venezuela, 106
Women in the Global Factory, 95
Women on the Global Assembly Line, 146
Women on the U.S.-Mexico Border: Responses to Change, 65
Women Workers in the Sri Lanka Plantation Sector: An Historical and Contemporary Analysis, 117
Women Workers' Resource Directory, 54
Women's Productive and Reproductive Roles in the Family Wage Economy: A Colombian Example, 119
Women's Work and Family Life: The Case of Electronics Workers in Singapore, 118
Women's Work in the Informal Sector: A Zambian Case Study, 116
Women's Work in Third World Agriculture: Concepts and Indicators, 115
Women, Men, and the Division of Labor, 105
Women, Men, and the International Division of Labor, 43
Women: The Last Colony, 41
Work and Workers, 141
Work Ethics, 82
Work History: Disaggregating the Changing Terms of Poor Women's Entry into Lusaka's Labor Force, The, 116
Workers and Revolution in Iran: A Third World Experience of Workers' Control, 65
Workers and Unions in the New Nicaragua, 136
Workers Are Coming, The, 136
Workers World, 84
Workers' Struggle in South Africa, The, 137
Workers, Unions and Popular Protest, 87
Working People of Central America, 141
World Alcohol Industry with Special Reference to Australia, New Zealand, and the Pacific Islands, The, 63
World Bank and Structural Transformation in Developing Countries: The Case of Zaire, The, 63
World in Their Web: The Dynamics of Textile Multinationals, The, 60
World of Women's Trade Unionism: Comparative Historical Essays, The, 46
World Steel Industry Today, The, 115
World's Largest Industrial Enterprises: 1962-1983, The, 53
Wrong End of the Rope, The, 137
Yellowcake: The International Uranium Cartel, 62

INDEXES   163

GEOGRAPHICAL AREAS

This index includes all references to countries and regions mentioned in this resource directory. Names are given as they appear in the resource and imply no political judgment about the legitimacy of national claims. Regional references (e.g., West Africa) are given only when there is a resource that treats the area as a whole. References are provided for organizations in chapter 1 only if they specify a concern for a particular country.

Africa, 14, 30, 52, 62-63, 115-16, 138-39
Algeria, 29
Angola, 116
Argentina, 22, 23, 30, 47, 64, 65, 118
Asia and Pacific, 14-16, 25, 63-64, 85, 117-18, 139-40
Australia, 2, 25, 64
Bahamas, 23
Bangladesh, 100, 102, 131, 135
Bolivia, 65, 92, 97
Brazil, 26, 36, 64, 82, 83, 89, 112, 118, 119, 126, 129, 133
Burkina Faso, 136
Canada, 43
Caribbean, 22, 26, 43, 91, 94, 109, 111, 126, 133
Central America, 9, 49, 85, 90, 119, 123, 141
Ceylon (Sri Lanka), 29
Chile, 23, 26, 29, 36, 64, 140, 141
China, 29, 45, 54, 126, 127, 128
Colombia, 23, 26, 34, 118, 119, 126, 128
Cuba, 26, 64, 65
Dominican Republic, 45, 126
Egypt, 97, 105, 108
El Salvador, 112, 118, 119, 133, 135
Europe, 16-18
Ghana, 130
Guatemala, 32, 64, 103, 106, 108, 112, 124, 134, 141
Guyana, 63
Haiti, 23, 34, 45, 112, 131
Honduras, 102, 112
Hongkong, 27, 30, 45, 64, 126, 132
India, 29, 37, 41, 50, 54, 63, 104, 114, 118, 139, 140, 144
Indonesia, 54, 136
Iran, 48, 65, 66
Israel, 66, 123, 142
Ivory Coast, 22
Jamaica, 26, 29, 64, 99, 114, 141
Japan, 99, 100
Kenya, 62, 116, 136

Latin America and Caribbean, 18, 64-65, 118-19, 140-41
Malaysia, 27, 43, 48, 54, 101, 118, 134
Mexico, 26, 30, 34, 64, 65, 95, 109, 114, 119, 131
Middle East, 65-66, 76, 96, 119, 141-42
Mozambique, 62
Namibia, 57, 104
Nicaragua, 112, 113, 119, 124, 136, 140, 141
Nigeria 29, 47, 62, 115
North America, 18-19
North Yemen, 108, 119
Pakistan, 100
Peru, 24, 26, 29, 64, 118, 123
Philippines, 11, 27, 35, 36, 52, 53, 63, 64, 79, 94, 98, 100, 112, 114, 117, 118, 122, 125, 131, 132, 134, 136, 139, 140, 145
Puerto Rico, 22, 29
Senegal, 116, 126
Singapore, 30, 101, 117, 118
South Africa, 29, 36, 40, 55, 56, 57, 63, 84, 88, 89, 94, 104, 114, 116, 124, 132, 135, 136, 137, 138, 142, 144, 145
South Asia, 63
South Korea, 22, 27, 30, 31, 88, 103, 117, 118, 130, 135, 143
South Pacific, 36, 44, 63, 64, 113
Southeast Asia, 40, 43, 44, 64
Southern Africa, 63
Southern Rhodesia (Zimbabwe), 29
Sri Lanka, 27, 47, 117, 126, 128, 137
Taiwan, 30, 31, 43, 45, 111, 117
Tanzania, 62
Thailand, 27, 54, 64, 118, 126, 131, 135, 139
Trinidad and Tobago, 119
Tunesia, 142
Turkey, 141
Venezuela, 23, 106
Vietnam, 104, 118
Virgin Islands, 22
West Indies, 26, 127
Zaire, 36, 63
Zambia, 36, 63, 116, 130
Zimbabwe, 110, 127, 136, 139

SUBJECTS

This topical index also contains references to organizations and individuals not directly related to the production and/or distribution of resources listed in this

164 INDEXES

directory. Keyword descriptions for the issue-focus of organizations in chapter 1 do not appear in this index.

advertising, 41, 92
AFL-CIO, 51, 80, 90, 112, 118, 123, 135
agribusiness, 30, 107, 116, 125, 139
AIFLD (American Institute for Free Labor Development), 95, 112, 123
Alcan, 44
aluminum, 60
Amax, 36
American Federation of Labor, 32
Anglo American, 36
Anti-Slavery Society, 44
apartheid, 10, 70, 116, 124, 132, 144
Aquino, Corazon, 35
arms trade, 61, 138
assembly operations, 34, 54, 95
banking, international, 24, 28, 60, 61, 62, 65, 82, 115, 116, 117, 141
biotechnology, 97
Booker McConnell, 31
boycott, 28, 77, 88, 134
Brascon, 44
Broken Hill Pty., 36
capital,
  internationalization of, 38, 59
  migration of, 25, 61, 62, 100
capitalism, 41, 60, 62, 64
cartels, 91, 115, 126
cash crops, 30, 45, 49, 102, 125
child labor, 116, 126
churches, 5, 6, 11, 54, 63
CIA, 135, 144
Ciba-Geigy, 115
Citibank, 116
Club Med, 56
Coca-Cola, 32, 64, 106, 124, 134
coconut, 35
CODELCO, 36, 81
Cominco, 44
consumer groups and issues, 7, 15, 33
Control Data, 88
corporations, 4, 33, 51, 52, 55, 56, 61
  actions against, 91, 103
  activities and roles of, 31, 53, 65, 137
  British, 52
  Canadian, 43, 57
  crimes of, 104
  development and, 51, 62, 115, 124
  environment and, 37
  European, 53
  history of, 38, 129
  impact of, 38, 40, 61, 79, 100, 116, 117, 118, 130
  in developing countries, 61, 74, 133
  investments of, 22, 48, 53
  policies of, 18, 77, 125, 130
  power of, 13, 33, 56, 62, 81, 103
  regulation of, 30, 37, 91
  research on, 71
  social accountability of, 28, 33, 70, 79
  social responsibility of, 4, 6, 12, 48, 55, 70
  Third World, 39, 62
  U.S., 4, 33, 56, 57
  unions and, 89
debt, 24, 62, 82, 115, 117
Del Monte, 131
dependency, 30, 44, 60, 62, 63, 64, 65, 82, 109
DepoProvera, 40, 96
development, 14, 28, 38, 51, 64, 74
  economic, 23, 31
  export-oriented, 30, 35
  strategies of, 22
"Dirty Dozen" campaign, 11
divestment, 116, 144
division of labor, 3, 25, 27, 43, 47, 60, 62, 63, 105
Dole, 139, 140
Dow Chemical, 143
drugs, 46, 61, 115
Duvalier, Jean-Claude, 45
economic dislocation, 34, 134
economy, global, 61, 72, 87, 90, 108, 122
environment, 2, 12, 16, 35, 37, 136
exports, 23, 54, 138
  agricultural, 49, 102, 116
  nuclear, 31
Falconbridge, 44
FAO, 49
free trade zones, 68, 122, 124
Gecomines, 36
General Motors, 90
German Overseas Institute, 39
global factory, 87, 95, 115, 131, 146
Gompers, Samuel, 32
hazardous products, export of, 37, 60, 61, 92
hazards, 29, 34, 37, 54, 61, 72
health, 17, 41, 54, 101, 119
Hesburgh, Theodore, 48
Hiram Walker, 44
human rights, 9, 10, 32, 48
hunger, 91, 102, 116, 125
Inco, 36, 44
industrialization, 47, 61, 64, 68, 101
industry,
  agricultural, 35, 58, 94, 97
  alcohol, 63
  alpaca, 35
  automobile, 37, 58, 64, 65, 99
  chemical, 92
  clothing, 60, 131
  coffee, 31, 102, 128, 145
  copper, 63
  diamond, 37
  electronics, 34, 43, 44, 54, 58, 72, 101, 118, 134
  fishing, 104
  gold, 37
  grain, 118, 138
  heavy machinery, 58
  nuclear, 32

oil, 61, 62, 66, 115
pharmaceutical, 39, 41, 46, 58, 59, 60, 92, 138
rice, 118
seed, 91, 107, 123
semiconductor, 34
steel, 106, 115
sugar, 64, 81, 98, 126, 127, 145
tea, 128, 135
textile, 26, 38, 43, 58, 60, 100, 123, 136
tin, 65, 93, 138
tobacco, 48, 110, 145
tourism, 59
weaving, 134
Institute of Health Policy Studies, 46
International Monetary Fund (IMF), 62, 65, 68, 141
International Power, 44
investments, 99, 100, 118
 socially responsible, 6, 22
 U.S., 65
Kennecott, 36
labor force, 35
labor movement,
 African, 74, 87
 Brazilian, 90
 Canadian, 79, 84, 94
 Central American, 9, 75, 90, 133, 141
 Filipino, 11, 79, 87, 140
 Hongkong, 64
 international, 75, 105
 Korean, 103
 Latin American, 23, 32
 Middle Eastern, 76
 Peruvian, 64
 South African, 116
 Third World, 42, 105, 115
 U.S., 9, 74, 119, 132
labor studies, 15, 42, 78, 84
labor,
 industrial, 52
 international, 42
 role of, in history, 23, 32, 84, 135
 social policy and, 73
Litton, 143
Lonrho, 31
MacMillan Bloedel, 44
maquiladores, 87, 95, 109, 119
Massey-Ferguson, 44, 90
Mercedes, 90
migration, 44, 64, 68, 96, 105, 108, 119, 132, 133
mining, 18, 28, 35, 63, 65, 81, 93, 132
Nestlé 91
New International Economic Order, 28, 41
New International Information Order, 41
Noranda Mines, 44
Northern Telecom, 44
nuclear,
 technology/energy, 31, 94, 139, 140
 weapons, 31, 56, 70, 144
occupational safety and health, 2, 27
organize, right to, 11
Pan-American Federation of Labor, 32

Peace Corps, 35
peasants, 28, 30, 34, 123
pesticides, 10, 60, 92, 115, 118, 145
plant closures, 19, 61, 73, 80, 83, 87, 89
political economy, 30, 35, 39, 60
Polysar, 44
poverty, 48, 61, 62, 64, 110, 131
production, 60
 agricultural, 30
 overseas, 34
 social relations of, 34
protectionism, 64
rainforests, 98, 108, 144
raw materials, 80, 130
Rio Tinto Zinc, 36
Scania, 90
Seagram, 44
Shell, 56, 88, 91, 124
socialism, 60, 62, 64
solidarity, 8, 9, 17, 40, 76, 108, 132
strikes, 27, 32, 132, 134
sugar, 31, 35, 44, 64, 81, 91
Sullivan principles, 57
Tate and Lyle, 31
technology, 3, 29, 59, 60, 64, 65, 117
toxic materials, 37, 61
trade, 3, 5, 60, 92, 126, 127, 129
Trade Union Congress of the Philippines, 80
trade, arms, 16
transnational corporations,
 role of, 14
 role of, in developing countries, 3
U.S. Agency for International Development, 95, 99
U.S. Export-Import Bank, 94
U.S. Steel, 125
unemployment, 76, 109, 117, 118
Unilever, 31, 56, 90, 129
Union Carbide, 144
unions,
 British, 12
 Chilean, 64
 El Salvadorean, 18, 135
 Filipino, 11, 87
 Iranian, 66
 Nicaraguan, 136
 repression of, 118
 South African, 40, 89, 94, 132, 136, 137, 138, 144
 trade, 2, 12, 20, 47, 54, 63
 women's, 46
United Fruit, 144
United Nations, 57
Upjohn, 96
Volkswagen, 90
wages, 25, 27, 44, 118
weapons, 9, 10, 70, 138
Westinghouse, 94
women, 14, 17, 18, 41
 Asian, 69, 89, 92, 101, 111, 117
 Central American, 124
 corporations and, 19, 34, 61, 85, 112
 discrimination against, 118, 130

pharmaceuticals and, 39, 96
role of, 119, 130, 136
rural, 29, 91, 102, 115, 118
sex industry and, 118
workers,
  agricultural, 27, 29, 91, 115, 117
  black, 89, 116
  control by, 65
  domestic, 26, 27, 34
  industrial, 27, 29, 83, 92, 107
  migrant, 96
  self-employed, 34, 114
  sugar, 8, 45, 81, 98, 111, 131
  Third World, 28
  urban, 64, 118
  women, 15, 18, 24, 25, 27, 43, 44, 50, 54, 64, 95, 97, 101, 106, 107, 109, 111, 114
working conditions, 25, 27
World Bank, 49, 62, 63, 98, 108
World Council of Churches, 13
ZIMCO, 36

DATA CENTER

Affiliate of the Investigative Resource Center
464 19th St., Oakland, CA 94612 USA (415) 835-4692

The Data Center is an independent, non-profit research and information center. Founded in 1977 the Center provides a range of products and services for the public-interest community on national and international issues of justice and peace.

Custom Research Services

Clipping Service: Data Center staff will monitor and clip any or all of the 400 newspapers and magazines they receive for those who need ongoing information about a given topic, such as human rights in the Philippines.

Search Service: Data Center researchers will search over 400 file drawers of periodical clippings and provide full-text photocopies of articles on corporations, countries, industries, labor issues, and a variety of other political and economic subjects.

Call or write for cost estimates on the Center's custom research services.

Publications

Latin America and Caribbean: The Center produces two regular publications on these regions: *Information Services on Latin America* (monthly) and the *Central America Monitor* (biweekly). Write for a free brochure. The Center has also compiled velo-bound collections of newsclippings on Grenada (1983, 150pp.), Jamaica (1985, 115pp.), and the Sanctuary Movement (1985, 70pp.). $10 each.

Corporate Information Services: The Center publishes two monthly 100-page collections of newspaper and magazine articles on corporate issues: *Corporate Responsibility Monitor* and *Plant Shutdowns Monitor.* Write for subscription rates. Data Center *Corporate Profiles* are custom-designed collections of articles from the media and of government and corporate documents on any of 5,000 U.S. and foreign corporations. Write for rates.

The Data Center also publishes well-organized and up-to-date collections of newsclippings on the political and religious right, terrorism, U.S. foreign policy, and environmental pollution.

The Data Center is a member-supported organization. Write for a schedule of fees and a list of benefits. Contributions are tax-deductible.

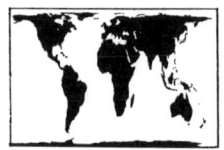

Third World Resources

464 19th Street   Oakland, CA 94612

Third World Resources gathers, catalogs, annotates, and publicizes education and action resources from and about the Third World.

Resource Directories

Twelve directories are being compiled on these subjects:

Third World general	Food, hunger, agribusiness
Africa	Human rights
Asia & Pacific	Militarism, peace, disarmament
Latin America & Caribbean	Native peoples & natural resources
Middle East	Nuclear arms & energy
Women in the Third World	TNCs & labor

Quarterly Newsletter

The *Third World Resources* newsletter contains notices and descriptive listings of organizations and newly released print, audiovisual, and other educational resources on Third World regions and issues. Inquire for subscription rates. Sample copy: US $1.

Each 16-page issue contains a unique 4-page insert with a comprehensive listing of resources on one particular region or subject. Inquire about discounts for bulk purchases.

Documentation Center

All resources are cataloged and integrated into the library collection of the Data Center where they are accessible to Center library users and Search Service clients. Bibliographical data are stored in a computerized data base to facilitate identification and retrieval of cross-referenced resources.

Third World Resources is a financially independent project of the Data Center, a non-profit, tax-exempt (501.c.3) resource center. Contributions to Third World Resources are tax-deductible.